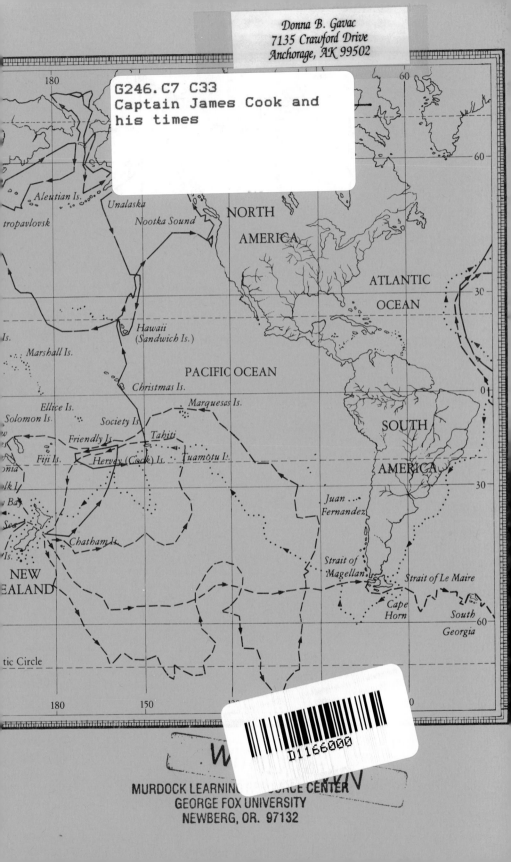

Donna B. Gavac
7135 Crawford Drive
Anchorage, AK 99502

G246.C7 C33
Captain James Cook and
his times

180                                                                    60

60

NORTH

AMERICA

ATLANTIC

30

OCEAN

Aleutian Is.

Unalaska

tropavlovsk          Nootka Sound

Is.

Marshall Is.                    Hawaii
                              (Sandwich Is.)

PACIFIC OCEAN

Christmas Is.

Ellice Is.                           Marquesas Is.

Solomon Is.          Society Is.                                        SOUTH

Friendly Is.      Tahiti                                          AMERICA

Fiji Is.      Hervey (Cook) Is.    Tuamotu I.                          30

onia                                              Juan
                                                Fernandez
lk I.

Bay

Sea                                                                    Strait of
                  Chatham Is.                                        Magellan      Strait of Le Maire

Is.                                                                            Cape
                                                                               Horn        South
NEW                                                                                        Georgia
EALAND                                                                                     60

tic Circle

180          150                                                     0

D1166000

MURDOCK LEARNING RESOURCE CENTER
GEORGE FOX UNIVERSITY
NEWBERG, OR. 97132

*Captain*
*James Cook*
*and His*
*Times*

# Captain
# James Cook
## and His
## Times

*Edited by*
ROBIN FISHER & HUGH JOHNSTON

UNIVERSITY OF WASHINGTON PRESS
Seattle

WITHDRAWN
MURDOCK LEARNING RESOURCE CENTER
GEORGE FOX UNIVERSITY
NEWBERG, OR. 97132

Copyright © 1979 by Robin Fisher and Hugh Johnston

Copyright of each paper resides with its author.

Published in the United States of America by
UNIVERSITY OF WASHINGTON PRESS, 1979
by arrangement with Douglas & McIntyre Ltd., North Vancouver


Library of Congress Cataloguing in Publication Data:

Main entry under title:

Captain James Cook and his times.

Eleven papers from a conference on Captain Cook's
explorations held at Simon Fraser University in
1978.
1. Cook, James, 1728-1779—Congresses. 2. Explorers—England—Biography—Congresses. I. Fisher,
Robin, 1946-     II. Johnston, Hugh J.M., 1939-
G246.C7C33     910'.92'4  [B]     78-73989
ISBN 0-295-95654-2

All rights reserved. No part of this book may be
reproduced or transmitted in any form or by any means,
electronic or mechanical, including photocopy, recording,
or any information storage or retrieval system,
without permission in writing from the publisher.

Design: Robert Bringhurst, Vancouver
Composition by The Typeworks, Mayne Island
Printed and bound in Canada

WITHDRAWN

It has not been part of my intention to discredit the achievements of Cook. My intention has been to suggest that it is timely that they be placed in a new perspective.

BERNARD SMITH

# Acknowledgements

The editors gratefully acknowledge the assistance of the MacMillan Family Fund. To the contributors they say thanks for making the task of editing as easy as possible; and to all the participants, organizers, and supporters associated with the Cook Conference at Simon Fraser University they express their appreciation. As all who attended know, special thanks are owed Prof. Phyllis Auty, director and driving spirit behind the conference, without whom the book would not have taken shape.

# Contents

List of Illustrations . . . . . . . . . . . . . . . . . . . . . . . . . . . . . . . . . . . . . . . viii

List of Maps . . . . . . . . . . . . . . . . . . . . . . . . . . . . . . . . . . . . . . . . . . . . . . ix

List of Tables . . . . . . . . . . . . . . . . . . . . . . . . . . . . . . . . . . . . . . . . . . . . . ix

*Robin Fisher & Hugh Johnston,* INTRODUCTION . . . . . . . . . . . . . . . . . . . 1

*Alan Frost,* NEW GEOGRAPHICAL PERSPECTIVES AND THE EMERGENCE
OF THE ROMANTIC IMAGINATION . . . . . . . . . . . . . . . . . . . . . . . . . . . . . . 5

*David Mackay,* A PRESIDING GENIUS OF EXPLORATION:
BANKS, COOK, AND EMPIRE, 1767 - 1805 . . . . . . . . . . . . . . . . . . . . . . 21

*Howard T. Fry,* ALEXANDER DALRYMPLE AND CAPTAIN COOK:
THE CREATIVE INTERPLAY OF TWO CAREERS . . . . . . . . . . . . . . . . . . . . 41

*Glyndwr Williams,* MYTH AND REALITY: JAMES COOK AND
THE THEORETICAL GEOGRAPHY OF NORTHWEST AMERICA . . . . . . . . . . 59

*Robin Fisher,* COOK AND THE NOOTKA . . . . . . . . . . . . . . . . . . . . . . . . 81 ✔

*Christon I. Archer,* THE SPANISH REACTION TO COOK'S
THIRD VOYAGE . . . . . . . . . . . . . . . . . . . . . . . . . . . . . . . . . . . . . . . . . . . . 99

*Terence Armstrong,* COOK'S REPUTATION IN RUSSIA . . . . . . . . . . . . . 121

*Sir James Watt,* MEDICAL ASPECTS AND CONSEQUENCES
OF COOK'S VOYAGES . . . . . . . . . . . . . . . . . . . . . . . . . . . . . . . . . . . . . . . 129

*Bernard Smith,* COOK'S POSTHUMOUS REPUTATION . . . . . . . . . . . . . . 159

*Rüdiger Joppien,* THE ARTISTIC BEQUEST OF CAPTAIN COOK'S
VOYAGES . . . . . . . . . . . . . . . . . . . . . . . . . . . . . . . . . . . . . . . . . . . . . . . . . . 187

*Michael E. Hoare,* TWO CENTURIES' PERCEPTIONS OF JAMES COOK:
GEORGE FORSTER TO BEAGLEHOLE . . . . . . . . . . . . . . . . . . . . . . . . . . . . 211

NOTES . . . . . . . . . . . . . . . . . . . . . . . . . . . . . . . . . . . . . . . . . . . . . . . . . . . 229

INDEX . . . . . . . . . . . . . . . . . . . . . . . . . . . . . . . . . . . . . . . . . . . . . . . . . . . 265

The Contributors . . . . . . . . . . . . . . . . . . . . . . . . . . . . . . . . . . . . . . . . . 277

# List of Illustrations

1. The *Resolution* and the *Discovery* anchored in Ship Cove, Nootka Sound, p. 82
2. Bird form rattle from Nootka Sound, p. 87
3. Indian village at Yuquot, Nootka Sound, p. 93
4. Engraving of house interior, Yuquot, p. 94
5. Indian man and woman of Nootka Sound, p. 102
6. Indian dance on the beach at Friendly Cove, p. 117
7. *The Death of Cook* by John Webber, p. 170
8. *View of Owhyhee one of the Sandwich Islands* by Francis Jukes, p. 170.
9. *Death of Captain Cook* by George Carter, p. 171
10. *Death of Captain James Cook* by D.P. Dodd, p. 171
11. *Death of Cook*, lithograph, p.172
12. Frontispiece to *The British Nepos*, p. 173
13. Frontispiece to Banke's *New System of Geography*, p.176
14. *The Apotheosis of Captain Cook,...*, p. 177
15. *The Death of Cook* by Johann Zoffany, p. 178
16. *Navigation, or the Triumph of the Thames* by James Barry, p. 181
17. "Persons and dresses of the inhabitants of the South Sea Islands," engraving, London, 1778, p. 189
18. Engraving from Teodoro Viero's *Raccolta di... Stampe*, p. 192
19. Crayon drawing done for Viero's *Raccolta di... Stampe*, p. 192
20. Engraving from *Raccolta di... Stampe*, p. 193
21. Engraving from St.-Sauveur's *Encyclopédie des voyages*, p. 193
22. Etching from St.-Sauveur's *Costumes civils*, p. 197
23. Pen and wash drawing for a plate in *Costumes civils*, p. 197
24. Etching from *Encyclopédie des voyages, p.* 198
25. *Tableau des découvertes du Cap^ne Cook & de La Pérouse*, p. 200
26. Wallpaper stripe from Dufour's series *Sauvages de la mer Pacifique (1804)*, p. 201
27. Aquatint from Stuart and Kuyper, *De Mensch...*, p. 201
28. Aquatint from Stuart and Kuyper, *De Mensch...*, p. 205
29. Illustration from Ferrario's *Il costume antico e moderno*, p. 208
30. Illustration from *Il costume antico e moderno*, p. 209
31. Pen and wash drawing, Lipperheidesche Kostumbibliothek, Berlin, p. 209

# List of Maps

1. Manuscript map (1729) of Bering's discoveries of 1728, p. 58
2. Detail from a Russian manuscript map of the voyage of Mikhail Gwosdev, 1732, p. 61
3. Map by Philippe Buache, Paris, 1752, p. 62
4. Gerhardt Müller's *Nouvelle Carte* (1758), p. 63
5. Russian manuscript map of the explorations of Peter Krenitsyn and Mikhail Levashev, 1767-8, p. 65
6. Spanish manuscript map of 1775, p. 67
7. A Map of the New Northern Archipelago by J. von Stahlin (1774), p. 69
8. Russian manuscript map of the explorations of Lieut. Ivan Synd, 1765-8, p. 78
9. Detail from *A General Chart exhibiting the Discoveries made by Capt. James Cook* by Henry Roberts (1784), p. 80
10. Sketch map of Nootka Sound, p. 95
11. Spanish map of Friendly Cove, p. 111

# List of Tables

1. Incidence of Sickness and Mortality on the Second Voyage, p. 134
2. Incidence of Sickness and Mortality on the First Voyage, p. 141
3. Incidence of Sickness and Mortality on the Third Voyage, p. 149
4. Early Signs of Some Vitamin B Deficiencies, p. 156

# Introduction

*Robin Fisher & Hugh Johnston*

THE essays in this volume are a selection from the proceedings of the conference "Captain James Cook and His Times" held at Simon Fraser University in the spring of 1978. The occasion for the conference was the bicentennial of Cook's arrival at Nootka Sound, on the west coast of Vancouver Island, on 29 March 1778. Over the past ten years a series of bicentennial celebrations has traced the path of Cook's great voyages of discovery to the south and the north Pacific. The call for commemorative lectures in New Zealand and Australia in 1969-70 brought from the New Zealand historian John Cawte Beaglehole the mild complaint that these celebrations were keeping him from doing more useful work on Cook.[1] Eight years later, at Simon Fraser University, the name that came into discussion almost as frequently as Cook was Beaglehole, and his work underlay the substance of every session.

J.C. Beaglehole, apprenticed in the history of New Zealand ("the only thing you could write a thesis about in those days"[2]), master of the dusty depths of colonial constitutional history, and a student of the eighteenth century, first tackled Cook in the context of writing *The Exploration of the Pacific*, which was published in 1934.[3] It was then that the idea of a full length study of the man first presented itself to him, a project that was finally launched in the late 1940s with the co-operation of the Hakluyt Society and the financial support of the New Zealand government. He threw himself into the task of editing a true text of Cook's journals, of undoing the mischief of Hawkesworth, the editor of the first voyage, and of improving upon Douglas, the more faithful editor of the second and third voyages. Thus in 1955, 1961, and 1967 the three successive volumes of *The Journals of Captain James Cook* were published, along with the two-volume *Endeavour Journal of Joseph*

*Banks* in 1962: a rich lode which other scholars immediately began to mine. He started drafting the life of Cook in 1967, the year in which he retired from Victoria University of Wellington, and, at this point, one can sympathize with his regret at any interruption. J.C. Beaglehole died on 26 March 1971, and his masterly and almost universally acclaimed *Life of Captain James Cook* appeared in 1974.[4]

Beaglehole's *Cook* offers as complete a study as one could expect a single scholar to produce. It is to be admired not just for its thoroughness but also for its erudition, style, and scholarly integrity. Having read Beaglehole, one might ask if there is anything else to say. The answer, as these papers show, is that Beaglehole's editions of the journals make possible a reassessment not only of Cook but, to some extent, of Beaglehole. He has paved the way, not closed it off. It is a measure of the power of his contribution that in the past few years much valuable scholarship has come to maturity.

Like any biographer, Beaglehole focussed on his subject. The lens of his scholarship threw an intense light on Cook, but sometimes cast a shadow on those who surrounded him. In his paper on "Cook's Posthumous Reputation," Bernard Smith has pointed out how the eulogists of the late eighteenth century excluded other individuals from their orations lest mention of their achievements diminish those of the hero. To some extent, perhaps, Beaglehole shared this tendency. Cook was his hero, and other men were sometimes judged harshly. David Mackay, Howard T. Fry, and to some extent Michael E. Hoare all assert the importance of men who were Cook's contemporaries. Joseph Banks, Alexander Dalrymple, and the two Forsters[5] made fundamental contributions to Cook's voyages. Clearly their careers were profoundly influenced by their association with Cook. But it is also true that Cook's stature was enhanced, not diminished, by the men that surrounded him. As the old Maori saying, which Beaglehole uses to sum up Cook, has it, "a veritable man is not hid among many."[6]

Perhaps surprisingly, given Beaglehole's exhaustive work, there are even some new perspectives emerging on Cook the man. Research prompted by bicentennial celebrations is producing new insights into Cook's early life in Yorkshire and the extent to which local connections explain his otherwise curious decision to join the Royal Navy in 1755. The last few years of Cook's life also bear re-examination, and Sir James Watt provides intriguing new evidence on the state of Cook's health on the third voyage and, therefore, on the often erratic behaviour that finally culminated in his death at Kealakekua Bay on 14 February 1779.

Beyond the man himself, there is his reputation, not limited to England but truly European. The dimensions of his influence emerge in the papers of Bernard Smith, Terence Armstrong, Christon I. Archer and Rüdiger Joppien. We see Cook mythologized and, through Smith and Armstrong, follow the fate of a reputation which, both in Europe and Russia, was attended by as many vicissitudes as his navigation. These papers suggest that history, like mythology, is the product of the time in which it is written, a point that is also taken up by Michael E. Hoare in his essay on Cook's biographers. In the areas of the imagination and art, as Alan Frost and Rüdiger Joppien show us, and in nearly every aspect of contemporary science, Cook's discoveries contributed to currents of thought that ran strongly for decades to come. Usually the influence was creative, but not always. Sir James Watt reiterates the point that Cook's conclusions actually retarded the search for a satisfactory treatment for scurvy on Royal Navy vessels.[7] But in other areas the new geography established by Cook was accompanied by the discovery of new intellectual worlds. Cook was, of course, the harbinger of a surge of imperial expansion that was to have a profound effect on the Pacific. But there was also a reverse flow of influence. The Pacific affected Europe, and the papers on this theme follow in the wake of Bernard Smith's extremely influential work on the *European Vision and the South Pacific*.[8]

It has been from the south Pacific that much of the best Cook scholarship has come, a trend that is confirmed in the pages of this volume. The antipodean domination is most clearly exemplified by Beaglehole. Indeed, T.H. Beaglehole has suggested in the Preface to his father's *Life of Captain James Cook* that it was a book that perhaps only a New Zealander could have written.[9] Certainly, down to the last poetic sentence, the *Life* reveals a great understanding of, and empathy for, the south Pacific and its people. J.C. Beaglehole, along with Bernard Smith, had a formative influence on a generation of younger scholars, some of whose work is contained in this book. Partly because, in the past, much emphasis has been laid on the south Pacific, our intention has been to assert the importance of the north. Clearly Cook was growing more and more weary on the third voyage, and although he was not as thorough as he might have been as he searched for the northwest passage, Glyndwr

Williams shows how he contributed to the emergence of a definite coast-line out of the clouds and fogs of cartographers' imaginings. As in the south, Cook's influence did not end with his departure, and Christon I. Archer explains how the appearance of his account of the third voyage taught the Spanish the importance of publicizing their own efforts to explore the northwest coast of America. By then, however, it was too late, for Cook's presence on the coast resulted in the development of the sea-otter trade and the influx of British and American traders.

Another aspect of Cook's explorations that demands attention, in both the north and south Pacific, is their consequences for the indigenous people. Here, in the tradition of Beaglehole's "Note on Polynesian History,"[10] the methods of historians and anthropologists need to be brought together in an effort to achieve some understanding of both sides of the relationship that developed between Cook's men and the people of the Pacific. Hitherto, European writing has been dominated to a considerable extent by the "fatal impact" view,[11] which tends to obscure any reciprocity that may have existed in the contact situation. The extension of this line of thought, sometimes expressed at the conference, is the notion that there are two points of view on Cook's presence in the Pacific—that of the European and that of the Pacific people—and that these views are necessarily distinct and different. In his paper, Robin Fisher tries to show that a reciprocal relationship, which neither group dominated and both benefitted from, developed between Cook's men and the Indians of Nootka Sound. If nothing else, both cultures also have in common the subsequent manipulation of Cook's memory to suit current social and political concerns.

As the prefaces and footnotes of his volumes indicate, J.C. Beaglehole, like all scholars, drew on the knowledge of others. Yet he dominated the field of Cook studies in a way that no individual now can or, perhaps, ought to do. To carry the task further, to better understand the full scope of Cook's explorations and their impact, it is necessary to bring together people from many disciplines, individuals with different expertise but with a common interest. Those who participated in Simon Fraser's Cook conference demonstrated that, like the voyages themselves, Cook studies are now very much a co-operative enterprise.

# New Geographical Perspectives
# and the Emergence of the
# Romantic Imagination

*Alan Frost*

COMMODORE John Byron's 1764 circumnavigation effectively began a second great age of modern European exploration which did not conclude until there was little left of the world to chart.[1] In the next forty years Wallis, Carteret, Bougainville, Cook, Phipps, La Pérouse, Bligh, Malaspina, D'Entrecasteaux, Vancouver, Baudin, and Flinders sailed to the edges of the world, often among reefs or on lee shores, often with ships crank, often short of provisions and almost every other necessary, greatly extending knowledge of the world's oceans, and raising another new world for Europeans to comprehend as an entity in time and space.[2]

These extensions of European knowledge involved much more than simple exploration. The second half of the eighteenth century saw the beginnings of scientific exploration and survey of, and collection in, vast regions of the globe. So thoroughgoing were their endeavours that large portions of Cook's and Vancouver's charts, for example, were superseded only in this century. Banks and Solander returned from Cook's first circumnavigation "laden with the greatest treasure of Natural History that ever was brought into any country at one time by two persons,"[3] and Cook's second and third voyages resulted in more such treasure. Pallas and his colleagues journeyed under the auspices of the Russian Academy of Science. Sparrman and Masson collected widely in southern Africa. The Bartrams botanized eastern North America. Humboldt sent back shiploads of specimens from tropical America. In the nineteenth century, analytical workers made these collections a basis of modern science.

James Cook stands at the head of these explorers. In the course of his three voyages between 1768 and 1779, he sailed farther, and farther out of sight of land, than any before him. He discovered and rediscovered islands and island groups in the Pacific Ocean. He charted the coasts of New Zealand, eastern Australia, and northwest America, and in doing so showed that the legendary *Terra Australis* did not exist. The first to do so, he crossed the antarctic circle not once only, but three times, reaching at his farthest point South 71°10'. He sailed through the Bering Strait into the Arctic Ocean, to reach 70°44' North. When he died at Kealakekua Bay, Hawaii, on 14 February 1779, "in an affray with a numerous and tumultuous body of the natives," he had, as a contemporary said, "fixed the bounds of the habitable earth, as well as those of the navigable ocean."[4]

Sometimes in fortuitous, but more often in deliberate ways, too, Cook's endeavour was central to the whole. The Royal Society and the Admiralty, for example, mounted Phipps's northern voyage in the wake of Cook's first and second ones, and Cook's voyages were subsequently models for those of La Pérouse, Vancouver, Baudin, and Flinders, among others. Sparrman, the distinguished Swedish naturalist, joined the *Resolution* at the Cape in 1772, and left it there in 1775. In the later 1770s, William Hodges went to India to pursue the interest in tropical scenes he had developed during Cook's second voyage. In 1786, the year in which he helped plan the British colonization of New South Wales, Banks sent Ledyard, who had also sailed with Cook, to walk across Siberia. He then sent A.P. Hove to collect in India, and Mungo Park to do so in Sumatra. The great naturalist took a leading part in the founding of the Association for the Exploration of the Interior Parts of Africa in 1788, and then oversaw the despatch of Ledyard and Park in search of the Niger River. Humboldt was impelled to his great journey by George Forster's stories from his voyage with Cook and by Hodges's painting of tropical nature. At the turn of the century, Banks sent Caley and Brown to collect in Australia.

The British public were greatly interested in the Pacific explorations. J.R. Forster wrote in 1772 that "circumnavigations of the globe have been of late the universal topics of all companies."[5] Hawkesworth's narrative of Bryon's, Wallis's, Carteret's, and Cook's voyages appeared in 1773 and was quickly reprinted, and a second edition appeared in the same year. Cook's *A Voyage to the South Pole* appeared in May 1777 and sold out on the first day; a second edition followed in the same year, a third in 1779, and a fourth in 1784. Cook's and King's *A Voyage to the Pacific Ocean* appeared in June 1784, priced at 4½ guineas, and sold out in three days. Other accounts of these voyages, by Cook's companions and compilers, also appeared quickly, as publishers took advantage of the public's interest, and there were more than one hundred editions and impressions of these between 1770 and 1800.

In the scenes they described, of course, but also to a significant degree in their outlooks and sensibilities, the authors of exotic voyages and travels differed from those who confined their progress, and descriptions, to Europe. Such latter authors as Thomas West, William Coxe, William Gilpin, and Horace-Bénedict de Saussure, for example, responded to European scenes within limits set by their social and aesthetic traditions, so that they praised in measure as they saw signs of established habitation, past or present (cities and villages, formalized vistas, cultivation, ruins), or as they saw nature, by "her own most beautiful exertions," forming herself into either "sublime" scenes, or "harmonious compositions of diverse effects."[6]

On the other hand, such explorers as Cook, the Forsters, Bartram, Bruce, Hearne, Vancouver, Park, and Humboldt knew that the human scenes they found differed radically from European ones and that the differences provided much food for thought about received notions concerning man and society.[7] As well, though they inevitably responded to natural scenes which reminded them of European ones, their curiosity, habits of scientific observation, and lack of formalized appreciation of landscape led them also to describe vistas which European aesthetic conventions did not accommodate—ones of vast ocean distances and continental masses, Edenic islands, tropical nature, and frozen arctic and antarctic wastes. In doing so, they themselves began to develop new and less intellectually limited modes of perceiving nature; at the same time, of course, they provided extensive materials for others soon to 'further this process.[8]

Whereas writers have described the place of the eighteenth century discoveries in the subsequent course of European politics, economics, and sciences, the influence of the new geographical perspectives on the European imagination is a much less charted area. A few adventurers (most notably, Bernard Smith) have touched its shores, but it remains very much a *terra incognita*. What is the extent of its coastlines, and the nature of its landscapes? Do reefs guard all its shores; are its beaches of crushed corals or black volcanic sand; do pines crown its headlands? What lies beyond the coastal mountains? Do great rivers cross it east to west, or north to south? Do glaciers freeze, or deserts waste, its interior? Are the inhabitants white, of a large Stature, strong, industrious, and courageous, who have neither King nor Prince, but all combine together in the Form of a Commonwealth, choosing Governors only to make the Lazy work, to punish Offenders, and to render Justice to every Man—or are they rather dreaded anthropophagi?

The first thing that he who seeks out this *terra incognita* discovers is that, unlike its historical progenitor, it is not just a transient conjunction of cloud and ocean, but is real. William Wordsworth, Samuel Taylor Coleridge, and Robert Southey, those leading members of the first generation of British Romantic poets, were all born during the decade of Cook's voyages (Wordsworth in 1770, Coleridge in 1772, Southey in 1774), and they grew up in the ethos of interest in the world beyond Europe that those voyages created. They learned of this world from stories they heard or read in early childhood, from books they studied, or from people who taught them at school, and from works they read for instruction or pleasure.[9] Not travelling in person beyond Europe, they became armchair travellers about the great globe, in the manner that their poetic mentor Cowper so nicely described:

> *[Man] travels and expatiates, as the bee*
> *From flower to flower, so he from land to land;*
> *The manners, customs, policy of all*
> *Pay contribution to the store he gleans;*
> *He sucks intelligence in every clime,*
> *And spreads the honey of his deep research*
> *At his return, a rich repast for me.*
> *He travels, and I too. I tread his deck,*
> *Ascend his topmast, through his peering eyes*
> *Discover countries, with a kindred heart*
> *Suffer his woes and share in his escapes,*
> *While fancy, like the finger of a clock,*
> *Runs the great circuit, and is still at home.*
> (*The Task*, Book IV, 11.107-19)

Either with the primary narratives, or via extracts in other works,[10] these poets ranged much about the world in the 1790s and early 1800s, sometimes in "realms of gold, and goodly states and kingdoms," but as often, as befitted their rather solitary dispositions, in waste landscapes and seascapes. Repeatedly, they saw themselves in terms of the experience they gained vicariously through their readings. Thinking of

Cook's perilous passage up the east Australian coast, for example, Southey wrote to G.C. Bedford, "Will you write soon upon this subject and believe me semper paratus—either boldly to launch the bark with full sails or creep along the coast in search of the bay of contentment, perhaps in danger of splitting upon a hidden rock."[11] In mind of Bligh, Coleridge wrote to Poole, "What am I to do then?—I shall be again afloat on the wide sea unpiloted & unprovisioned."[12] Southey founded his dream of pantisocracy in the European experience of Tahiti.[13] Applying one of Bartram's descriptions, Coleridge described Wordworth's mind as a towering beech tree.[14] Knowing the feelings of all those who go down to the sea in ships, he asked Poole to "pardon the childish impatience which I have betrayed. The Sailor, who was borne cheerily a circumnavigation, may be allowed to feel a little like a coward, when within sight of his expected & wished for port."[15]

Across the 1790s, too, these poets developed a theoretical place for the literature of exotic travel in their poetics. Coleridge wrote to Joseph Cottle in April 1797, "I should not think of devoting less than 20 years to an Epic Poem. Ten to collect materials and warm my mind with universal science. I would be a tolerable Mathematician, I would thoroughly know Mechanics, Hydrostatics, Optics, and Astronomy, Botany, Metallurgy, Fossilism, Chemistry, Geology, Anatomy, Medicine—then the *mind of man*—then the *minds of men*—in all Travels, Voyages and Histories."[16] Wordsworth told Tobin concerning his projected masterwork, *The Recluse*, in March 1798, "I have written 1300 lines of a poem in which I contrive to convey most of the knowledge of which I am possessed. My object is to give pictures of Nature, Man, and Society. Indeed I know not any thing which will not come within the scope of my plan.... If you could collect for me any books of travels you would render me an essential service, as without much of such reading my present labours cannot be brought to a conclusion."[17] And Southey's poetic practice in the years 1794-1805 shows that he, too, then developed the view which he later expressed via Montesinos: "There are now few portions of the habitable earth which have not been explored, and with a zeal and perseverance which had slept from the first age of maritime discovery till it was revived under George III. In consequence of this revival, and the awakened spirit of curiosity and enterprise, every year adds to our ample store of books relating to the manners of other nations, and the condition of men in states and stages of society different to our own. And of such books we cannot have too many."[18]

With their intrinsic interest in the literature, and with their theoretical views concerning its use, the first Romantics returned from their voyages and travels with rich freights of images, which they used extensively in their poetry from the mid-1790s onwards. Wordsworth, for example, borrowed for *The Borderers* (1796-7) from Bligh; for "The Complaint of a forsaken Indian Woman" (1798) from Hearne; for "Ruth" (1798-9) from Bartram; for "The Affliction of Margaret" (1801?/1804) from Keate; for "To H.C. Six Years Old" (1802) from Carver; and for moments of *The Prelude* (1797-1805) from Bartram and other accounts of North America from Barrow, Bruce, Dampier, Park, Purchas, and others.

The very strange case of Captain Bligh, Fletcher Christian, and the mutiny on the *Bounty* provided the poets with a powerful *exemplum*. Wordsworth had it in mind when he wrote *The Borderers*, for he made Rivers's fall into misanthropic vengeance turn on his mutiny against, and abandonment of, his captain during their voyage to Syria:

> On our voyage
> *Was hatched among the crew a foul Conspiracy*
> *Against my honour, in the which our Captain*
> *Was, I believed, prime Agent. The wind fell;*
> *We lay becalmed week after week, until*
> *The water of the vessel was exhausted;*
> *I felt a double fever in my veins,*
> *Yet rage suppressed itself;—to a deep stillness*
> *Did my pride tame my pride;—for many days,*
> *On a dead sea under a burning sky,*
> *I brooded o'er my injuries, deserted*
> *By Man and nature;—if a breeze had blown,*
> *It might have found its way into my heart,*
> *And I had been—no matter—do you mark me?*
> *. . . . . . . .*
>
> *One day in silence did we drift at noon*
> *By a bare rock, narrow, and white, and bare;*
> *No food was there, no drink, no grass, no shade,*
> *No tree, nor jutting eminence, nor form*
> *Inanimate large as the body of man,*
> *Nor any living thing whose lot of life*
> *Might stretch beyond the measure of one moon.*
> *To dig for water on the spot, the Captain*
> *Landed with a small troop, myself being one:*

*There I reproached him with his treachery.*
*Imperious at all times, his temper rose;*
*He struck me; and that instant had I killed him,*
*And put an end to his insolence, but my Comrades*
*Rushed in between us: then did I insist*
*(All hated him, and I was stung to madness)*
*That we should leave him there, alive!—we did so.*
### Act IV, ll. 1689-1720

The parallels between Rivers's story, and Christian's, are of course extensive. Both are introspective characters who feel humiliation deeply. Both have a harsh captain who goads them into rebellion and whom they abandon. Both are pawns of other crew members. Both are tormented by guilt. And, as Jacobus remarks, Rivers's "I had been deceived.... I had been betrayed" echoes Christian's comment, as reported by Bligh: "I am in hell—I am in hell."[19]

We may also see that Coleridge had the *Bounty* mutiny somewhere in mind when he wrote "The Ancient Mariner." He had previously been interested in Christian's story, for he included an "Adventures of *Christian*, the mutineer" amongst his projects in 1795/6. In June 1797, he heard Wordsworth read *The Borderers* (and notice how many of the images in the just-quoted passage reappear in Coleridge's poem). In November, he and Wordsworth planned the ballad while walking to Linton—he mentioned his friend Cruickshank's dream of the skeleton ship, and Wordsworth suggested the ideas of the guilty sailor and the albatross.[20] "A soul in agony" describes Christian as aptly as it does the Mariner. And as well, there is the distinct and fascinating prospect that Coleridge may have modelled the Mariner's secret return on a like one by Christian—but confirmation of this must of course await proof that Christian did indeed return.[21]

Such borrowings give some indication of the poets' interest in, and use of, the literature of exotic travel, but they suggest only inadequately this literature's more general influence in the poetry. These overt borrowings are rather the tips of the iceberg visible above the water, or the fragments which have crumbled from it. The bulk of the iceberg—at once the profoundest, and the least tangible, aspect of the influence on the new geographical perspectives on the Romantic imagination—lies in the presence of a distinctive motif of the voyage or journey.

In eighteenth-century literature, the voyage or journey motif usually functions only as action. The typical eighteenth-century venturer is imbued with the spirit of the Grand Tour. There are strange sights to behold, and foreign countries to see, but he beholds and sees from the perspectives which he brought to the voyage. He is a tourist, and he remains essentially unchanged by the experiences of his voyage.

In Romantic literature, on the other hand, the motif functions both as action and as a profound psychological pattern. Physically, the Romantic voyage or journey is one in which the protagonist proceeds into an unknown or "unnatural" world for which his previous experience has not prepared him, in the end to reach a haven (sometimes, a paradisal island), or to return home. Imaginatively, it is a progress from inherited and conventional views of reality to the perception of a new and very different reality. The Romantic venturer, as he proceeds, relinquishes received truths and comfortable ways of knowing experience. Beginning his travels with little imagination or sensitivity, by their end he has become aware of his own humanity, of the humanity of his fellow men, of their mutual kinship, and of the variousness of the world. The Romantic venturer is a man in active search of reality and, much more than his eighteenth-century counterpart, he is involved in, and altered by, what he experiences on his way.[22]

Cook, and such fellow explorers as Bougainville, Bligh, Bruce, Dampier, La Pérouse, Vancouver, and Park set forth this motif in its physical aspect (and sometimes, interestingly, in its imaginative or spiritual one) as they penetrated previously unexplored oceans or territories and faced their un-European realities, and as they reached island or inland havens or returned home. And Wordsworth, Southey, and Coleridge all instinctively acknowledged the presence and primacy of these models in their poems of Romantic journeying and voyaging.

Wordsworth presented one version of the motif in *The Prelude* when he described his progress from his Cumberland childhood and his conventional education into the chaos of London and the failing French Revolution, then to his return to rural simplicity and the realization of his creativity. His use of the journey motif of course most relates to the facts of his own life, but he also drew upon exotic travel literature at various points as he developed it—for example, upon Bartram, Bruce, and Columbus, Park, and Dampier.

Coleridge borrowed similarly for "The Rime of the Ancient

Mariner." The larger pattern of Cook's second voyage, to the point of his deciding to cross the Pacific by following in Quiros's path, is England southward to antarctic seas, eastwards to the mid-Pacific, then northwards to the equator. The Mariner's voyage shows this same pattern: "How a Ship having passed the Line was driven by Storms to the cold Country towards the South Pole; and how from thence she made her course to the tropical Latitude of the Great Pacific Ocean ... " And there are close parallels between each section of Cook's voyage and the Mariner's voyage, until the Mariner's ship is becalmed and the narrative becomes increasingly psychological and symbolic.

The opening stanzas of Part II of the poem, for example, describe the Mariner's ship's leaving the desolate antarctic regions for tropical waters and the attendant changes in the weather; and just as every feature of the Mariner's antarctic voyage has its parallel in Cook's voyage so, too, does every feature of the Mariner's course northward have its parallel in Cook's course northwards from 71°S latitude to Easter Island and the Marquesas, and in precisely the same sequence.

The Mariner tells first how they have swung north, and how (in the 1800 version) the bad weather continues:

> The Sun now rose upon the right,
>   Out of the Sea came he;
> Still hid in mist; and on the left
>   Went down into the Sea.
> (1800: ll. 81-4)

Cook writes of 30 and 31 January 1774, when he had turned north: "thick fog continuing with showers of snow, gave a coat of ice to our rigging of near an inch thick. In the afternoon of the next day the fog cleared away at intervals; but the weather was cloudy and gloomy, and the air excessively cold" (Cook, I, 269). The Mariner tells of how "the good south wind still blew behind" (l. 85); Cook, of how the wind blew "very fresh" from the WSW from 6 to 12 February (I, 272). The Mariner tells of calms: "For all averr'd, I had kill'd the Bird / That made the Breeze to blow" (ll. 91-2); Cook, of how there were light breezes and calms from 12 to 15 February (I, 272). The Mariner tells of a sudden, and significant change in the weather:

> Ne dim ne red, like God's own head,
>   The glorious Sun uprist:
> Then all averr'd, I had kill'd the Bird

> That brought the fog and mist.
> 'Twas right, said they, such birds to slay
> That bring the fog and mist.
>
> *(ll.93-8)*

Cook tells of how "As we advanced to the North, we felt a most sensible change in the weather. The 20th, at noon, we were in the latitude of 39°58′ South, longitude 94°37′ West. The day was clear and pleasant, and I may say, the only summer's day we had had, since we left New Zealand. The mercury in the thermometer rose to 66" (I, 273). The Mariner tells how "The breezes blew, the white foam flew, / The furrow follow'd free" (*ll.* 99-100); Cook, how they had good winds for five days (I, 273). The Mariner tells of calm: "Down dropt the breeze, the Sails dropt down" (*l.*103); Cook, of having "a calm for near two days together, during which time the heat was intolerable" (I, 275). The Mariner remarks that "We were the first that ever burst / Into that silent Sea" (*ll.*101-2); and Cook, of course, was at this point coming north from the Antarctic Ocean in which he had been the first man to sail, into an area of the southern Pacific where, again, no man had been before him.

To this basic pattern, Coleridge added details and images from many other works. For the flashing watersnakes, for example, he drew on Bourzes, Cook and King, Bartram, Dampier, and Purchas; for the Hornèd Moon, from Bruce, Cook, James, and Hawkins; for the lightning, from Bartram and Hawkesworth; for the ice, from Benyowszky, Cook, and James, among others; for the albatross, from Shelvocke.[23] The result was a magical poem of romantic voyaging in which he traced a man's desperate progress to an awareness of community, a realization of love.

In their early writings, the Romantic poets drew upon the literature of the European tour for numbers of their natural descriptions. As they found their authentic voices, however, they turned from the intellectually based, and limited, modes of perception which inform this literature, and sought to realize instead an "immediate, visual, ... sensuous," and encompassing apprehension of nature and of reality.[24] As they did this, they turned increasingly to the literature of exploration, and from the mid-1790s onwards, images, scenes, and motifs from this literature crowd their poetry and inform some of their most significant pieces.

There are extensive and profound links between the geological perspectives which explorers presented in the second half of the eighteenth century and the poetry which Wordsworth, Coleridge, and Southey wrote c. 1795-1805, and these are present as a consequence of shared perception and purpose.

As Lowes points out,[25] the direct, lucid, and concrete vocabulary of the explorers offered the poets examples of that language which they sought, in which men "convey their feelings and notions in simple and unelaborate expressions" and which, "arising out of repeated experience and regular feelings is a more permanent and far more philosophical language than that which is frequently substituted for it by Poets."[26] Cook, for example, told his readers that he lacked "the advantage of much school education" and therefore asked them to excuse the inaccuracies of his style. He wrote, however, in the manner that the Royal Society fostered from its inception, of vigorous and unembellished observation and report.[27] In what other might he (or anyone else) have better described man's endurance than when he told how, on 23 December 1773, in 67°S latitude, longitude 138°E, they "made sail to the West, under double reefed top-sails and courses, with a strong gale at North, attended with snow and sleet, which froze to the rigging as it fell, making the ropes like wires, and the sails like boards or plates of metal. The sheaves also were frozen so fast in the blocks, that it required our utmost efforts to get a top-sail down and up; the cold so intense as hardly to be endured; the whole sea, in a manner, covered with ice; a hard gale, and a thick fog (I, 257)." How better might one show a man in the agony of knowing that he places himself beyond redemption than by quoting Christian when Bligh has asked him, on being forced from the *Bounty*, "if this treatment was a proper return for the many instances he had received of my friendship?" Christian, wrote Bligh, "appeared disturbed at my question, and answered, with much emotion, 'That,— captain Bligh,—that is the thing;—I am in hell—I am in hell" (p. 8). How better to show such agony, unless it be in Coleridge's way in "The Ancient Mariner"?

Again, since the explorers described without strong intellectual or aesthetic presuppositions, the poets found in their narratives images, situations, and motifs appropriate to the delineation of what they saw to be mankind's fundamental emotional and spiritual states. Equally with such "incidents of common life" as Wordsworth's escapade in the stolen boat, his experience on Salisbury Plain, his return to the Wye, his meetings with Cumberland shepherds, or Coleridge's confinement with his scalded foot, for example, Christian's setting Bligh adrift, Bruce's finding the springs of the Nile, or Cook's navigating the Antarctic Ocean revealed "the primary laws of our nature." Sometimes, even the poets found the explorers' moments to be of such power and import as to be, in effect, "spots of time," possessing "A vivifying Virtue, whence . . . / . . . our minds / Are nourished and invisibly repaired."

The moments which the poets found in the explorers' narratives did of course differ in important ways from those which they encountered in their daily lives. The explorers' vistas were exotic and not familiar or homely ones, and, in offering parallels to European situations and experiences, they inevitably suggested what might be universal. Yet the manner and detail of the explorers' descriptions meant that their vistas were not abstract ones, and the use of these therefore allowed the poets to depict essential emotion in, at once, both a particularized and a general way. Hearne's description of the northern Indians' savage custom of abandoning their weak, for example, allowed Wordsworth to show "the last struggles of a human being at the approach of death, cleaving in solitude to life and society."[28]

Again, in being defined in books, the explorers' vistas were not subject to the vicissitudes of the poets' personal remembrance and revaluation. In such poems as "This Lime-Tree Bower My Prison," "Frost at Midnight," "Tintern Abbey," and *The Prelude*, the poets identify themselves as individuals in time and place by commingling present with past, and envisaged future, moments and scenes (and that they can do so is of course of great comfort to them).[29] The moments which they recur to in Bartram, or Cook, or Hearne, or Bruce, however, exist independently of their personal continuums and are therefore, in a sense, timeless. And the poets realized and took advantage of this difference. As Keats found with Ruth, and Arnold with Sophocles, for example, Wordsworth, Coleridge, and Southey found that the explorers' experiences helped them to know that which they shared with all others.

We see well the intimate connection which these poets felt between what was ultimate in their experience, and the displays of humanity in the explorers' narratives, in such poems as "Ruth" and "The Complaint of a forsaken Indian Woman," "The Ancient Mariner" and "Kubla Khan," and *Madoc*. Nowhere is it clearer, however, than in Wordsworth's early drafts of "The Ascent of Snowdon," a passage which we find, perhaps even more than Coleridge's ballad, to be the quintessential one of Romanticism, enacting as it does the union of the individual psyche with the "mighty Mind" that suffuses the universe.

The drafts[30] show that as he developed his evocation of his experience on Snowdon, Wordsworth kept himself aware of other moments of the "analogy betwixt / The mind of man and nature." Two of these, as we would expect, are from his childhood and in their imagery and import clearly rank as "spots of time."[31] The others, though, are of distinctly different origin. "To these appearances which Nature thrusts / Upon our notice, her own naked work / Self-wrought, unaided by the human mind, / Add others more imperious," he writes, and continues:

> those I mean
> Which on our sight she forces, calling man
> To give new grandeur to her ministry,
> Man suffering or enjoying. Meanest minds
> Want not these monuments, though overlook'd
> Or little prized; and books are full of them,—

He then describes Columbus and his sailors "in unknown seas / Far travell'd," seeing their compass needle "take / Another course, and faltering in its office/Turn from the Pole"; Sir Humphrey Gilbert giving himself up to the waves; Mungo Park's extremity; and Dampier, adrift in a canoe, threatened with the eternal conjunction of sea and sky:

> Kindred power
> Is with us, in the suffering of that time
> When, flying in his Nicobar Canoe
> With three Malayan Helpers, Dampier saw
> Well in those portents of the broken wheel
> Girding the sun, and afterwards the sea
> Roaring and whitening at the night's approach,
> And danger coming on, not in a shape
> Which in the heat and mettle of the blood
> He oft had welcom'd, but deliberate
> With dread and leisurely solemnity.
> Bitter repentance for his roving life
> Seized then upon the ventrous mariner,
> Made calm, at length, by prayer and trust in God.
> Meanwhile the bark went forward like an arrow

*Shot from a bow, the wind for many hours*
*Her Steersman. But a slackening of the storm*
*Encouraged them at length to cast a look*
*Upon the compass by a lighted match*
*Made visible, which they in their distress*
*Kept burning for the purpose. Thus they fared*
*Sitting all night upon the lap of death*
*In wet and starveling plight, wishing for dawn,—*

Wordsworth did not include these analogies in his finished text, but, clearly, they helped him to define the quality of his individual experience, and to understand, and to convey, its universal aspects.

The first Romantics, then, used the new geographical perspectives to find the universal moments in the flood of those they knew individually, and to develop their evocation of these. Wordsworth moved towards saying this explicitly when he told Tobin that he needed travel books in order to make his pictures of "Nature, Man, and Society." Coleridge did likewise when he told Cottle that he would know "the *mind of man*—then the *minds of men*—in all Travels, Voyages and Histories." But William Gilbert, for all his chaos, put it best. In a work that Wordsworth, Coleridge, and Southey each praised, because in it he spoke for them, Gilbert observed:

A man is supposed to improve by going out into the *world*, by visiting *London.* Artificial man does; he extends with his sphere; but alas! that sphere is microscopic: It is formed by minutiae, and he surrenders his genuine vision to the artist, in order to embrace it in his ken. His bodily senses grow acute, ever to barren and inhuman pruriency; while his mental become proportionately obtuse. The reverse is the Man of Mind: He who is placed in the sphere of Nature and of GOD, might be a mock at Tattersall's and Brookes's, and a sneer at St. James's: He would certainly be swallowed alive by the first *Pizarro*, that crossed him:—But, when he walks along the River of Amazons; when he rests his eye on the unrivalled Andes; when he measures the long and watered Savannah; or contemplates from a sudden Promontory, the distant, Vast Pacific—and feels himself a Freeman in this vast Theatre, and commanding each ready produced fruit of this wilderness, and each progeny of this stream—His exaltation is not less than Imperial. He is as gentle too as he is great; His emotions of tenderness keep pace with his elevation of sentiment; for he says, "These were made by a good Being, who unsought by me, placed me here to enjoy them." He becomes at once, a Child and a

King. His mind is in himself; from hence he argues and from hence he acts; and he argues unerringly and acts magisterially: His Mind in himself is also in his GOD; and therefore he loves, and therefore he soars.[32]

Contemporaries saw James Cook as a "British Columbus" and made his achievements yardsticks to measure those of others. One reviewer saw that the astronomer Herschel, "from whom more important discoveries may be expected," "may justly be deemed among astronomers what Cook is among navigators, the first of his profession, the explorer of worlds unknown, and the illustrator of the celestial, as our great navigator was of the terrestrial, globe." La Pérouse told the British officers in New South Wales that Cook had "left nothing to those who might follow in his track to describe, or fill up." After news of Bligh's open-boat voyage had reached England, William Windham exclaimed to James Burney, "But what officers you are! you men of Captain Cook; you rise upon us in every trial." Coleridge's friend Thomas Poole told Henrietta Warwick that his trivial affairs filled his fleeting moments "as effectually as the sublime pursuits of a Cook, or the pernicious politicks of a Pitt." Vancouver saw that Cook's labours would "remain a monument of his pre-eminent abilities, and dispassionate investigation of the truth, as long as science shall be respected in the civilized world; or as long as succeeding travellers, who shall unite in bearing testimony to the profundity of his judgment, shall continue to obtain credit with the public."[33]

When we think of the majesty and mystery of this extraordinary man's achievements—who being constantly at sea from his youth, proceeded without the advantage of much school education; who, with the assistance of a few good friends, passed through all the stations belonging to a seaman, from an apprentice boy in the coal trade, to a post captain in the Royal Navy; who set himself to be the first discoverer, even was it nothing more than sands and shoals;[34] and who therefore ranged the Pacific Ocean, from Australia and New Zealand in the southwest, to the northern coasts of America, from the antarctic to the arctic circles—we may also know that, in giving the reality he did to the world beyond Europe, he marked the imagination of his age in the manner of a Newton or a Darwin.

# A Presiding Genius of Exploration: Banks, Cook, and Empire, 1767-1805

## David Mackay

IN the bleak winter of 1799 the naval storeship *Porpoise* had a tempestuous passage between the Downs and Spithead. The master was alarmed about what he described as the "extreme crankness" of the vessel and he was pessimistic about her chances of reaching the final destination in New South Wales. In a stiff breeze the *Porpoise* was unable to carry her mainsail or topgallant sails, while with all her sails set in lighter winds she lumbered along at a slower pace than much smaller craft. According to the master, the reason for her predicament was obvious. Situated square in the middle of the quarter deck was a thirteen-foot by seven-foot "plant cabin" weighing five tons.[1] Why was a naval vessel encumbered with such an odd construction? Sir Joseph Banks, we may safely conclude, was once again messing about with boats.

You will remember that more famous incident twenty-seven years earlier when there had been alterations to another vessel bound for the Pacific. Cook's *Resolution* had had her waist heightened and an additional upper deck built with a raised roundhouse on top. On that occasion, too, the modifications made the ship "so exceedingly crank" that she seemed likely to capsize in a moderate breeze with only reefed topsails, jib and main topmast sails set. Although Lieutenant Clerke professed his willingness to "go to Sea in a Grog Tub, if desir'd or in the *Resolution* as soon as you please," the commander, and presumably the rest of the crew, were more circumspect and the *Resolution* was removed to Sheerness to be restored to her original state. The alterations had been made for Joseph Banks and his large retinue, but on seeing that they were to be removed the scientist raged a little and then abruptly withdrew from the expedition after crossing swords with the Admiralty, the Navy Board, Sir Hugh Palliser and even James Cook.[2]

Notwithstanding this foolishness, Banks's travelling experiences over the previous six years had elevated him from the stolid ranks of the landed gentry and laid the foundations for a remarkable career. While most young men of his background chose to complete their education in the salons of Paris and art galleries of Italy, he ventured into that nursery of seamen around the coast of Newfoundland in the company of his young naval friend, Constantine Phipps. Undaunted by the continual seasickness and occasional fever which that voyage produced, Banks on 25 August 1768 set out with James Cook on a journey around the world in the bark *Endeavour*. Given the comfortable alternatives which lay open to him, this was a remarkable step. Perhaps too much emphasis has been placed on the "effortlessly superior" way in which Banks foisted himself upon the *Endeavour*: "He simply, we may say, walked on board the *Endeavour*, elbowed her officers out of the way, and was made welcome."[3] If the manner of doing this was characteristic of the English gentlemen of fortune of that age, the decision itself was not. Few men of fortune would have given up the leisure of their estates to sleep in a hammock in the six-foot square cabin of a tossing ex-collier. The naturalist Gilbert White was dismayed by his fortitude: "The circumnavigation of the globe is an undertaking that must shock the constitution of a person inured to a sea-faring life from his childhood: & how much more that of a landman?"[4]

This three-year voyage was to colour the young scientist's experience and leave an impression which strongly influenced his later life. His views on exploration, plant transfer, and imperial expansion were to be profoundly affected by it. Although so much on the voyage was new, Banks's curiosity was never satiated; he was a voracious observer and collector whose enthusiasms baffled or bemused his shipmates. Throughout the Pacific and East Indies he encountered new plant and animal species, many of which seemed to have considerable economic value. Some of the new lands seemed suitable for European settlement, or to offer prospects for lucrative trade.

Although his journal is unrevealing about shipboard life, later events make clear that Banks learned an enormous amount about ships and seamen. Despite an unfortunate but shortlived breach in their friendship in 1772, Banks had a deep respect for the resolution, skill, and authority of the commander. The social gulf between Banks and Cook was comfortably bridged by their common and complementary talents. Both were in

their way practical men: down to earth, efficient, professional, concerned for accuracy and probity. Cook accepted and exploited Banks's
greater learning; the scientist admired and depended upon the commander's experienced judgement of ships and men. Although there
were occasional minor differences, Cook was generous in terms of men
and materials whenever Banks wished to collect natural history specimens or visit indigenous peoples. By the time he landed at Deal on 12
July 1771, Banks's tutelage aboard the *Endeavour* had made him one of
the best informed laymen on the subject of navigation.

How then do we explain the crisis over the refitting of the *Resolution*?
The *Endeavour* voyage had also inflated his ego. The young man had
been carried away by his own enthusiasm and overwhelmed by a sense
of self-importance. Historians have generally accepted J.C. Beaglehole's
stern irony: "[Banks] had come to conceive of himself as a sort of presiding genius of exploration. From the moment it was known that he was
to go on a second voyage communications descended upon him as if he
were another department of state. . . . "5

By the time of the *Porpoise* voyage, I wish to suggest, Banks was the
"presiding genius of exploration" and he had virtually become "another
department of state." The voyage with Cook had provided the crucial
early boost to his career, but it was the intellectual and administrative
context in which the voyages of Cook and his followers went forward
that enabled Banks to achieve his extraordinary authority. In this
sense he is a representative figure. His career tells us much about the
nature and role of science in the eighteenth century; the particular
legacy of Cook's voyages; the expansion of governmental functions; the
problems of imperial administration following the American War of Independence. To untangle these threads it will be useful to return to the
subject of the plant cabin on the cumbersome vessel *Porpoise* in the
winter of 1799.

In contrast to the Home Office, Banks from the outset had regarded
New South Wales as a potential supplier of valuable commodities to the
mother country. On his suggestion, the first fleet had carried a number
of useful plants to Botany Bay, and Governor Phillip had collected specimens of cotton, indigo, coffee, and the cochineal insect in Brazil on the
passage out.6 The storeship *Guardian* was the first vessel bound for New
South Wales to carry a "plant cabin," "garden hutch," or "botanic
conservatory," as it was variously called, and the initiative again came

from Banks. In April 1789, he pointed out to the Undersecretary of State, Evan Nepean, that the infant colony was sparsely supplied with European fruit trees and other plants "as are useful in Food or Physic," and there were few indigenous productive species. Drawing on his experience on the *Endeavour*, he suggested a range of plants that would do well in the colony and yet survive a long sea voyage.[7] Despite its own inertia on such colonial matters, the ministry welcomed his initiative, and the *Guardian* was remodelled according to Banks's plans to carry a considerable quantity of plants and numerous animal specimens. By the time the ship had collected more plants at the Cape in November 1789, she was a veritable ark, but she came to rest not in Botany Bay but on an iceberg in 44° South. While the waterlogged vessel managed to survive a gruelling nine-week voyage back to the Cape, most of its precious live cargo was lost.[8]

Although Banks raised the possibility of shipping live plants on subsequent sailings, it was not until the selection of the *Porpoise* that a suitable ship presented itself. Once again Banks's proposal was readily accepted by the Home Office and the Admiralty; a plant cabin was constructed, plants purchased, a gardener appointed, and after some unforeseen changes of plan the bulk of the cargo eventually reached New South Wales.

Banks had been remarkably persistent in this endeavour over the years. The Admiralty had been surprisingly tolerant, and the Pitt Ministry receptive and co-operative. Apart from the grumbles of Mr. Scott, commander of the *Porpoise*, the enterprise seems to have been accepted as a rational and routine undertaking. But can we view it with such equanimity? Consider the problems. The *Guardian*'s encounter with an iceberg points not only to the perils of the voyage, including storms and violent seas, but also to the enormous climatic variations the plants would be subject to during the voyage of six months or more. Eighteenth-century sailors were a rough lot and not likely, one would have thought, to have shown great concern for a collection of greenery taking up valuable space on the quarterdeck. Salt spray would have been destructive to live plants, but in the tropics the cabin would need to have been well ventilated and watered. An eighteenth-century storeship was infested with cockroaches, mice, and rats, as well as an assortment of dogs, goats, cats, hens, monkeys, and parrots belonging to the crew.[9] The obstacles to a successful trans-shipment would seem to be enormous, and yet most of the delicate cargo survived the arduous journey.

By the time of the *Porpoise* voyage, however, such transfers of plants had become almost routine. The plant cabin on the vessel was identical to that which Banks had erected on Vancouver's *Discovery*. Long before Bligh's *Bounty* voyage, Banks had accumulated a wealth of information about the care of plants at sea, and in 1773 he had synthesized a list of instructions for the shipping of tropical varieties.[10] The breadfruit expeditions testify to the remarkable success of his methods and the willingness of some commanders to follow them. He was also concerned with attempts to introduce a variety of food and cash crops into India to avert the problem of famine and to provide commodities for the European investment. Under the Board of Trade's auspices he planned and directed an expedition to the Gujarat to procure the seeds of fine cotton for transplantation to the West Indies.[11] Throughout the world an extraordinarily large contingent of Banksian collectors were busy gathering plant specimens and shipping them back to their mentor in Soho Square. The *Porpoise* voyage was therefore only one part of a large Banks-directed movement to exploit botanical knowledge for productive purposes within an imperial framework.

Clearly his own voyage with Cook provided much of the inspiration for these enterprises, but Banks was also working within a tradition which had much earlier origins. There was a strong utilitarian and empirical strain to eighteenth-century science, and by the time of Cook's voyages this had begun to influence maritime exploration and the development of empire. Two most notable achievements of the English branch in the scientific revolution of the seventeenth century were: firstly, the acceptance that the practical benefits to be gained from scientific knowledge were the true measure of its worth; secondly, the rejection of knowledge based on teleological or metaphysical explanations.

Francis Bacon's *New Organon* had eschewed the pursuit of science for transcendent goals and pushed activity towards establishing dominion over nature and understanding the operation of natural laws. Once natural forces were understood and controlled, they could be redirected to benefit mankind as a whole. From the foundations of the Royal Society onwards, these essentially utilitarian aims of science, and especially natural history, were preserved. The *Philosophical Transactions* of the Royal Society strongly emphasized this concern, and it was reflected in the charters of the provincial societies which proliferated in the eighteenth century: the Gentlemen's Society of Spalding, Lunar Society of Birmingham, Derby Philosophical Society, and many smaller bodies.[12] The express aim of the Royal Society of Arts, Manufactures and Commerce, formed in 1754, was to exploit scientific knowledge for practical purposes, and it pushed this forward with generous offers of bounties and premiums.[13] On 9 March 1799, during a meeting at the home of Sir Joseph Banks, the Royal Institution was founded with the purpose of "diffusing the knowledge and facilitating the general introduction of useful mechanical inventions and improvements; and for teaching, by courses of philosophical lectures and experiments, the application of science to the common purposes of life."[14]

The emphasis on observation and experiment can also be traced back to the seventeenth century and is seen in Newton's acceptance that science should be established on the basis of facts derived from close observation and experimental verification. This empiricism in the sciences suggests a clearly defined and accepted approach to any particular problem. Detailed observation of natural phenomena; accurate measurement; study of behavioural change; description of phenomena exclusive (insofar as it was possible) of value judgements and in a mode that was recognizable to and accepted by other scientists; classification and categorization of phenomena; the formulation from the accumulated data of general principles which were to be checked by experiment and reexamination—this was the preferred methodology of the eighteenth century.

The Baconian influence and empirical strain was particularly powerful in botany, and in a sense reflected its origins as a science. The first accurate observation and description of plants had been by those wishing to exploit them for medicinal purposes, such as the Greek Dioscorides, whose *De Materia Medica* represented an early attempt to standardize and systematize plant names. Although in the seventeenth century several men came close to developing a universal system of classifying plants, the real breakthrough came from the Swede Carl von Linné in the 1730s. His comprehensive system, based on the characteristics of the reproductive organs of plants, is no longer of great importance, but in its time it produced order and reason where undifferentiated and incomprehensible chaos had previously reigned. Linné did botany another great service, one symbolized by the Latin styling he always gave himself (Linnaeus). He introduced an international botanical nomenclature, giving all plants a generic and a specific name in Latin, and publishing all his works in that language. More than any other science, botany exhibited the co-operative and public aspects which Bacon had tried to infuse into all the sciences.

As I have already suggested, Banks was very much heir to this strong Baconian tradition, and his earliest associations with botany were in this mould. It was also to be expected that someone with his impeccable gentry origins would be naturally drawn to such a philosophy of science. The fortunes of his family had advanced substantially as a result of "scientific" farm management in the early eighteenth century, and Banks himself sustained the improving impulse when he came into the inheritance in 1764. Arthur Young held up his estates at Revesby as an ideal model for the innovative landowner.[15] This interest in agricultural progress manifested itself in some of Banks's later activities: his introduction of the merino sheep into England, and management of the first flocks; his promotion of new strains of wheat and other grains and his researches into diseases in corn; his further efforts for the drainage of the fens.[16]

After 1770, Banks was England's most prominent disciple of Linnaeus and the most enthusiastic proselytizer of his system. The botanical work on the *Endeavour* voyage and the substantial collections which Banks and Solander had brought back reinforced the ecumenical significance of the Linnean taxonomy. Gradually, however, the sphere of his scientific influence extended, until by the time of Cook's death he (BANKS) was the doyen of British applied science generally. He became virtual "Director" of Kew Gardens at about the time the *Resolution* sailed on its first voyage, and from that base he presided over the collecting and distributive functions of a vast botanical *imperium*. From the time of his election to the presidency of the Royal Society in 1778, his powers of patronage were used to the full to promote the interests of science and scientists. It was in this area that his great strength lay. He published little. His individual contribution to scientific knowledge after Cook's voyages was insubstantial. But his natural history collections and Soho Square library were rich in material and always open to the curious and dedicated.[17] He had enormous capacity to generate enthusiasm in others, and the power, wealth and generosity to give that enthusiasm full reign once aroused. Although botany was his first interest, no scientific endeavour was outside the bounds of his own curiosity and therefore beyond his patronage.

However, it is in his belief in the economic importance of plant transfer that Banks's Baconian philosophy is most clearly revealed, for he believed that it was in the imperial context that natural history could be exploited to the best advantage. This global approach was a legacy of his involvement with Cook's voyages and a tribute to the vistas those voyages had opened up. Scientific knowledge coupled with enterprise and industry could be exploited to augment the resources of British colonies for the aggrandizement of the mother country. One can easily understand the attractions of such a philosophy in the years following American independence. Apart from the Spanish imports of bullion from their South American dominions, the wealth of the colonies from the sixteenth century onwards had derived from their tropical vegetable products: spices, sugar, tobacco, dyes, medicinal drugs, tea and coffee, oils. Some of these new products had been introduced into Europe: vegetables such as potatoes, tomatoes and spinach to supplement the diet: exotic trees such as the rhododendron, plane, and cedar to grace the parklands of the nobility and gentry. In such cases botanical gardens provided the reception centres where plants could be acclimatized, propagated and studied.

Many plants, of course, would not grow in temperate climates but could be transferred from one tropical country to another. All European countries with Asian or American empires attempted the introduction of exotic tropical plants to their dominions, the French being particularly active. But in the eighteenth century it was for England that it held the greatest appeal, because she had been something of a latecomer in the scramble for colonies and it often seemed that she got the worst of the pickings. Now spices, dyes, coffee, cocoa, tea and cotton could all be introduced into British colonies and distributed to interested planters, eventually supplying the British market and undercutting European competitors.[18]

Banks was the foremost exponent and proponent of such schemes and he pointed to the vital imperial economic function of botany. He would select species that could be readily transplanted; recommend regions where they might thrive; advise on methods of transporting plants and caring for them at sea; advise on propagating and processing plants, and maintain botanic gardens as reception centres. In this way he was the eighteenth century's most powerful agent in translating the Baconian scientific philosophy into practical realities. More than this he had become the imperial agent of the industrial revolution, fossicking the world for cotton, dyes, coal, and flax for an increasingly mechanized society. I have chosen to dwell on his botanical interests in the colonial setting because these may be seen as a direct outgrowth of his involvement in Cook's voyages, but Banks's function as a scientific entrepreneur extended to almost every area where science could be exploited for practical advantages: from deciding on the coinage of the realm to the organization of voyages of discovery.

It is to the organization of voyages of discovery that I now wish to direct my attention. Lieutenant James King remarked to Banks in October 1780, "it is with real pleasure & satisfaction that I look up to you as the common Center of we discoverers."[19] This was not simply the idle flattery of a man appealing to a powerful patron. From Cook's death onwards, Banks shaped the course of British maritime discovery and managed its practical implementation. Between the return of the *Resolution* and the *Discovery* in 1780 and the capture of Mathew Flinders in December 1803, he played a major role in every significant government expedition and in many private ones as well. In the last years of his life he was still able to influence the voyages of Ross, Parry, and Franklin in search of a Northwest Passage. From the time of the foundation of the African Association in 1788, Banks used his office as president to direct the exploration of that continent, including the travels of Mungo Park.

The pattern of Banks's involvement in the scientific side of such expeditions is well enough known. Apart from his own direct participation in Cook's first voyage, and the withdrawal from the second, he began to place scientific appointees on subsequent expeditions, beginning with the botanist David Nelson on Cook's third sailing. From this point onwards, his influence with the Admiralty was assured. In 1785 a Pole, Anton Hove, was installed on the ship *Nautilus* that was sent out to search for a suitable site for a convict settlement in southwest Africa.[20] Two years later David Nelson was placed in the *Bounty* going out on Bligh's first breadfruit expedition: Christopher Smith and James Wiles were appointed to the second.[21] When the merchant fur trader, Richard Cadman Etches, proposed an expedition to the northwest coast of America in pursuit of sea otters, Banks persuaded him to take along Archibald Menzies as botanist/surgeon to the enterprise.[22] This experience qualified Menzies for a Banks-sponsored place on the *Discovery* under Captain Vancouver.[23] The Admiralty also approached him to find a suitable astronomer for the expedition.[24] The entire scientific party on Flinders's *Investigator*, including a botanist, miner, gardener, astronomer, botanical draughtsman, and landscape painter were appointed by Banks. He also, of course, placed gardeners and plant cabins on the *Guardian* and *Porpoise*.

The willing acceptance by the Admiralty of these adjuncts to maritime exploration requires some explanation. After all, Captain George Vancouver resented the presence of Menzies on his vessel and initially doubted the need for an astronomer. Even Cook had sometimes lost his patience with the men of science.[25] However, successive British governments after 1780 accepted such supernumeraries as a matter of course.

One of the reasons for this must be Banks's powerful advocacy of the scientific role in voyages of discovery. His voyage on the *Endeavour* had pointed to the productive conjunction of exploration and scientific enquiry. He therefore tempted the governments away from a narrow interpretation of geographical discovery, towards a wider view which looked to a general advancement of knowledge on a broad front. The voyages should have as their purpose not only maritime discovery but also the gathering of information which would be of potential value to England, and it is clear that he viewed his own travels in this way. They were evaluating exercises in which the economic and resource potential of new lands was to be carefully analysed. His philosophy in this sense was decidedly imperialistic. On the return of his protegé, Mungo Park, from an expedition to West Africa, Banks told a meeting of the African Association that

> by Mr. Park's means [we have] opened a Gate into the Interior of Africa into which it is easy for every nation to enter and to extend its Commerce and Discovery.... As increased Riches still increase the wants of the Possessors, and as Our Manufacturers are able to supply them, is not this prospect, of at once attaching to this country the whole of the Interior Trade now possessed by the Moors, with the chance of incalculable future increase, worth some exertion and some expense to a Trading Nation?[26]

In pursuit of this object he pressed the government to occupy the whole coast of Africa from Arguin to Sierra Leone.[27]

The instructions that Banks issued to scientists reflected such utilitarian views. They were enjoined to note any new or useful products; to assess the resources in terms of timber and pasture; to examine exposed strata for mineral deposits. The instructions to Matthew Flinders, based on a draft by Banks, ordered him to have an eye for "anything useful to the commerce or manufactures of the United Kingdom."[28] The instructions to Archibald Menzies in 1791 emphasized the need to evaluate the productive potential of all countries the ships visited, and he was also advised to search for deposits of coal, limestone, or other valuable minerals.[29] Menzies's own journal shows how faithfully he attended to his brief, and reveals his constant concern for the intrinsic value of what he found. In the area of King George's Sound in southwest Australia, he described forests and woodlands

> capable of affording an excellent range & good feeding to domestic animals of every denomination,... New Holland has a delightful & promising appearance & we therefore conceive it an object well worth the attention of government in a more particular investigation of it, as it offers fair to afford an eligible situation for a settlement which on account of its nearness & easy access to our settlements in India possessed peculiar advantages not to be derived from the opposite shore.[30]

All the data Menzies gathered were to be handed over to Banks for analysis and report to the government. The gout-bound scientist with his network of collectors and observers therefore acted as a scientific information agency which processed material and made recommendations to ministers.

Banks's role in the scientific side of such expeditions is generally recognized; his function in their general organization is less clearly established, although in this area his association with Cook's voyages left its strongest imprint. Some enterprises, such as the breadfruit expeditions and the voyage of the *Investigator*, were directly instigated by him, and he supervised them from beginning to end. The original plan for the breadfruit expedition was outlined in a letter to Pitt in February 1787, and from this point onwards the government turned the entire organization of the enterprise over to Banks.[31] His part in the management of Bligh's second voyage was equally extensive.[32]

More surprising, perhaps, is his role in Vancouver's voyage. During the height of the Nootka crisis in February 1790, Lord Grenville, the new Secretary of State for Home Affairs, asked Banks for background information on the Spanish voyages up the northwest coast of America and the legitimacy of Spanish claims.[33] When the crisis blew over he was automatically involved in the decision to switch the destination of the *Discovery* from the south Atlantic to the northwest coast of America. Once that decision had been taken, the Home Office and the Admiralty drew heavily on his knowledge in planning the new voyage. Nepean drafted the preliminary plan with the assistance of a note on surveying by Banks.[34] A collection of articles for barter was supplied from a list that he had drawn up for the earlier punitive expedition.

The real depth of his involvement is evident in the drafting of Vancouver's own instructions. As a result of a request from Grenville, Banks provided three sets of instructions for the Secretary of State. The first set gave advice on how Vancouver was to treat Archibald Menzies. The other two were prefaced by a note:

> Enclosed your Lordship will receive the opinions you did me the honor to require from me, concerning the mode of carrying on the intended survey of the N.W. Coast of America in the most Speedy & Effectual manner consistent with the degree of accuracy required in an undertaking intended to be of a General nature.[35]

The first part of these instructions consisted of a technical paper on surveying drawn up after consultation with the geographer James Rennell and Captain Bligh. The second part set out the broader objectives of the expedition and formed the basis for the surveying section of the final instructions of 8 March 1791.

Banks's control of such expeditions undoubtedly reached its peak with the voyage of the *Investigator*. A proper exploration of New Holland had been on his mind for some years, but in November 1800 he persuaded Earl Spencer, First Lord of the Admiralty, to equip a surveying expedition for that purpose, and to give the command of it to Mathew Flinders.[36] From this point onwards the management of the voyage lay in his hands. He appointed the members of the scientific party, stated their salaries and allowances, ordered their equipment, and wrote their instructions and conditions of appointment. He kept regularly in touch with the fitting of the *Investigator*, and installed yet another plant cabin on yet another quarterdeck. Whenever Flinders required substantial alterations, he applied in the first instance to Banks. At one point Banks felt obliged to explain his role, in somewhat understated terms, to the chairman of the East India Company:

It may be necessary to explain to you as a reason for my interfering in this last question which seems wholly out of my way that owing to the present heavy pressure of business in the Admiralty that board have from time to time intrusted me with the execution under their orders of almost every detail of the lesser articles of the outfit of the Ship, hence it is that every part of her affairs are well known to me.[37]

The specialized navigation instruments, charts, accounts of earlier voyages, and articles of barter with indigenous peoples were supplied from lists drawn up by Banks. Those hoping for a place on the vessel knew it was to him that they could most profitably apply. When in February 1801 Flinders was promoted to the rank of commander, he wrote to his mentor that this was something "for which, Sir Joseph, I feel myself entirely indebted to your influence and kindness."[38] When Banks wrote to the Admiralty asking if his suggestions relating to the fate of the journals and plant and animal specimens would be approved, the secretary, Evan Nepean, replied: "Any proposal you make will be approved. The whole is left entirely to your decision."[39] When the time came to draw up Flinders's instructions, Banks again played a substantial role, and he subsequently had alterations inserted at the commander's request. His involvement even extended as far as the naming of the vessel.[40]

Why had the government, and the Admiralty in particular, entrusted the management of such official concerns to a civilian? The explanation, I believe, can be linked to two things: firstly, Banks's position as virtual guardian and exemplar of the Cook tradition; secondly, his general advisory role to government at a time when its functions were expanding beyond the competence of its own administrative resources.

Undoubtedly it was his experience on the *Endeavour* which established Banks as the general director of exploration in the late eighteenth century. By the end of the second voyage, Beaglehole suggests, Banks "had not yet become the general manager of the reputation of Cook, but the way was open to him."[41] By the end of the third voyage his position in this respect was secured. But he achieved more than this. Cook's voyages became the model for subsequent expeditions. Banks became the custodian of that model: the general repository of all the surviving and accumulated knowledge and experience that the great navigator had bequeathed. In developing the overall conceptions of particular voyages, Banks alone retained the respect, authority, and bound-

MURDOCK LEARNING RESOURCE CENTER

less geographical knowledge which inspired governmental trust. Alexander Dalrymple, that difficult character, had been tried and found wanting. Despite the fiasco at the time that Cook's second voyage was being organized, Banks was one of the few persons outside the Navy Board with comprehensive information about the outfitting of ships for maritime exploration, and from the first breadfruit expedition onwards, the Navy Board generally sought his advice.

What were the components of the Cook model insofar as they related to voyages of exploration involving Banks in this period? Although the vessels employed in the Pacific after 1780 were not all Whitby colliers, they were all capacious merchantmen, and "sloops" in naval parlance. In its search for a ship to carry breadfruit the Admiralty specified a "roomy Ship both as to accommodation as well as stowage."[42] The *Discovery*, the *Providence* and the *Investigator* were also beamy merchant ships selected for the same qualities. In the fitting, equipping and manning of the vessels, Cook's example served the Navy Board until Flinders's voyage. When the *Bounty* was being fitted in September 1787, Bligh reported to Banks that "Capt. Cook's supplies are a president [sic] the different boards are govern'd by, and I shall not give them any trouble unless in essential points."[43] Victualling followed the same pattern, the general view being that of "great benefit having been received by the Crews of His Majesty's Ships employed under the late Captain Cook on voyages to the South Seas."[44]

Similarly, in Vancouver's voyage, the *Discovery* was ordered to be fitted, stored, and victualled in the same way as the *Resolution* had been for Cook's second voyage. The same list of ineffective antiscorbutics was put aboard.[45] Almost ten years later the *Investigator* of Flinders conformed to the pattern, although by that time the model had become almost institutionalized by the weight of precedents built up.[46] In some areas this could have positive disadvantages, and Banks reported to Nepean that the astronomer was unhappy about having his salary set at the level that had attained during Cook's voyages.[47]

Even private merchant adventurers paid lip service to Cook's achievement. This was partly so that they might attract the support and patronage of men like Banks, and to give some bogus air of respectability to their often shaky enterprises. Richard Cadman Etches used this as a lever to attract Banks's support for his fur trading expeditions to the northwest coast of America.[48] He could even boast that his commanders,

Dixon and Portlock, had served on Cook's third voyage. The trading voyage of James Strange was undertaken in two ships named the *Captain Cook* and the *Experiment*, and the leader of the expedition approached Banks in 1785 for advice on exploration. The prime objective of this voyage was fraudulently stated to be "exploration for the benefit of navigation," and Strange asked for any instructions which would "in the most distant degree gratify either Public or private Curiosity in so far as related to Science."[49] Robin Hallet has suggested that the influence of Cook's voyage extended to the exploration of Africa under Banks's direction after 1788.[50]

More powerfully perhaps, Cook's influence could be seen in the example and standards that he set. His surveying work and seamanship were held up as the touchstones of quality and industry, and it was so that they should be aware of these standards that Banks loaned his *Endeavour* journals and records to men like Portlock, Bligh, and Flinders.[51] Cook had also lifted something of a psychological barrier. His ships had always returned from their arduous and sometimes perilous voyages with their crews substantially intact.[52] Scurvy, long the fatal deterrent to such expeditions, became less of a barrier to the penetration of the Pacific. Published accounts of his voyages were widely read and appreciated, and became standard manuals for the exploring navigator. He had opened up the world in a geographical sense, making its most distant corners seem accessible and even familiar.

Cook had also shown that the empirical strain which was a strong element in eighteenth-century science could be carried over into the practical arts of seamanship. In this sense he was, like Banks, in tune with the spirit of the age. He was an astute, curious, and yet objective observer. He showed unusual but consistent concern for detail and accuracy—the charts that he drew of Newfoundland were used well into the nineteenth century. He eschewed conjecture and never firmly laid down a coast that he had not seen or traced; every geographical fact had to be verified, and he showed a gentle scorn for the theorizing of geographers such as Dalrymple. Boswell made a laboured effort to describe the quality: "a plain, sensible man with an uncommon attention to veracity. My metaphor was that he had a ballance in his mind for truth as nice as scales for weighing a guinea."[53]

Some of his crews, products of that stern school of seamanship, inherited these capacities and the traditions that went with them. His disciples in this regard infused a whole era of navigation. All the great remaining voyages of the eighteenth century drew on Cook's officers. Bligh, Portlock, Vancouver, Colnett, Riou, and Hergest all got their commands and served with great distinction. These men then passed on their skills and training to a second generation of men such as Flinders and Broughton.

To this body of men Banks became mentor and protector, as Charles Burney pointed out to him in 1791: "You have been such a constant Patron & Friend to all deserving Circumnavigators, who in the late voyages on discovery ventured their lives with Captain Cook & other commanders...."[54] He found them jobs, secured them promotion, helped publish their journals, rescued them from debt and debtors' prison, obtained them pensions, looked after their wives, widows and children, and generally maintained their spirits and skills. Throughout his life he held it as a strict duty to give the officers and relations of Cook first call on his patronage.[55] Cook's own career had illustrated the importance of personnel for successful voyages of exploration, and Banks's knowledge of these men made his advice invaluable in the selection of officers and commanders. The men themselves welcomed his role, aware that he was sustaining a certain *esprit de corps*. He was the patron of discovery, the first line of approach to government on any enterprise. Even foreign explorers approached him for instructions. One of Malaspina's crew members wrote of him in 1789: "No person in the world is so well qualified to give direction & proper counsels in a voyage like this. His experience, his success, & his zeal for the improvement of Natural History make him the proper model for future travellers."[56]

Ultimately, Banks was one of the few men to see beyond the voyages themselves to the prospects which they held out. In this way too he was ensuring that Cook's achievement be fully recognized. Exploration represented an investment in men, materials, and enterprise which should not be squandered. New resources had been discovered in the form of timber, flax, whales, seals, and sea otters, as well as numerous trading goods for the eastern markets. Some of the new countries were suitable for European habitation and could be turned into valuable colonial assets. The discoveries had opened the Pacific to British ships and given a new flexibility to commercial as well as to naval enterprise. In the opening chapter of his account of the *Bounty* voyage, William Bligh clearly expressed this philosophy:

The Object of all former voyages to the South Seas, undertaken by command of his present majesty, has been the advancement of science, and the increase of knowledge. This voyage may be reckoned the first, the intention of which has been to derive benefit from these distant discoveries.[57]

That Banks was able to give some practical expression to this philosophy was due to the increasing weight that he carried in the counsels of His Majesty's ministers.

In October 1791 Banks wrote to a French botanist: "I have also myself been for some time more than I ought diverted from the study of Botany, my favourite occupation by having undertaken other occupations Chiefly of a public nature."[58] Between 1785 and 1805 he frequently complained about the burden of such official work. As early as 1788 he asked Lord Hawkesbury to intervene with the prime minister so that he might be excused from the office of high sheriff of Lincolnshire:

Occupied as I am here in the Scientific Service of the Public & ready nay happy to find time to do anything I might be thought capable of by those who are intrusted with the Executive Government of the Country I have if I do not flatter myself a claim for my discharge.[59]

From the middle of the 1780s onward he regularly attended meetings of the Privy Council Committee for Trade and Plantations to give evidence on scientific and colonial matters. In 1797 he was made a full member of the Privy Council so that his status might be formalized.[60] As a matter of course the government consulted him on the supply of raw cotton, naval stores, explosives, dyestuffs, corn supplies, the coinage, mineral supplies, the East India trade, whaling, and of course voyages of discovery. He became the government's principal advisor on colonial affairs until well into the nineteenth century and became the East India Company's acknowledged counsellor on all matters relating to natural history and vegetable products. No other man outside government in this period exercised such a pervasive influence over such a wide area of official activity. Sir Joseph Banks, as his own letter to Hawkesbury suggests, had become "another department of state."

His links with the government and his considerable supply of patronage never depended on political power. Although he dabbled in his legitimate sphere of influence in Lincolnshire elections, he avoided being drawn into central politics. When offered some official position relating to New South Wales in February 1789, he turned it down in the belief that the colony's interest would best be served by his own impartiality.[61] In a letter to a French correspondent in 1798 he described what seems to have been an unwritten agreement: "The ministers of my Government Sometimes allow me to influence their Decisions in matters of science, but it is an implied Compact between them & me that I am never to meddle with their opinions of Political measures."[62]

The government's preparedness to draw on Banks's advice can be ascribed to causes other than his own energies and talents. It is clear that in the changed political circumstances after the American War of Independence, the administrative tasks confronting the government temporarily outstripped the capacity and resources available to handle them. The traditional, limited conception of the functions of government were being replaced as a result of pressures forcing ministries to take a broader view of their responsibilities. In these circumstances, bodies such as the Board of Trade, Home Office and the Treasury often found themselves helplessly out of their depth and they showed a willingness to call on specialist advice and professional expertise from outside the ranks of government.[63] Sir Joseph Banks in this way became a one-man department of scientific and industrial research, to be consulted and employed on practically all matters relating to science, exploration, and the colonies.

In colonial affairs especially, the government was eager to have Banks's assistance. There his views were decidedly mercantilist and imperialist. Given his Baconian learnings, it was perhaps inevitable that he should view the acquisition of colonies as the logical consequence of discovery. As I have tried to show, this was the underlying assumption behind the instructions that he wrote for scientists such as Menzies and Robert Brown. He believed that colonies should produce raw materials for consumption by the growing industries of the mother country, and his plans for plant interchange and even convict colonies buttressed this philosophy.

Drawing on his experiences on board the *Endeavour*, Banks in 1779 testified before a Commons Committee on the suitability of New South Wales as the site for a convict colony. Later he supported a private plan recommending Botany Bay for this purpose, and he certainly had a hand in the planning of the first fleet. The scientist regarded the penal settlement with paternal affection, conscious of the fact that it was pretty much his own brainchild. There was more than just nostalgia and wishful thinking in his remark to Governor Hunter that he would like to be able to settle down to a peaceful existence on the banks of the Hawkesbury.[64]

In the years after 1787 the Pitt government became dependent on Banks for the administration of that territory, which became Cook's most substantial legacy in colonial terms. In almost every aspect of the running of the colony they deferred to his opinion. His illness or a sojourn at Revesby could throw colonial affairs into confusion and hold up the despatch of business. In January 1802, changes in the colonial administration caused some dislocation, as one correspondent wrote to the botanist Robert Brown in Sydney: "The confinement of S. Jos. B. to his bed for this month past has prevented him from setting the new department of State, to which the colonies are since Mr. Addington's administration alotted, to work...."[65] Banks had come a long way since the days spent collecting plant specimens in Botany Bay as a supernumerary on Cook's *Endeavour*.

Banks's role in sending plants to New South Wales on the *Porpoise* can therefore be explained in several ways. And there is a final, perhaps symbolic twist to our tale. We left the *Porpoise* at the beginning of this paper in an exceedingly crank state, the consequence, her testy commander argued, of the five-ton plant cabin on her quarterdeck. When the Navy Board referred the problem to Banks, he was calm and conciliatory, agreeing that the plants could be safely stowed below decks but quietly questioning the commander's estimate of the plant cabin's weight. His own calculation suggested it was only three tons three hundredweight. Perhaps the unstable state of the ship was due to other causes and would remain, with or without the plant cabin?[66] Banks's surmise proved to be correct. Lieutenant Governor King remembered seeing the *Porpoise* in frame, when he had observed that she was about twelve feet too short for her breadth, giving her sailing qualities more like those of Lieutenant Clerkes's grog tub than those of a transport vessel. King reported to the comptroller of the Navy Board that even without the plant cabin the ship was top-heavy, and she was hard to bring about.[67] On lee shores such as those in New South Wales she would be a disaster. Eventually the vessel was condemned and a captured Spanish ship was adapted for the purpose, renamed *Porpoise*, equipped with plant cabin and contents, and despatched to Botany Bay. Banks's association with the Navy Board had become so close following Cook's voyages that the irony of the situation may have escaped him.

# Alexander Dalrymple
# and Captain Cook: The Creative
# Interplay of Two Careers

## Howard T. Fry

ALEXANDER Dalrymple's lifelong commitment to British commercial expansion, which was to be seen in the mid-nineteenth century as a principal cause of the country's prosperity at that time, began when he was preparing to take over the responsibilities of the secretaryship at Fort St. George, Madras. He came to dream of founding an emporium in the Malay Archipelago whose tentacles would reach out as far as the northern coasts of New Guinea and of the Australian continent, and it was to enable him to take personal control of a preliminary voyage of reconnaissance, in furtherance of this project, that Dalrymple had persuaded the governor at Madras to allow him to forego the succession to the lucrative post of secretary.

This decision was reached at the moment when Commodore Wilson arrived at Madras determined to seek a new Eastern Passage to Canton via the northwest coast of New Guinea. It was thereupon decided that Dalrymple's forthcoming voyage should include a close survey of this passage, and though wartime developments were to cause the cancellation of this part of his mission, nevertheless the close attention that he now paid to earlier voyages along the northern coast of New Guinea was the origin of the theory that he first put forward in 1762, and which was later adopted by Captain Cook, that the Solomon Islands and Dampier's New Britain were one and the same group of islands.

Since Dalrymple had never been trained for the sea, his friend Captain Thomas Howe, a younger brother of Admiral Howe, gave him some intensive training in practical navigation. Combined with his own flair for mathematics, this was to result in his becoming, over the next five years, a highly skilled navigator who was both able and willing to adopt the new scientific methods that were then coming into use.

At first Dalrymple shared the command with an experienced seaman named Captain George Baker, but it was this early experience of a divided command which convinced Dalrymple that this was an unsatisfactory basis upon which to run any such expedition, and which was to persuade him to turn down a similar proposal for the *Endeavour* in 1768. It needs to be stressed, however, that Beaglehole was mistaken in his assertion that Dalrymple "had never, in the technical sense, commanded a ship," but had merely served for "two or three years in the schooner *Cuddalore*, sailed by Captain Baker."[1] In fact, Dalrymple had had sole command of the *Cuddalore* from 24 November 1759, when Baker had returned to Madras to take command of the *London*. Dalrymple remained in positions of command during the next five years, and was given a captain's certificate by the East India Company in 1764.

This whole enterprise was a remarkable achievement on the part of a young man who was only twenty-two years of age at the time that he first set sail on the *Cuddalore* in 1759. The Sulu project, which was very much his own brainchild, introduced the free-port system to the Malay Archipelago and was the forerunner and conscious inspiration of the later free port of Singapore.[2] Clearly Dalrymple was a man of proven powers of leadership and of rare imaginative insight and originality of mind.[3]

*The preparations for 1768*

When Dalrymple returned to England in 1765, a vigorous program for the exploration of the Pacific was already under way. For years he had specialized in the history of exploration, and his name had already been drawn to the attention of the First Lord of the Admiralty. He could not hope to be employed in any purely naval enterprise, but he knew that the Royal Society would be sending an expedition to the Pacific to observe the transit of Venus in 1769, and if it could be induced to combine astronomical observations with exploration, then he might indeed aspire to play a major role. For even in a purely nautical sense, his comparative inexperience as a seaman was counterbalanced by his proven abilities in the new scientific methods of navigation[4] as well as in cartography, hydrography, and surveying, skills in which the common run of seamen did not excel. Furthermore, in addition to his unchallenged historical expertise, there was the important consideration that the area to be explored lay within the monopoly of the powerful East

India Company. Since any new discoveries in the Pacific would inevitably be intimately linked with existing trade in the Orient, and Dalrymple had already played the leading role in initiating an extension of the company's trade in the Malay Archipelago, this combination of skills and circumstances made his claims to lead the new expedition very strong indeed. All in all, his qualifications were highly competitive.

To strengthen his claims, Dalrymple now concentrated upon preparing the most authoritative collection of voyages relating to the South Pacific yet published, in the conviction that a thorough knowledge of what had previously been achieved was an essential prerequisite for a successful program of exploration. Dalrymple realized that apart from serving as a dependable reference, his work would also have to avail as a piece of promotional propaganda to show both the Royal Society and the public at large the unique opportunity that the 1769 expedition would provide for exploration of unprecedented significance. For Dalrymple knew that many were opposed to further expansion,[5] while within the Royal Society itself some could be expected to fear that the risks inherent in exploration might jeopardize the success of the scientific program. In fact, as late as 18 December 1767 Maskelyne was anticipating a voyage of two years' duration, an estimate that was clearly based upon the supposition that it would be occupied with astronomical observations alone.[6]

To overcome the inertia emanating from such circles, Dalrymple therefore set himself the task of making out so strong a case for the existence of a southern land, or lands, that his contemporaries would feel that the risks and expense involved would be fully justified by the likelihood of substantial rewards to follow.

The failure of later historians to appreciate the need for such promotional propaganda has led to much misconceived criticism about the "woeful lack of scepticism" that abounded. It is nonsensical to depict Dalrymple as being "pursued by a profound fatality" because he had the courage to put forward theories that he knew full well might be proved wrong. It was the cautious and noncommittal scepticism advocated by his leading twentieth-century detractor which was precisely the attitude that Dalrymple saw as the greatest threat to action, since, as he himself said, "it is so much easier to treat with derision than to investigate."[7] His own attitude was that "errors may lead to truth." Like all successful promoters, he spoke with conviction, keeping any secret doubts to himself.

The important point was that his theories should be sufficiently in accord with the knowledge of his time so as to be plausible, and sufficiently enticing and challenging to inspire further exploration. In stirring up interest and enthusiasm, in attempting to locate previous discoveries from the very inadequate data available, in demonstrating the size and necessary location of any landmasses posited by the traditional counterpoise theory, thus giving Cook precise problems to investigate, and in bringing together the most authoritative accounts then known of earlier voyages, Dalrymple was performing an invaluable public service. The triumphs of Cook's first two voyages were to be his vindication.

## Cultivating the Royal Society

To press his claim, Dalrymple made himself known to the Royal Society, and on 20 March 1766 he attended his first meeting at a time when plans were already being formulated for observing the transit of Venus.[8]

On 12 November 1767 the Royal Society set up a strong committee to work on the preparations for observing the transit. Included among its members were Captain (later Vice-Admiral) John Campbell, Nevil Maskelyne, and Dr. Bevis, an astronomer who had formerly worked with the celebrated Dr. Halley. Such a committee could be relied upon to set exacting standards for anyone who aspired to lead its expedition. When this committee met on 17 November 1767 in order to decide upon the most suitable sites from which to observe the transit, and draw up a preliminary list of qualified observers, among those selected was Dalrymple, described as "a proper person to send to the South Seas, having a particular turn for discoveries, and being an able navigator, and well skilled in observations." Coming from such an able committee, that recommendation speaks for itself.

On 3 December this committee met to finalize the list of observers, and Maskelyne reported that Dalrymple had already expressed a willingness to go. This prompted the latter to clarify his position. Three months earlier, the directors of the East India Company had once more begun to give serious consideration to Dalrymple's far-reaching Sulu scheme, for which he was the obvious choice for leader. If he were offered that position, it would give him the chance to refashion the whole pattern of the East India Company's trade with China. In view of that challenging new opportunity, on 7 December he wrote to the Royal Society to express his enthusiasm for its forthcoming expedition but to stress that he was not prepared to serve "as a Passenger going out to make the observation or on any other footing than that of having the management of the ship intended for the service."[9]

Apparently the Royal Society was already anticipating that it would have to rely upon the Royal Navy to transport its scientific observers to the Pacific.[10] The nearest precedent for this was the voyage of 1698-1700, "the first sea voyage undertaken for purely scientific purposes,"[11] when the scientist in charge, Edmund Halley, had been given the command of the vessel; this precedent would not have been lost upon Halley's old collaborator, Dr. Bevis, a member of the committee. Furthermore, if exploration was also undertaken, there was the further example of Dampier who, despite his civilian status, had been given the command of a naval vessel because of his expertise regarding the area to be explored.

These were pertinent historical precedents for the part that Dalrymple hoped to play. This was a role that had been commonplace in Tudor times[12] and which still prevailed in France, where Bougainville, with far less nautical experience than Dalrymple, had been given command of his notable voyage of circumnavigation on exactly the lines that Dalrymple envisaged. In this light, he would control the strategy of the voyage and the general management of the ship, while the master would sail the vessel. In 1769, when discussing the planned expedition to Sulu, Dalrymple spelled out his concept. Arguing that if he were to be in charge of that expedition, then he must also have command of the ship, he wrote: "I have a commission of five years' standing as captain of a ship in the Company's service: although I consider myself well enough qualified to navigate a ship . . . I am very far from pretending an equal ability in every branch; . . . I would therefore be better pleased to have a master than a chief-mate appointed under me."[13]

Captain Campbell, who had been suggested for the command, clearly did not want it, so the committee of which he was a member now accepted Dalrymple's application for the post. Thus on 18 December 1767, when those who had been selected attended the Royal Society to receive their official appointments, the president of the society formally recommended that Dalrymple be given command.[14]

Captain Campbell now began to play a key role. It was he who acted as

Dalrymple's first host when the latter began his regular attendance at the weekly meetings of the Royal Society. Furthermore, Campbell was a personal friend of Sir Edward Hawke, the First Lord of the Admiralty, and after King George III had instructed the Admiralty to provide a suitable vessel for the expedition, it is reasonable to suppose that it was Campbell's influence which at first persuaded Hawke to accept Dalrymple as commander of the vessel despite his civilian status.

On 10 March 1768, the very day on which the Navy Board began to widen its search for a suitable vessel, Dalrymple was the president's guest at a meeting of the Royal Society when the choice of ship was presumably an important topic of conversation.[15] Eleven days later, the Royal Navy, finding no proper vessel of its own, turned its attention towards the purchase of a merchant ship, and Campbell's influence is again suggested in the decision to investigate one of the "cat-built" vessels in the Thames that were similar to the ship on which he had begun his own seagoing career.[16]

Thereafter, according to Dalrymple's own account, "the Admiralty approving of his being employed for this service, [he] accompanied the surveyor of the Navy to examine two vessels that were thought fit for the purpose. The one he approved was accordingly purchased." There is every reason to believe this account. As the appointed captain, Dalrymple was the obvious man for the surveyor to consult, and his statement agrees exactly with the recorded evidence, which shows that two, and not three ships (as stated by Beaglehole) were examined and reported upon.[17] Furthermore, Dalrymple, a strictly truthful man, first made and later repeated his claim in the most public manner possible, yet even Hawkesworth, while seeking to answer Dalrymple's various criticisms, quoted but did not challenge this particular claim. If it had been untrue, he would surely have done so. Dalrymple explained his preference for the *Endeavour* on the ground that the ability to carry an extra anchor and cable might prove a matter of "the utmost consequence."[18] The importance of this choice of ship was given heavy emphasis by Captain Cook himself when he wrote: "I am firmly of opinion that no ships are so proper for discoveries in distant, unknown parts ... as was the *Endeavour*. For no ships of any other kind can contain stores and provisions sufficient.... Little progress had been hitherto made in discoveries in the Southern Hemisphere. For all ships which attempted it before the *Endeavour*, were unfit for it."[19]

It was only now that Hawke was forced to change his mind about the command, yet it is noteworthy that Dalrymple, although the one to lose most by the change, went out of his way to clear Hawke of all personal responsibility for what followed. It was due, he said, to threats that Hawke "would be exposed to a parliamentary impeachment if he employed any but a Navy officer."[20] Thus a power struggle had now broken out between the Royal Navy and the Royal Society for the overall control of this scientific and exploratory expedition. Since it was crucial to have co-operation rather than rivalry, Hawke proposed a compromise whereby Dalrymple would retain command of the scientific party, while the naval commander would "be positively ordered to follow (Dalrymple's) opinion, on the compliance with which his promotion was to depend."[21] This was a significant concession in the direction of the precedents of Halley and Dampier, but Dalrymple turned down this proposal, since he was convinced that a divided command was incompatible with success. This is what the President of the Royal Society meant when he stated that Dalrymple declined to go "unless he could be vested with the *free* command" (my italics). This was certainly the right decision, however difficult it was to take, and Dalrymple deserves great credit for having made this sacrifice.

## The years 1768-1771

A month was to pass before Cook was appointed to the command. Meanwhile, having no further part to play with the voyage himself, Dalrymple gave to Banks, who was now the senior representative of the Royal Society on board the *Endeavour*, a description of the Arias Memorial that he had acquired with its account of the voyage of Torres, and a copy of Dalrymple's own preliminary volume[22] with its map showing the route of Torres through the strait separating New Holland from New Guinea.

Dalrymple now concentrated upon completing his *Historical Collection*,[23] the first volume of which appeared in January 1770, and it was on the strength of that work that he was elected a Fellow of the Royal Society on 14 February 1771. Dalrymple had been present, as Franklin's guest, on the occasion of Bougainville's visit to the Society in May 1770, and he was likewise present on 30 May 1771 when Cook's letter from Batavia was read, outlining the course of his voyage and including a copy of his journal and some charts.

The *Endeavour* reached the Downs on 12 July, and within a month Dalrymple was learning about the voyage at first hand, as Banks's guest at the Royal Society Club. He was also able to hear Cook speak about the voyage on the occasion of the tabling of the manuscripts and journals on 21 November. Thus Dalrymple would have learned how those on board the *Endeavour* had debated upon their future moves once the circum-navigation of New Zealand had been completed. As Banks remarked in his journal, the best plan would have been to cross the Pacific in high latitudes[24] and so return to England by way of Cape Horn, but this had reluctantly been rejected since the sails and rigging were too worn for such a voyage after "the blowing weather" that they had had to endure off New Zealand.

New Zealand alone of Cook's landfalls and discoveries on that first voyage had shown promise for future development.[25] Yet it was a country whose natural assets were counterbalanced by the fact that the people, though "mild and gentle by nature, [were] frequently in danger of perishing by famine." This was because they were totally devoid of livestock and dangerously dependent upon their supplies of fish and vegetables.[26]

Benjamin Franklin and Alexander Dalrymple were among a group who were discussing the results of the voyage when Franklin urged that it would be a policy of enlightened self-interest for Britain to intervene because "a commercial nation particularly should wish for a general civi-lization of mankind, since trade is always carried on to much greater extent with people who have the arts and conveniences of life, than it can be with native savages." The result was a proposal to organize "a voyage by subscription, to carry the conveniences of life, as fowls, hogs, goats, cattle, corn, iron, etc... and to bring from thence such productions as can be cultivated in this kingdom to... advantage." Dalrymple was to be in command, and it is noteworthy that the type of ship that he specified as most suitable for the voyage was exactly the same as the *Endeavour* (which he always claimed to have selected), namely "a Catt or Bark, from the coal trade, of 350 tons."[27]

Once it became clear that this scheme was not going to get off the ground, Dalrymple turned his attention to another project. He knew that the government, in those early years of industrialization, was beginning, in Harlow's words, "to seek out and establish an all-British supply of animal oil in the Arctic Seas and in the southern regions of the Atlantic and Pacific Oceans to lubricate the new machines and light the streets of London and the new industrial towns."²⁸ It was also well known that there had been reports of the discovery of "a very temperate and pleasant country" in the South Atlantic Ocean associated with the voyages of La Roché in 1675 and of the ship *Léon* in 1756. This land was reportedly situated somewhere in the vicinity of 45°S, and Dalrymple realized that if these reports were well founded this would prove a very favourable location from which to carry on "the whale and other fisheries, and also for the prosecution of any commerce which may be found in the countries to the South."²⁹ He therefore planned a preliminary voyage of reconnaissance which, if it was successful in its search, would be followed by the establishment of a colony.

Such an enterprise needed prior governmental approval, but when Dalrymple had an interview with Lord North he found the minister affable but noncommittal, and this failure to obtain official approval eventually brought the project to an end. Nevertheless, before that happened, Dalrymple, in his customary manner, had been preparing the way for the voyage of exploration by collecting the most authoritative accounts available of previous voyages in the area. He got his friend M. D'Aprés de Mannevillette, the distinguished French geographer, to obtain a copy of Bouvet's voyage of 1738-39 from the archives of the French East India Company, as well as the manuscript journal of the voyage of the *Léon*. From the Board of Longitude he obtained the original manuscripts relating to the voyage of Edmund Halley, who had also reported signs of land in the area in question, and he had obtained observations on the winds of the Falkland Islands from his friend Philip Stephens, the secretary of the Admiralty. These materials formed the basis of his new collection and of his *Chart and Memoir of the Southern Ocean*.

The latter was intended not only to be the most accurate chart of the south Atlantic yet published but also to show where the tracks of Bouvet and Halley had proved that there was no land—and where the accounts of the La Roché and the ship *Léon* had suggested that there might be land. To this end, Dalrymple, like his French contemporaries Buache and Danville, included in his chart the "gulph St. Sebastiano" taken from the Ortelius world map of 1586, Ortelius in turn having taken it from Mercator's "Sea Chart of the World" (1569). This was a reminder of an ancient report which might prove to be an earlier sighting of this possible land or island. Thus the map was intended as a standing invitation and challenge to seamen in the area to go and investigate. No navigator could be misled, since the accompanying *Memoir* clearly stated whence this gulf had been derived.[30]

To Beaglehole, who completely misunderstood the intention of these geographers, this action was "very rash."[31] Cook, however, thought otherwise, and after he had searched for this land in vain, he expressed his appreciation that Dalrymple and Danville had included this feature in their maps. Theirs, he wrote, were "the only two charts I have seen it inserted in:... I will allow them the merit of leading me to the discovery [of the Isle of Georgia]."[32] Beaglehole only saw this practice as "the sort of thing that inevitably turned Cook into a sort of executioner... of misbegotten hypotheses," and failed to perceive that Dalrymple and Danville had achieved their purpose in getting a search made. In fact, of course, Cook had performed the very reconnaissance that Dalrymple had wished to undertake himself, had Lord North given him the authority to act.

## The dispute with Hawkesworth

When Cook set out on his first voyage to the Pacific, the power struggle between the Royal Society and the Royal Navy over the command of the *Endeavour* (and over the expedition as a whole) had inevitably left a residue of bitterness on both sides. In addition, Captain Cook, like many other practical seamen, had a natural tendency to distrust speculative geography.[33] This combination of influences seems at first to have caused Cook to underestimate the man whom he had replaced, so that during the voyage of the *Endeavour* he paid more attention to the *Memoir* and map of Pingré[34] than to the book and map by Dalrymple.

When Hawkesworth's official account of the first voyage was at last published in 1773, Dalrymple was understandably upset. In a work that was certain to be an international best-seller, he found himself not only denied credit for the choice of the *Endeavour* or for the important unearthing of evidence about Torres's voyage[35] but also accused, as he put it, of having "misrepresented the Spanish and Dutch voyages to support my own ill-grounded conjectures."[36] Having been recently elected a Fellow of the Royal Society on the strength of his *Historical Collection*, which was indeed a landmark in the historiography of the south Pacific, he found it intolerable that his reputation for scholarly integrity should have been so unjustly and thoughtlessly jeopardized.

The main target of his anger was Hawkesworth. His initial criticisms of Cook were confined to dissatisfaction with his failure to make a more determined effort to prove or disprove the reported sightings of the *Orange* when the *Endeavour* was sailing from Cape Horn to Tahiti, and with the failure to probe more thoroughly that part of the south Pacific which lay to the eastward of New Zealand—because of the choice of the equinox for this part of the voyage. It was only after Hawkesworth had assured him that he had faithfully repeated the very words of Cook in the passages that had understandably caused offense, and had then chided him with criticizing so great a navigator, that Dalrymple, an arch opponent of all forms of flattery, added a further criticism of the events that had culminated in the grounding of the *Endeavour*.

The first of these letters was written on 22 June 1773, the second on 18 September 1773.[37] These are the only two occasions on which Dalrymple, to my knowledge, attacked Cook. How can any objective historian, upon such flimsy evidence, deduce therefrom a lifelong enmity between them? In point of fact, influences were at work to bring the two men closer together. On the professional level each had cause to treat the other with added respect. Cook, who carried with him, on his second voyage, Dalrymple's newly published *Historical Collection*, could no longer doubt the scholarship that underlay the geographical speculations, and these two volumes were in Beaglehole's words "a guide-book always in his hand." Similarly, after that second great voyage Dalrymple had no further grounds for complaint, since the south Pacific had now been very thoroughly investigated, as he had wished, and in the most masterly manner imaginable. There were also personal factors at work. When Dalrymple used to travel from London to Edinburgh to visit his family, he was in the habit of calling in at Great Ayton, Cook's boyhood home, to visit his old friend and Cook's new one, Commodore Wilson, now the village squire. We also know that Cook was a personal friend of Alexander's brother, Captain Hugh Dalrymple of the Royal

Navy, under whom James Burney, the future admiral and Pacific historian, had first served before he sailed on Cook's second voyage. And as fellow Pacific historians, Burney and Alexander Dalrymple worked closely together. We also know that one of Alexander Dalrymple's sisters sent Cook a personal gift shortly before he set sail on his last voyage. These incidents do not prove a closer relationship between Captain Cook and Alexander Dalrymple, but in view of the close-knit and affectionate bonds that linked the various members of the Dalrymple family, they are at least suggestive.

### The third voyage of Captain Cook

Dalrymple, then in India, was to play no direct role in the preparations for Cook's third voyage, although it is very possible that his influence was felt through his writings on the commercial potentialities of Korea, the Ryukyu Islands, and Japan.[38] Now the very fact that no one was at hand to prepare the way for this new expedition in the manner that Dalrymple's volumes had served the first two, was probably a major factor in its more limited success. Dalrymple had always insisted that careful preliminary historical analysis was an essential prerequisite for success, and this was precisely what Cook lacked on his third voyage. At that stage, nobody had completed a careful survey either of the Russian or of the Spanish voyages in the north Pacific Ocean. Instead, Cook was faced with the baffling problem of trying to unravel the disparate and contradictory studies of Müller and Stählin. This must have added considerably to the strain imposed upon him, and it is reasonable to assume that it was a major contributory cause of that new sense of tiredness that Beaglehole detected in Cook, that "less sureness of touch" and those "inner tensions" which helped to produce "a perceptibly rather different man."[39]

Though he had had no share in the preparations for the voyage, Dalrymple, who had just been appointed hydrographer of the East India Company, was closely involved with its aftermath. He and Banks were invited to help with the preparation of the official account, and within a few days of the ships' return to England he was entertaining Captain King to dinner at the Royal Society Club, an occasion that he repeated a month later. Thus in the winter of 1780 he was already in possession of the most authoritative available information on the voyage.

*The consequences of the opening of the Pacific Ocean*

The official account of Cook's last voyage was not published until 1784 when the war was over, and it was not until 1785 that the fur-trading voyages between the northwest coast of America and China began. By that time Dalrymple had had five years in which to ponder the outcome of Cook's opening up of the Pacific Ocean, and he saw much cause for concern. Instead of the discovery of extensive new lands and an increase of trade, which he had confidently anticipated in 1768, a relatively empty ocean had been revealed in the south Pacific which promised vast new opportunities for the whalers but at the cost of greatly increasing the vulnerability of the East India Company's trade with China. Cape Horn and the Cape of Good Hope were generally recognized as providing the only possible outer limits for the preservation of a trading monopoly in the Orient, and the supporters of the East India Company reasonably argued that the maintenance of such a monopoly was essential for a large-scale, orderly, and peaceful trade with China. Yet this monopoly was now under serious threat, not only from the whalers but also from the proponents of the Botany Bay project, the "country trade," the effects of the American Revolution, and from the adherents of the influential new economic school of laissez-faire free trade.[40] Similarly, in the north Pacific the future of the Hudson's Bay Company now seemed to be threatened by the developing trans-Pacific fur trade.

Having played a significant part in unwittingly helping to create some of these new conditions, Dalrymple now devoted his attention to suggesting a series of countermeasures whereby the two companies could meet the new challenge without any sacrifice of the expansion of trade.

The initial crisis was in the western Pacific, and here the first task was seen as the defensive one of keeping the intruders at bay. On the one hand Dalrymple therefore advised against making concessions to the whalers, and on the other he advocated a determined effort to terminate the Botany Bay project, which he saw as a likely source of arms and ammunition for the increasingly numerous pirates of the Malay Archipelago and as a general threat to the peaceful development of the China trade. Apart from arguing that Tristan da Cunha would provide a better answer to the convict problem, he also sought to frighten the government by suggesting that the narrative of Nicolas Struyck and the

Dauphin map both provided evidence that Britain had no legal title to the east coast of New Holland by right of prior discovery. For this reason, he noted, "some men have suggested that the Plan of sending the convicts to New Holland, may involve us in disputes with other European Nations, who may claim the right of antecedent discovery." In writing these words Dalrymple was fully aware that the authorities were particularly concerned at that moment with the implications of a possible diplomatic confrontation with the Dutch.[41]

There was, in fact, a clash of views between the government, which was seeking a political compromise with the Dutch, and the East India Company, which was only concerned with increasing its trade in the Malay Archipelago. Though the company could not act in defiance of the government's wishes after the establishment of the Board of Control in 1784, nevertheless its directors, in 1786, expressed the view that a post in the vicinity of the northwest coast of New Guinea would serve the twofold purpose of "awing the Dutch to prevent a rupture with them, or in case of its taking place...[providing] shelter and refreshment, for our ships which make [the eastern] passage, was well as for promoting the most important operations in case of future war." It was in this context that Dalrymple prepared his *Collection concerning Papua* and then initiated the important survey of that coast by John McCluer (1790-92) after the final failure of the government's efforts to negotiate a settlement with the Dutch had become apparent.[42]

Having done his best to help contain these dangerous incursions by competing interests into the western Pacific, Dalrymple next turned his attention to the American continent. Here the reports from successive fur traders were making it imperative that a new close survey of the northwest coast should be undertaken to discover whether any germ of truth might be found to underlie the legends of de Fuca and de Fonte, a matter not clarified by Cook's last voyage. For Dalrymple was becoming convinced that only a joint marketing operation by the Hudson's Bay and East India companies, employing an overland route that utilized large rivers and extensive inland waterways, would enable Britain to retain control of the fur trade and at the same time maintain intact the chartered privileges of these two great companies.

So once more, as preparation for a new voyage of discovery, Dalrymple combined the roles of scholarly investigator and promoter. First he delved into the archives of the Hudson's Bay Company in order to construct the most authoritative account that it was possible to devise from such complex material of the geography of the North American continent, accompanying this with his notable "Map of the lands around the North Pole" (1789). Then, as promoter, he marshalled all the evidence he could find to support the legends of de Fuca and de Fonte, and published it all in his *Plan for promoting the fur-trade...* (1789).

The Nootka Sound crisis, however, showed that the Spaniards would not allow British intrusions in this area to go unchallenged. Dalrymple thereupon not only engaged in the ensuing pamphlet War,[43] but also proposed that Britain should exploit this crisis by establishing a free port off the Pacific coast of Latin America, on one of the Galapagos or other islands. Such a port would not endanger the East India Company's privileges in the Pacific Ocean, since it would lie within the zone allotted to the South Sea Company. The Admiralty, having already despatched Vancouver to make a close survey of the northwest coast, also took up this new suggestion, in 1793, by sending James Colnett on an expedition that combined another search for the elusive Isla Grande in the southern Atlantic with a survey of the Galapagos and neighbouring island groups.[44]

## The false lead of Frédéric Metz

These successive moves by Dalrymple show how he was undertaking for his own era tasks similar to those which had been performed by Richard Hakluyt and John Dee in an earlier age. In 1805, however, an obscure Frenchman named Frédéric Metz thought that he saw enmity towards Cook, not the expansion of trade, as the motivation behind Dalrymple's activities.[45] This false lead was carelessly and uncritically adopted by R.H. Major in 1859, and has been followed by writers ever since.

Metz's theory was derived from a footnote found in Dalrymple's *Memoir concerning the Chagos Archipelago* (1786), in which he had first suggested that the Dauphin map contained evidence of a sixteenth-century European discovery of the east coast of Australia.[46] Metz read into this theory an insinuation that Cook was familiar with the map when he fell in with the east coast of Australia. This, Metz argued, was absurd, since it would mean that Cook "exposed himself and his crew to an almost certain death in order to have a plausible excuse for applying a name similar to that which this coast had already received from the un-known and anonymous navigator who had previously discovered it." Metz went on to attribute this supposed insinuation, which was in reality a figment of his own imagination, to Dalrymple's assumed irrita-tion that Cook had "demolished beyond hope of recovery, [Dalrymple's] theories of the existence of the southern lands, and the northwest passage of America."[47]

That was a careless suggestion to begin with, since Dalrymple did not write about the northwest passage until after Cook's death. Further-more, had Metz read Dalrymple's *Memoir* and footnote for himself, he could not have supposed that the Dauphin map had been discovered, as he asserted, in the British Museum, since Dalrymple, writing in 1786, specifically stated that it was then in the possession of Sir Joseph Banks.

In 1807 the French geographer M. Barbié du Bocage acknowledged that "the English claim that none of these charts were discovered till after the death of Captain Cook,"[48] and circumstantial evidence sup-ports that claim. According to James Burney in his *Chronological History of the Discoveries in the South Pacific Ocean* (1803), the Dauphin map had formerly been "part of the collection of the Earl of Oxford, but at his death it was taken away by one of his servants, and remained in con-cealment until it was discovered by the president of the Royal Society, Sir Joseph Banks, who purchased it and restored it to the Harleian Library."[49] Since Banks became president in 1778 and was knighted in 1781, a literal reading of that statement makes 1781 the earliest date for its discovery. There is other circumstantial evidence that points the same way. Thus when Dalrymple was writing his *Historical Collection concerning Papua*, not earlier than 1781,[50] he referred to the voyage in 1705 of the *Vassenbosch* to New Holland, as recorded by Nicolas Struyck, and commented that "by his expression, it seems the East-Coast of New Holland was then examined."[51] In such a context it seems certain that Dalrymple would have drawn attention to the Dauphin map, just as he did in his 1786 pamphlet on Botany Bay, had he yet studied it and come to the conclusion that it depicted a still earlier European visit to this same coast.[52]

Similarly, Metz was ignorant as to what Dalrymple was really saying in his *Memoir*. As the hydrographer of the East India Company, Dal-rymple was describing his attempt to recover lost knowledge of the Chagos Archipelago and the Maldive Islands, which had been among the earliest Portuguese discoveries in the East. He was complaining that this task was made unnecessarily difficult by the tendency of successive navigators to use various names for what were, in fact, the same islands. He therefore recommended the use, wherever possible, of native names, a viewpoint with which Captain Cook himself agreed.[53] Dalrymple then added the footnote which has been the cause of all the controversy. After noting the similarity of names on the relevant coastlines of the Dauphin map and on Captain Cook's chart, Dalrymple added: "[This] correspondence [of names] shows, that when native names cannot be had, the fittest names are descriptive." In other words, because both the ancient navigator and Captain Cook had adopted this wise procedure of using descriptive names along a coastline where the native names were not known, men now studying these two maps, made quite independently of one another two-and-a-half centuries apart, were able to realize that these two navigators had in reality been describing one and the same coastline. It is strange indeed that Dalrymple's commendation of Cook's use of descriptive place names should have been torn from its context, quoted only in part, and then distorted into a supposed innuendo that Dalrymple did not make and could not have made.[54]

Thus we see that a supposed resentment against Cook had nothing to do with the shaping of Dalrymple's career. On the other hand, his work was of the greatest significance for the planning, execution, and outcome of the voyages of Captain Cook. For it was he who gathered the evidence and posed the problems for Cook to resolve in his first two voyages, and then in the aftermath of all three of Cook's voyages helped his generation to live with the results. The motivation throughout was the expansion of British trade. This truth, however, has been obscured for far too long through the stultifying influence of Metz's false theory of 1805, which was adopted and given wide and long-enduring currency by R.H. Major in 1859. V.T. Harlow began the much needed reappraisal of Dalrymple as a major figure in British imperial development in the second half of the eighteenth century. It is high time for a similar reassessment to be made with regard to Dalrymple's role in the opening of the Pacific Ocean.

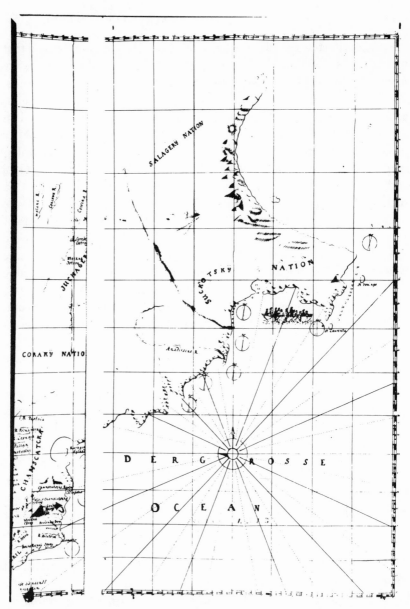

MAP 1. A 1729 manuscript map of Bering's discoveries of 1728. British Library, London: K. Top. 114. 43(1). This is the German version of a map which exists in several variant forms in the Russian and Swedish archives. It shows Bering's crucial voyage of July/August 1728 to the eastern tip of Asia (Cape Dezhnev). Although this is clearly marked, there is no hint of land to the east. The first published version in western Europe of this map came with du Halde's *Description géographique de la Chine* (Paris, 1735).

# Myth and Reality: James Cook and The Theoretical Geography of Northwest America

## Glyndwr Williams

In his first two Pacific voyages James Cook destroyed the illusion fostered by the theoretical geographers of his and earlier times that a large temperate continent existed in the southern hemisphere, offering untold opportunities for European settlement and exploitation. His journals demonstrate that Cook preserved a detached scepticism about the intriguing and entrancing hypotheses put forward by geographers and propagandists. Before he sailed on his second voyage he wrote, "as to a Southern Continent I do not believe any such thing exists unless in a high Latitude... hanging clowds and a thick horizon are certainly no known Signs of a Continent."[1] In his own inimitable, dogged fashion he sailed through the areas where cartographers had suggested solid land; he showed that their straits were closed, their land bridges were open, and that only their imaginations were unbounded. In the precise impartiality of the detailed charts he brought back with him, Cook demonstrated the reality of the south Pacific: the great ice barrier of Antarctica; the relationships of Australia, New Zealand's twin islands, and New Guinea; the position of a host of lesser islands. The south Pacific emerged from the mist behind which guesswork and fantasy had flourished; within the space of a few years it moved from the world of Télémaque and Gulliver to that of James Cook, professional explorer.

The evidence which Cook provided in such abundance between 1769 and 1775 of the unreliability of theoretical geography makes the events of the third voyage the more puzzling. It is true that the quest was different, and arguably more difficult: instead of the looming haystack of a southern continent, Cook was searching for the slim needle of a Northwest Passage. It is true also that Cook was older, tireder, certainly more irascible, on his final expedition. But even before the ships sailed, Cook was in a sense behaving out of character. By now he virtually drew up his own instructions, and those instructions, dated 6 July 1776, reveal a degree of reliance on theoretical cartography which it took a season of frustrating exploration in 1778 to dispel. There was enough of the old Cook to reject with derision the fantasies of the French school of theorists about the geography of northwest America, but in accepting the equally fallible prognostications of what may be termed the German school, Cook sent himself off in a pursuit of a will-o'-the-wisp. The year 1778 was a grim reminder of the truth of Bougainville's pronouncement: "La Géographie est un science de faits; on n'y peut rien donner dans son cabinet à l'éspirit de système, sans risquer, les plus grandes erreurs qui souvent ensuite ne se corrigent qu'aux dépens des navigateurs."

The eighteenth-century explorations of the north Pacific before Cook had brought great advances to Europe's knowledge of that remote area, but they had also brought confusion and speculation.' At the beginning of the century no European knew what lay between California and Kamchatka. The trend of the Pacific coast of America north of Cape Blanco in latitude 43°N was unknown; how far eastward Asia stretched from the peninsula of Kamchatka was equally doubtful. In the intervening five thousand miles there could lie ocean or land, islands or continent, a land-link between Asia and America, or the entrances of the Northwest and Northeast passages. Slowly and hesitantly the Russians began to resolve the mystery. In 1728 Bering sailed to the strait since named after him, and the first maps of his voyage show the eastern extremity of Asia—but with no hint of land across the water to the east (map 1). Within four years Gwosdev had supplied this information, in firm enough form for it to be recorded on a manuscript map drawn under the direction of one of Bering's officers, Martin Spanberg (map 2). The map indicates Cape Prince of Wales on the American side of Bering Strait, and stretching away to the east the unexplored reaches of *bolshaya zemlya* or "great land." Maps of Bering's expedition were soon published in Europe, but Gwosdev's discovery remained a dim rumour, and Spanberg's accurate representation of the northwest tip of America was never circulated. In 1741, after ten years of arduous preparations, Bering sailed again, this time for America, but followed his instructions

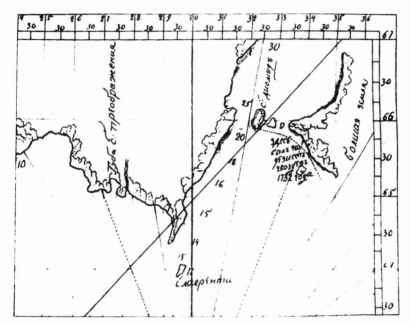

MAP 2.    Detail from a Russian manuscript map of the voyage of Mikhail Gwosdev, 1732. Central State Archives of Military History, Moscow: printed in A.V. Yefimov, *Atlas geograficheskikh otkrytiy v Sibiri i v severo-zapaduoy Ameriki XVII-XVIII vv* (Moscow, 1964). One of the most important maps of the period, it shows Cape Prince of Wales on the American side of the Bering Strait, and Gwosdev's track in Bering's old vessel the *St. Gabriel*. The legend east of Gwosdev's landfall near Cape Rodney is significant: "bolsháya zemlyá" or "great land." No better representation was to appear until Cook's voyage almost half a century later; but like so many Russian maps of the period this one was never published.

in heading first southeast from Kamchatka to clear up the mystery of those lands—Yedso, Staten Land, Company Land, and De Gama Land—thought to lie between Asia and America. In searching for these fictitious realms, Bering's two vessels became separated, and bereft of the security of each other's company, Bering and his second-in-command, Chirikov, made few reliable discoveries. Bering made his landfall at Mount St. Elias in Alaska and put boats ashore on Kayak Island before turning back to sail through the Shumagin and Aleutian islands. Chirikov sighted the American coast (or, to be more exact, the coast of Prince of Wales Island) farther to the southeast in latitude 55°21′N before swinging back for home, well to the south of the Alaskan peninsula, and touching only at one of the Aleutians.[2]

Map 3. *Carte des nouvelles découvertes entre la partie orient^le de l'Asie et l'occid^le de l'Amérique* by Philippe Buache (Paris, 1752). With its spider's web of straits, channels and island seas allegedly discovered by de Fuca, de Fonte and the Russians, this is an example of theoretical geography at its most undiscriminating, and was sensibly rejected by Cook as any sort of guide to the northwest coast.

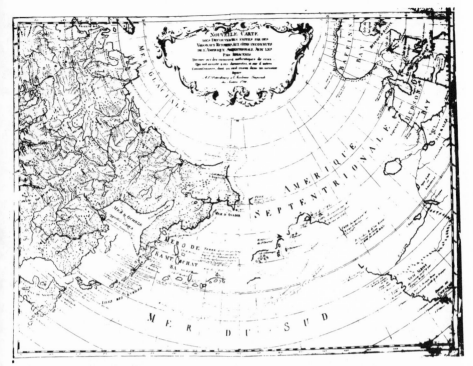

MAP 4. Gerhardt Müller's *Nouvelle Carte*, constructed in 1754 at the St. Petersburg Academy of Sciences, published in 1758, and then widely circulated in Europe. The tracks of both Russian vessels in 1741 are marked (Buache's map of 1752 showed only Chirikov's track); the Shumagin, Aleutian and Kurile islands indicated; and the imaginary lands such as Yedso eliminated. The map illustrates the view that the land sighted by Bering's men at their farthest east, on their return voyage, and that seen by Gwosdev in 1732 were all contiguous parts of the American mainland—a supposition which led to the bloated Alaskan peninsula of this map which was to intrigue and baffle Cook.

For all its defects, the voyage was a momentous one, but its pinprick discoveries threw little light on the geography of the vast area approached. Whether the landfalls of 1741 were continental or insular in character, and whether they were a continuation of the coastline sighted by Gwosdev in 1732, were now to become matters for endless altercation in Europe. Foremost in the debate were the French geographers Joseph Nicolas de l'Isle (younger brother of the great Guillaume) and Philippe Buache. When de l'Isle, who had been involved in the planning of Bering's second expedition, returned to France in 1747 he shared his information on the Russian discoveries with Buache, one of the foremost geographers of the day, and the two scholars concocted for the edification of the Académie Royale des Sciences in Paris a series of extraordinary maps in which they linked the recent Russian discoveries with the quite apocryphal explorations alleged to have been made in latitude 53°N by a Spanish admiral, de Fonte, in 1640, and the earlier discovery of a strait in latitude 48°N supposedly made by Juan de Fuca in 1592 (map 3). In an ascending spiral of publishing zeal, maps, memoirs, books, and atlases were produced by the two Frenchmen and their followers to prove that North America was penetrated by inland seas and straits which provided a continuous water passage from the Pacific to Hudson Bay or Baffin Bay.[3] From the Russian side came a powerful counterblast in the shape of a detailed narrative by Professor Müller of the St. Petersburg Academy of Sciences, *Nachrichten von Seereisen und zur See gemachten Entdecktungen* ... (1758). Translated into English (1761) and French (1766), the third volume provided a coherent and generally reliable account of the Bering voyages. The fictions of de l'Isle and Buache were properly rejected, but in their place Müller inserted another, for in a general map of the Russian explorations published in 1758 he tentatively expressed in cartographical form the official Russian conviction that most of the landfalls made by Bering's ships were continental in character (map 4). This led to a grossly enlarged Alaskan peninsula which south of Bering Strait bulged far to the west, stretching to within a few hundred miles of Kamchatka. It was among the maps which Cook took with him on this third voyage, and to which we shall return.

Official Russian exploration was followed by unofficial and generally obscure trading ventures as the *Promyshlennik* moved from island to

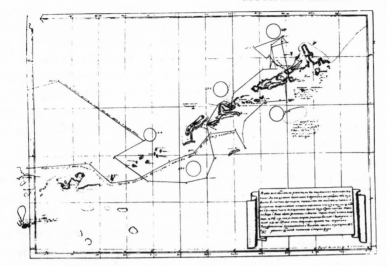

MAP 5. Russian manuscript map of the explorations of Peter Krenitsyn and Mikhail Levashev, 1767-8. Archives of the Central Cartographic Establishment of the Navy, Leningrad: printed in Yefimov, *op. cit.* The tip of the Alaskan peninsula (though without any interior shown, so there is no certainty whether it is island or mainland), the Shumagin Islands, and the larger islands of Unimak and Unalaska are now clearly marked.

island along the Alaskan coast in search of furs.[4] A brief renewal of government interest led to some important survey work by Captain Krenitsyn and Lieutenant Levashev in 1764-71, and on one of their maps the tip of the Alaskan peninsula, the Shumagin Islands, and the large islands of Unimak and Unalaska were clearly marked in a way that showed the errors of Müller's map (map 5). But their discoveries remained unpublished until William Coxe's *Account of the Russian Discoveries between Asia and America* (London, 1780), as did those of Lieutenant Ivan Synd, who combined surveying and escort work in those waters between 1764 and 1768. This failure to publish the working charts of the Russian explorers, and the eagerness of the speculative geographers to fill the void with their own eccentric productions, were to exercise a profound influence on Cook's future voyage to the region.[5]

If the Russian movements in the far north did not produce reliable maps, they were enough to provoke feelings of nervous apprehension in Spanish government circles, and the 1760s and 1770s saw a belated effort by the Spaniards to move north from lower California. The outrunners of this activity were seaborne expeditions which took the Spaniards, if fleetingly, as far north as Alaska. In 1774 Juan Pérez in the *Santiago* reached the Queen Charlotte Islands and sighted the southern tip of the Alaskan panhandle in latitude 55°North. On his return voyage he anchored off Nootka Sound, although he did not land there. The next year Juan Francisco de la Bodega y Quadra in the *Sonora* sailed farther north, discovering and naming Bucareli Sound on the west coast of Prince of Wales Island, and glimpsed the imposing snow-covered cone of Mount Edgecombe before turning back in latitude 58°30' North.[6] A map of the expedition's track traced the fifteen hundred miles of coastline from Monterey to the Alaskan coastline in latitude 58°N, although the lack of detail in the middle section of the map shows that Bodega was out of sight of land for much of the voyage, and farther north he gives no indication that his discoveries were of islands, not the mainland (map 6). Like most Spanish maps of the period, this one was never published, with the result that Cook has often been given credit for being the first European in a region which in fact had been visited several years earlier by the Spaniards. In 1790 such considerations were shown to be of more than academic interest when at the time of the Nootka Sound crisis questions of first discovery and occupation became matters of international consequence.

One reason for this spurt of Spanish enterprise was a series of alarmist reports from Spanish diplomats in London, matching those from St. Petersburg about Russian movements, to the effect that the English were making for the northwest coast. In 1776 the reports took on more substance and urgency, for Cook's third expedition was being prepared. The agitation for such a voyage had begun while Cook was still in the south Pacific searching for a nonexistent southern continent. British interest in the Northwest Passage had revived in the 1740s, when discovery expeditions had been sent to Hudson Bay only to find a closed western shoreline which offered little hope of a way through to the Pacific. Hudson's Bay Company slooping expeditions in the 1760s had confirmed this, but a remarkable overland journey by a company servant, Samuel Hearne, in 1770-72 had shifted the centre of attention for those interested in the possibility of a Northwest Passage. Hearne struck northwest from Churchill across the tundra until in July 1771 he became the first European to sight the northern coastline of the

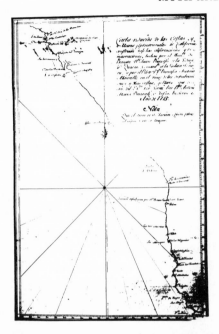

MAP 6.  Spanish manuscript map of 1775, "Carta reducida de las Costas, y Mares Septentrionales de California." Museo Naval, Madrid. The map, which remained unpublished, has a fair amount of information in its southern part, and to the north around the area of Bucareli Sound. The lack of detail in the middle section shows that, like Cook's vessels, Bodega's *Sonora* in 1775 was sailing out of sight of the coast of (modern) British Columbia for most of the time, and there is certainly no awareness here for the insular nature of the land to the east of the schooner's track. Even so, the voyage represented a bold stroke north by Spain three years before the much-publicized expedition of Cook reached the coast.

American continent. He had crossed no saltwater strait, and his journey proved that the passage from ocean to ocean through the North American landmass which many of the theoretical geographers had marked on their maps did not exist. But his sighting of the Arctic Ocean, though he placed it almost four degrees too far north, in latitude 71°54′ N, raised new hopes that a passage might be found across the top of the American continent. The period was one in which several scientists were arguing that the polar seas were ice-free, since seawater could not freeze, and that the ice encountered by earlier northern explorers must therefore be coastal and freshwater in character, coming for the most part from the arctic rivers as they broke up in the summer. The failure of naval vessels commanded by Phipps in 1773 to get beyond latitude

80°N in an expedition given orders to sail towards the north pole did not shake this belief, expressed in its most detailed form by the Swiss geographer Samuel Engel, who in 1765 had published his *Mémoires et observations géographiques et critiques sur la situation des pays septentrionaux de l'Asie et de l'Amérique,* much of which was taken up by an attempt to prove "la possibilité d'un passage par les mers septentrionales" (pp. 188-268). Engel had his followers in England, notably that enthusiastic amateur scientist Daines Barrington, who in the mid-1770s published several pamphlets on the subject and used his friendship with Sandwich, First Lord of the Admiralty, and his position on the council of the Royal Society to urge on the government the desirability of sending an expedition to find a polar passage into the Pacific. In 1774 a formal approach was made by the Royal Society to the government, advocating an expedition to the northwest coast of America to search for the Pacific entrance of the Northwest Passage.[7] Enthusiasm among influential geographers for this approach was increased by the publication in London in 1774 under the auspices of Dr. Maty, secretary of the Royal Society, of a book written by his opposite number in Russia, von Stählin, secretary of the St. Petersburg Academy of Sciences. This was accompanied by a map which claimed to show the discoveries in the 1760s of Lieutenant Synd and the Russian traders (map 7). It marked Alaska not as a peninsula but as a large island, and between it and North America lay a wide strait in longitude 140°W through which ships could apparently sail into the Arctic Ocean. A letter in the papers of Lord Dartmouth, Secretary of State for the American Colonies from 1772 to 1775, pointed to the obvious conclusion. It argued on the one hand that, "To suppose that an immense body of ice can Exist in a compact, fix'd, and solid body, without being supported, by Land at its Extreme Ends, or by a fix'd body at its Centre, is to suppose an impossibility," and in complementary fashion, "that the separation between Asia and America, Consists of an Archipelago; on the Respective Shores of each Continent, and that between these Archipelagos there is a large, wide, and open passage, not less than from sixty to an hundred leagues in Breadth."[8] Although Hearne's journey was not as yet public knowledge, the Hudson's Bay Company had passed on details of it to the Admiralty, which was thus able to fix the approximate location of the northern coastline of the American continent.[9] Even if the ice fields which had almost trapped Phipps in latitude 80°N extended across the polar regions (and Barr-

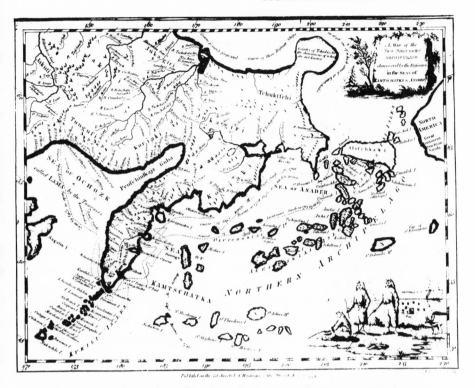

MAP 7. *A Map of the New Northern Archipelago* by J. von Stählin (London, 1774, based on the St. Petersburg issue of 1773). This representation, or rather misrepresentation, of Synd's explorations in the 1760s is theoretical cartography at its most irresponsible. Clusters of islands are scattered around the map in random fashion; Unalaska, Kodiak and other major islands are wildly displaced; Alaska is shown as a great island, separated from the American mainland by a strait to the polar sea 15° east of Bering Strait in latitude 65°N and longitude 140°W. It was this map which had a decisive effect on Cook's instructions in 1776, though even a cursory glance at it shows that Synd's vessel is not marked as sailing anywhere near the supposed strait between America and "Alashka."

ington insisted that Phipps had been sent in a "bad year"), their southern edge seemed to be several hundred miles north of the latitude in which Hearne had placed the American coastline.

The effect of these converging narratives and arguments is clearly seen in Cook's instructions. The beguiling theories centred on the apocryphal voyages of de Fuca and de Fonte were sternly ignored. No time was to be wasted looking for imaginary straits on the northwest coast in latitude 48°N and latitude 53°N; there was no repetition of the orders given to Byron in 1764 (uselessly, as it transpired) to search the coast between latitudes 38° and 54°North. Instead, Cook was "not to lose any time in exploring Rivers or Inlets, or upon any other account, until you get into the ... Latitude of 65°."[10] This was the latitude where Stählin's wide strait between Alaska and America opened into the polar sea, and that strait was the primary objective of Cook's third voyage. Once through the strait, if the current scientific theories were correct, Cook should find an open sea, glimpsed at midpoint by Hearne in 1771. Unstrengthened to meet ice, Cook's vessels were to sail eastward in the sea and out into the Atlantic, presumably through Baffin Bay, where other naval expeditions were being sent on exploratory missions in 1776 and 1777. Among the books and maps which Cook took with him, he is known to have had those of Engel, Müller, and von Stählin. His journal also shows that he knew that Spanish vessels had recently been along the northwest coast, information probably gathered from a short and garbled report printed in the London press at the end of May 1776.[11]

Cook's motives in setting off on a third voyage, to unfamiliar waters, so soon after returning from the great circumnavigation of 1772-75, are impossible to determine. A private man, he has left little indication of his thoughts at this time, save an evident restlessness at the prospect of early retirement. For Cook, the lure of the Northwest Passage was perhaps irresistible. To add to the lustre that would come to the first discoverer of the passage was the consideration—stressed to the crews on more than one occasion—of the £20,000 reward offered by an Act of Parliament in 1775.[12] It is fair comment to suspect that Cook was reasonably confident of success; of routine surveying work, even he had surely had his fill, and it is doubtful if the thought of *dis*proving the existence of a Northwest Passage was tempting enough to take him into the Pacific once more. It was at this time that Boswell met Cook, and wrote later, "I catched the enthusiasm of curiosity and adventure...."[13] The evidence of the journals is that the expedition approached its task in a mood of sanguine expectancy, and it is to the writings of Cook and his officers that we turn for an account of the hopes and disappointments of the 1778 season.

The expedition arrived on the northwest coast in March 1778, almost two hundred years after Drake had first sighted New Albion. The journals of Cook's officers reflected their interest as they strained for a glimpse through the rain and mist of that mysterious coastline where de Fuca was supposed to have discovered the great opening marked by a pillar in 1592. But the entrance now known by Juan de Fuca's name was passed unseen in the darkness, and a week later the ships anchored at Nootka Sound, their crews unaware of the fact that they were on not the mainland of North America but an island. At the end of April the expedition set sail for the north, keeping well out to sea because of bad weather, and land was not sighted again until latitude 55°20′N, well beyond the location of de Fonte's supposed strait. In his journal Cook was dogmatically sceptical about the existence of either de Fuca's or de Fonte's discoveries. On 23 March, just north of latitude 48°N, he wrote: "It is in the very latitude we were now in where geographers have placed the pretended *Strait of Juan de Fuca*, but we saw nothing like it, nor is there the least probability that iver any such thing exhisted."[14] Cook, unusually, had prejudged the issue, since he had seen nothing of the coastline between Cape Flattery and Nootka Sound. When sailing north from Nootka, out of sight of land as he passed latitude 53°N, Cook regretted in his journal that the squally weather kept him so far offshore, "especially as we were now passing the place where Geographers have placed the pretended Strait of Admiral de Fonte. For my own part, I give no credet to such vague and improbable stories, that carry their own confutation along with them nevertheless I was very desirous of keeping the Coast aboard in order to clear up this point beyond dispute...."[15]

As Cook kept steadily north, passing and naming Cape Edgecombe, Cross Sound, and Cape Fairweather, so the shoreline became bleaker and harsher; but the excitement on the ships mounted. On 11 May Lieutenant King wrote:

It may naturally be supposed that Mullers account of Berings expedition was often read and examin'd; and also a short account of later Russian Navigators published under the Inspection of Dr. Maty, with what is call'd an accurate Map affixd, tending to prove that Beerings Ideas of a continued Continent extending from the Latitude we are now in to the S.W. is false; we doubtless hop'd to find this last account here, and the broken land raises our Expectation that it will be so; but with all our pains we are not able to reconcile Mullers account and his Chart of where Beering landed, either with one another, or with what we observed....[16]

The next day King continued:

We have Dr. Matys map of the N°ern Archipelago constantly in our hands, expecting every opening to the N°ward will afford us an opportunity to separate the Continent, and enable us to reach the 65° of Lat.<sup>de</sup> when we understand that we are to examine accurately every inlet. We are kept in a constant suspense. Every new point of land using to the S<sup>o</sup>ward damps our hopes till they are again reviv'd by some fresh openings to the N<sup>o</sup>ward.[17]

That morning a large inlet opened before the vessels. Cook entered in his journal: "We had reason to expect that by the inlet before us we should find a passage to the North, and that the land to the West and SW was nothing but a group of islands."[18] His optimism was shared by others. "Between this western land and the Cape [Hinchinbroke], no land was seen to the North, which gave us some hope that here would be found the western termination of America." (Burney)[19] "... at nine in the morning, opened a large strait, the entrance of which appeared to be about four miles; probably the same called on our maps the Straits of Anian." (Rickman)[20] "... this being the first opening we had seen in the Land since we left King George's [Nootka] Sound our Hopes of a Passage were somewhat revived especially as the entrance here is wide and it had at first a very promising appearance." (Samwell)[21]

Cook named the inlet Sandwich Sound (it was later renamed Prince William Sound), and for five days the vessels followed it deep inland. On 17 May the land closed in, and Cook sent boats under Lieutenant John Gore and Lieutenant Henry Roberts to investigate. On their return, Gore and Roberts disagreed about their findings. Roberts was convinced that he had seen the end of the inlet; Gore, by contrast, wrote in his journal that "we found Deep water and Bold Shores in this Inlet, its wedth so far as I went up between 5 and 6 Miles."[22] The next morning, however, Cook turned back, explaining, "as the wind in the Morning came favourable for geting out to sea I resolved to spend no more time in searching for a passage in a place that promised so little success. I, besides, considered, that if the land on the west should prove to be islands agreable to the late Russian descoveries, we could not fail of getting far enough to the north and that in good time.... [23]

Leaving the sound, the ships sailed southwest until a high point of land was reached which Cook named Cape Elizabeth. Cook entered in his journal for 21 May: "Beyond it we would see no land so that we were in hopes that it was the western extremity of the Coast, but not long after we got sight of land bearing WSW." There was still room for optimism, for this land appeared to have no connection with Cape Elizabeth, and moreover:

In the Chart above mentioned [Müller's] there is here a space where Behring is supposed to have seen no land; it also favoured the account published by Mr Staehlin, who makes Cape St Hermogenes and all the land Behring discovered to the SW of it to be a cluster of islands, and places St Hermogenes amongst those which are destitute of Wood and to all appearance it was; so that every thing inspired us with hopes of finding here a passage Northward.... [24]

By 26 May Cook's hopes were shattered, for in the morning, as visibility improved up the inlet to the northwest, and

we clearly saw that what we had taken for islands were the summits of Mountains that were every where connected by lower land, which the haziness of the horizon had prevented us from seeing at a greater distance. This land was every where covered with Snow from the summits of the hills down to the very sea beach, and had every other appearance of being part of a great Continent, so that I was fully persuaided that we should find no passage by this inlet and my persevering in it was more to satisfy other people than to confirm my own opinion.[25]

Among these others, needless to say, was the irrepressible Gore, entering in his journal on 29 May, "Came to Sail Plying with the Tide of the Northward in a Gulf River or Streight—The Latter I hope."[26] He seems to have clung to hopes of a way through to the north longer than any, though he was supported by a few other journal writers. On 30 May, midshipman Edward Riou wrote, hopefully if confusedly, "A fine Even swell from Noward which is still in our favor of this place being an opening into the Sea of Anadir...."[27] In his published account, Rickman wrote, "On the 27th we found the river to widen as we advanced, and the land to flatten. We continued under an easy sail all day and the following night, grounding as we advanced from 30 to 40 fathom, shelly bottom and white sand. We were once more flattered with having found the passage, of which we were in pursuit, being now in the latitude of 60 degrees north."[28] As late as 1 June, Burney was able to raise a faint glimmer of hope even as the inlet narrowed and the water freshened: "The narrowness of the Channel forbids any great expectations; yet there was in its favour besides the depth of water this circumstance, that from the NbW to the NW points of the Horizon no high land was seen at the back of the lowland which was a swampy flat though in almost every other direction there was Land in sight of a height, sufficient to be seen 15 or 20 Lgs. dist."[29]

Cook was in an inlet (named Cook Inlet after Vancouver's explorations) but he was convinced that he was in a river. In a log entry of 6 June, tinged with bitterness, Cook explained:

> I was induced, very much against my own opinion and judgement, to pursue the Course I did, as it was the opinion of some of the officers that we should certainly find a passage to the North, and the late pretended Discoveries of the Russians tended to confirm it. Had we succeeded, a good deal of time would certainly have been saved but as we did not, nothing but a triffling point in Geography has been determined, and a River discovered that probably opens a very extensive communication with the Inland parts.... [30]

As Beaglehole remarks in his edition, for Cook to regard any point of geography as "triffling" was remarkable in itself; it was a clear sign of Cook's growing impatience and irritation. Trapped between an increasingly uneasy reliance on the printed maps, his own realization that the season was fast passing, and the conflicting views of his officers, Cook was showing an understandable but uncharacteristic lack of certainty. In his thoughtful journal, King reflected on the effect of the theoretical geography of the area on Cook's decisions:

> It may be asked why we tryed and Afterwards perserver'd so long in this Inlet; to those who have heard the Russian Accounts (since Beerings time) of these parts and who chose to place even the smallest confidence in a Map of their late discoveries publish'd under the eye of Dr Matty, must allow, that it was highly probable if not certain that a good deal of what Beering supposed to be continent was broken into Islands, (which even now if it proves so in part, we may yet not be too late) in which case it might have appeard strange not to have tried all large openings, and certainly would have been said, that every one we did leave unsearch'd was a Passage, which would have led us to our Wishes.... [31]

Once out of the entrance of Cook Inlet, the vessels were again forced away in a southwesterly direction, edging their way along the tongue of the Alaskan peninsula before at last turning north. On 9 August a strait was found, but to identify it was not easy. The eastern side was presumably America, but at first Cook referred to the Asian coast on the opposite side of the strait as "The Island of Alaschka or the Westland." The strait's appearance fitted neither Müller's map nor Stählin's: the first showed a strait more than one hundred miles across, the second showed *two* straits, with the great island of Alaschka lying between. The journals indulged in mild speculation about this, but most had long given up the attempt to reconcile the maps of the area with the reality, and in any case the question now seemed of only academic interest. What was important was that at last a way through to the north had been found. As King wrote: "Which conjecture is right we cannot determine, but we are in high spirits in seeing the land to the N°ward of those Extremitys trend away so far to the NE, and the other NW, which bespeaks an open Sea to the N°ward free of land, and we hope of Ice."[32] These hopes were soon ended, for as the ships bore northeast in an effort to sail along the northern edge the American continent they encountered an unbroken field of ice, ten or twelve feet high at the edge, and higher away from the water. It was moving slowly towards the coast, and as Cook got his ships away before they were crushed between this massive wall of ice and the shore, he reflected in his journal on the sanguine theories that the arctic ice was a coastal phenomenon, and that away from the land it would soon give way to open sea and easy navigation:

> It appeared to be intirely composed of frozen Snow and had been all formed at Sea, for setting aside the improbability or rather the impossibility of such masses floating out of River[s] in which there is hardly water for a boat, none of the productions of the land was found incorporated, or fixed in it. . . . It appeared to me very improbable that this ice could be the produce of the preceding Winter alone, but rather that of a great many. . . . [33]

As the ships returned through Bering Strait, Cook decided on one last attempt to find Stählin's great island of Alaschka, but an investigation of Norton Sound proved that the American coastline was continuous. As for the other islands scattered around on Stählin's map, Russian traders encountered at Unalaska were as baffled as Cook's men had been: "Nor had they the least idea of what part of the World *Mr Staehlins* Map referred to when leaid before them."[34] King grumbled, "We felt ourselves not a little vext and chagrind at the publication of such a Map, under the title of an accurate one, and the attention we had paid to it."[35] Cook was even more severe in his final summary: "If *Mr Staehlin* was not greatly imposed upon what could induce him to publish so erroneous a Map? in which many of these islands are jumbled in regular confusion, without the least regard to truth and yet he is pleased to call it a very accurate

little Map? A map that the most illiterate of his illiterate Sea-
faring men would have been ashamed to put his name to."[36]

Cook's reaction to the theoretical geographers had led him into two
fundamental errors. Before leaving England he had rejected, quite correctly, the de l'Isle/Buache school which constructed its maps of the northwest coast from the supposed discoveries of de Fuca and de Fonte; but
he had pushed his rejection of their bizarre maps to the extent that he
committed himself to the belief that the coastline north of Cape Flattery
was mainland rather than a series of islands. This error is easy to understand by anyone who has seen that coast. Professor Beaglehole wrote
after his first experience of Vancouver Island that it "is built on vast proportions: no one approaching it from the sea, or even flying down its
coast, would take it for an island—the scale of the hills behind hills is too
great, the snowy mountains inland recede too far, the line of breakers is
too long; the very clouds are almost too massive."[37] And if Cook did not
appreciate the insular character of the shoreline of modern British Columbia, with its maze of straits, inland waterways, and islands, because
he had no time to examine it, he, like the Spanish expeditions in 1774
and 1775, laid down reasonably enough the general trend of that coast.
The lapse of judgement which is more difficult to understand is Cook's
evident reliance on the maps of Müller and Stählin. Cook, after all, was
an explorer who had in the south Pacific demonstrated the unreliability
of the maps and theories of the speculative geographers. Over the years
he had developed a nose for the spurious, the exaggerated, and the erroneous; and no very close scrutiny was needed to throw doubts upon
the authoritativeness of the work of Müller and Stählin. Müller described his efforts at cartography in deprecating and revealing terms: "The
annexed map of the new Kamtschatka discoveries, lately published by
the academy of sciences, was made under my inspection.... As to that
part of the map which exhibits the American discoveries, they are taken
from drawings made on board the ships.... My work herein has been no
more than to connect together according to probability, by points, the
coasts that had been seen in various places...."[38] The form of the map
illustrates this quite clearly, with the use of broken lines to show
Müller's conjectures. If William Coxe is to be trusted (and he was
writing before firm news of Cook's discoveries was received), "Mr
Müller has long ago acknowledged, in the most candid and public manner, the incorrectness of the former chart, as far as it relates to the part

which represents America, as contiguous to Kamtchatka: but he still
maintains his opinion concerning the actual vicinity of the two continents in an higher latitude."[39]

That Cook should place any credence in Stählin's map is even more
incomprehensible. Stählin's published account is vague to the point of
meaninglessness. He wrote how trading vessels under the convoy of
Lieutenant Synd reached the east coast of Kamchatka, and

> then next year they pursued their voyage farther northward; and in that
> and the following years, 1765 and 1766, by degrees discovered a whole
> Archipelago of islands of different sizes, which increased upon them the
> farther they went, between 56th and 67th degree of north latitude; and
> they returned safe, in the year 1767. The reports they made to the
> Government's Chancery at Irkutzk, and from thence sent to the Direct-
> ing Senate, together with the Maps and Charts thereto annexed, make a
> considerable alteration in the regions of the sea of Anadir, and in the
> situation of the opposite coast of America . . . still more visible in the very
> accurate little Map of the new discovered North Archipelago hereto an-
> nexed, which is drawn up from the original accounts.[40]

The actual type of map brought back by Synd is shown here, and it
bears no resemblance to Stählin's masterpiece (map 8). Cook had not
seen the Russian manuscript charts, but even so credulous an enthusiast
as Daines Barrington remarked of the Stählin map in a paper read to the
Royal Society in December 1774 that "all this bears so little of the look
of truth, and is so unlike the notion Behring conveys of these straits, that
no credit can be given to it. . . . "[41] Coxe had certainly received, though
perhaps not by 1776, news of Synd's voyage which made it clear that
although members of the expedition landed on the American shore of
Bering Strait they stayed there only a short time and made no attempt to
explore eastward. A glance at the Stählin map adds to the puzzle of why
its representation of Alaska as an island was taken seriously; it marks
Synd's track only as far as the *western* coast of "Alaschka," and no
voyager is shown venturing through that eastern strait which seemed to
hold out such exciting possibilities of a short route into the polar sea.

Finally, there was the question of the ice. For almost three hundred
years, expeditions in search of a Northwest Passage had been forced
back, or frozen in, by ice. Each year the Hudson's Bay Company seamen
hurried out of Hudson Strait before the ice closed in, and the whalers
out of Baffin Bay; and it was not ice formed in the relatively small and

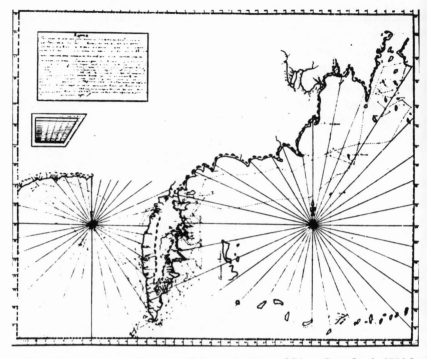

MAP 8. Russian manuscript map of the explorations of Lieut. Ivan Synd, 1764-8. Library of the Academy of Sciences of the U.S.S.R., Leningrad: printed in Yefimov, *op. cit.* A series of separate voyages by Synd is represented here, one of which had taken him to Bering Strait and to a landing on the American continent in the Cape Douglas or Cape Rodney area. There is nothing here to justify Stählin's representation of 1773/4.

shallow rivers of the region, but sea ice. Cook had known at first hand the dangers of navigation in the ice of the Baltic and off Newfoundland, and more recently he had in the southern hemisphere seen for himself fields of ice, permanent and unyielding, sixteen to eighteen feet in height.

Cook's instructions were based on two major fallacies: the theory that there was a short strait through to Hearne's sea east of Alaska, and the insistence that ice would not present a serious obstacle to navigation in the polar sea. Cook had set himself an impossible task, and his journal and those of his officers illustrate growing frustration as this was realized. It was a frustration which stemmed from the early hopes that a navigable passage would be found, the reward claimed, and the honour shared. Cook, it must be said, lacked the professional detachment which normally was one of his great strengths; he had been misled by theoretical geographers whose evidence was even flimsier than that used by the cartographers of the south Pacific whose representations Cook had treated with reserve if not derision. The hopeful excitement engendered by the fantasies of the scholars of Europe gave an undoubted stimulus to exploration, but the imaginative detail of their maps often exerted a perverse, even malign, influence on the tracks of the discovery expeditions. Cook's third voyage was not a surveying mission in the normal sense; it had one overriding objective, to find the Northwest Passage. To do this, Cook decided to test the hypotheses of theorists who claimed to show that such a passage existed and was navigable. What is striking is Cook's suspension of disbelief, and his evident failure to subject the maps in front of him to critical scrutiny. He was not to know that in the Russian government departments were unpublished charts of the Gwosdev, Krenitsyn, Levashev, and Synd voyages which among them laid down realistic if crude likenesses of the region between the Alaskan peninsula and Bering Strait, but his experience of the products of the Académie Royale des Sciences at Paris might have warned him that the Academy of Sciences at St. Petersburg was no guarantor of the accuracy of the maps of Müller and Stählin which were issued under its auspices. He had been imposed upon to the world's advantage, Beaglehole has written,[42] and the results of Cook's single season of exploration were indeed impressive. He charted the American coastline from Mount St. Elias to Bering Strait and beyond, determined the shape of the Alaskan peninsula, and touched on the coast of modern British Columbia. He closed the gap between the Spanish probes from the south and the Russian fur trading activities in the north. The maps brought home by Cook's officers after his death, and published with the official account of the voyage of 1784, showed the reality of his achievement (map 9). In outline, at least, the shape and position of the northwest coast of America were known; for the first time the region takes recognizable shape on the map, but it was not the shape that Cook had anticipated when he sailed from England in the summer of 1776.

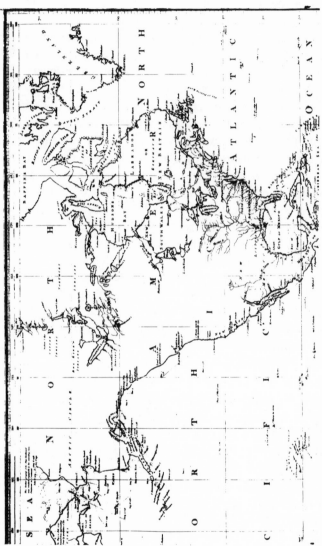

MAP 9.    Detail from *A General Chart exhibiting the Discoveries made by Capt. James Cook* by Henry Roberts (London, 1784). This map, constructed by one of Cook's lieutenants for the official account of Cook's last voyage, provided the most accurate survey to date of the northwest coast of America. The tracks of Cook (in 1778) and Clerke (in 1779) reveal the repeated attempts the ships made to force their way through the ice north of Bering Strait. The shape of northwest America shows that Cook thought that he was skirting the mainland on his long haul north from Nootka; in fact, for most of the time he was off the outer coasts of the island chain which runs from Vancouver Island to the Alaskan panhandle. For the first time on a widely-known published map the Alaskan peninsula is shown. The map also demonstrates the relation between Cook's coastal explorations and Hearne's in the interior—erroneously so, because Hearne's discoveries are placed too far north and west.

*NOTES, p. 242*

# Cook and the Nootka

*Robin Fisher*

THIS VOLUME CO-EDITOR; ASSOC. PROF OF HIST., SIMON FRASER U. & CHAIR OF 'COOK' CONFERENCE SPRING 1978 WHEN PAPERS PRODUCED.

UNDERLYING much of the writing on European exploration of *(SEE P. 277)* the Pacific is the assumption that, because the newcomers were able to dominate the contact situation, their arrival meant the beginning of the end for the peoples of the Pacific. The thesis has been put in its most blatant form by Alan Moorehead in *The Fatal Impact...,*[1] but others, who have examined the evidence more closely, have made the same case.[2] J.C. Beaglehole would appear to concur when he writes that on the day that Samuel Wallis came to Tahiti, "the knell of Polynesia began to sound."[3] Commentators on James Cook's landing on the northwest coast of North America have sometimes put similar conclusions in rather fanciful terms. Cook's arrival is described as the dawning of "the evil star of European civilization" in the standard ethnography on the Nootka, and a more recent generalizer has called Cook "the white messenger of doom."[4] *P. DRUCKER, 1951*

Cook's two ships the *Resolution* and the *Discovery* bore into what was later to be Nootka Sound on the evening of 29 March 1778.[5] They were to stay for exactly four weeks. On 31 March the ships were warped into Ship Cove, now called Resolution Cove, on the south end of Bligh Island. Refitting the vessels and gathering supplies began immediately, and the expedition was almost ready to leave by 5 April when it was discovered that the cheeks at the head of *Resolution*'s foremast were rotten. Repairing the defective parts took several days, and three days later, to add to the troubles, the mizzenmast broke during a gale. Consequently the vessels did not depart from the sound until 26 April. The unexpected delay was perhaps unfortunate for a captain anxious to probe northward, but it was also fortunate for at least two reasons. As Cook remarked drily in his journal, "It was lucky these defects were discovered in a place where wood, the principal thing wanting was to be

FIGURE 1.   The *Resolution* and the Discovery anchored in Ship Cove, Nootka Sound.
Pen and wash drawing by John Webber, National Maritime Museum, London.

had."[6] The prolonged stay also served the interests of ethnography, since it enabled some of the crew members to follow in greater detail the instructions "to observe the Genius, Temper, Disposition, and Number of the Natives and inhabitants."[7]

The visit of Cook and his men may have been the first contact between Europeans and the Indians of Nootka Sound, and it was certainly the first of any length. The Spanish navigator Juan Pérez had been in the vicinity four years earlier and had traded with some Indians. But no one had landed, and neither Pérez nor later historians could be quite certain of the precise location of this encounter. It is from Cook, not Pérez, that we have the first ethnographic account of the Nootka and the first detailed description of their reactions to the alien presence.

It would appear that the Nootka did not regard the Europeans as superior or more powerful than themselves and so they approached with confidence rather than diffidence. Certainly there was none of the submissive behaviour described in Tahiti,[8] and Cook was not deified as some have said that he was in Hawaii. It is always tempting to see any culture contact situation in terms of two entities interacting as opposites, with one emerging as dominant.[9] This deeply entrenched habit of mind is revealed by words like "civilized" and "primitive," "inferior" and "superior," and in descriptions of one culture's impact on another. Even more insidiously, some appear to want to see Cook's arrival at Nootka in terms of "good" and "evil." There were no such extremes at Nootka Sound in the spring of 1778. There was a balance in the relationship that developed between Cook's crews and the Indians. It is true that opposites can be balanced, but at the point of contact at Nootka Sound each group was subject to the culture of the other, each found things that were alien in the ways of the other but also things that were familiar, and each had to comply with demands made by the other. Neither group asserted a dominance, neither perceived the other as superior and, therefore, neither responded with submission.

A reciprocal relationship was established at Nootka Sound but, unfortunately for the historian, there is no such reciprocity in the evidence left by each group. We can learn a good deal about the seamen who came to Nootka Sound, but much less about the Indians who received them. With contact each group began to study the other, and what the Europeans thought about the Indians is recorded in their journals. What the Indians thought about the Europeans is more elusive. Here, like Cook and his men, we must embark on the often perilous course of trying to deduce their thoughts from their actions. We are often helped by the ethnographic literature but, by their own admission, the authors of these works are describing the Nootka culture of at least one hundred years later.[20]

The logs and journals of Cook's crews described the day-to-day encounters with the Nootka with varying degrees of accuracy and detail. There are a few exceptions, as at least two crewmen managed to spend the entire four weeks at Nootka without recording even the presence of the Indians.[11] Following the departure of the expedition, several of the officers wrote longer accounts of Nootka and its inhabitants. There was some tendency to make racial generalizations, to describe the Indians as being unlike Europeans or, in one case, like the Indians of other parts of America.[12] The observable characteristics and material culture received close attention and were described in some detail. William Anderson, the surgeon on the *Resolution*, collected a vocabulary of the Nootka language which, in the unfortunate absence of his journal for the period, is recorded in several others, including Cook's.[13] By all accounts Anderson was a skilled and perceptive ethnographer and his vocabulary was evidently compiled with considerable care. With the interesting exception of the word "Nootka" itself, it was praised for its accuracy by another student of the language nearly a century later,[14] and it remains a valuable document for the study of Nootkan languages. The daily life of the Indians was difficult to describe, partly because the ships were deliberately anchored out of sight of any Indian village, but also because, as Lieutenant James King realized, the presence of the Europeans altered their patterns of behaviour. They spent so much time visiting the two vessels that the usual daily activities were neglected.[15] There is disagreement in the journals on some aspects of Nootkan behaviour that perhaps ought to have been established by observation. The Europeans were intrigued by the question of whether the Nootka were cannibals, and many decided, on the basis of dubious evidence, that they were. Others, quite rightly, were suspicious of this evidence, Lieutenant John Williamson so much so that he conducted his own piece of empirical research. When he was unable to persuade an Indian to eat human flesh by offering him large quantities of iron and brass, he was satisfied that he had found conclusive evidence.[16] Even the population of Nootka villages that were visited was difficult to determine accurately, and so estimates varied wildly. It was not easy to decide, on the basis of the number of canoes pulled up on the beach, how many lived at Yuquot, for example;[17] a point that subsequent writers who have used inflated figures of the pre-contact Indian population ought to have kept in mind.

If there were problems in investigating observable characteristics, it was often impossible to inquire into less obvious things such as the social organization or the religious beliefs of the Indians. Apart from the language barrier, some recognized that describing the "tempers & manners" of an unfamiliar group of people like the Nootka on the basis of brief individual experience was likely to lead to widely differing, or even diametrically opposed, conclusions.[18] Then there was the fact that some of the information that the Europeans sought was the privately owned property of the heads of families, knowledge that only retained its potency if it was not shared. Yet, all the impediments notwithstanding, the journals are often remarkably perceptive and do convey important insights into the nature of the Nootka and their response to European contact.

The artifacts collected by the voyagers also give glimpses of late eighteenth-century Nootkan culture. Cook and his men were rather random collectors, and they tended to see the pieces that they acquired as functional and utilitarian. Cook commented that most of the masks were "both well designed and executed," but was noncommittal about their possible use. Other crew members concluded that they either served as hunting decoys or to protect the face during battle.[19] But Nootkan artists had already probed far beyond mere utility. The seabird rattle now in the Huntarian Museum, Glasgow, is one of the masterpieces of the period, and its clean, sweeping lines are indicative of a deep and strong artistic tradition at the time of Cook's arrival.[20]

As has been said of Columbus on the eastern shore of the Americas, Cook in the west "did not discover a new world; he established contact between two worlds, both already old."[21] Living in a seasonally abundant environment, and probably existing in relative isolation prior to European contact, the Nootka had evolved a culture of great richness and complexity. Cook's closest association was with the Moachat group which had a summer village at Yuquot. As the vessels entered Nootka Sound, canoes were seen coming off the point of land to the northwest, the location of Yuquot, and the journalists later noted that it was with these people that they continued to have dealings.[22] Following their an-

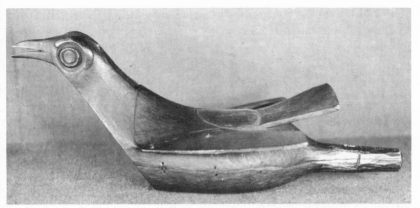

FIGURE 2.  Bird form rattle from Nootka Sound. Cook collection, Hunterian Museum, University of Glasgow.

nual pattern, these Indians had left their winter village at the head of Tahsis Inlet sometime in March in order to be at Yuquot in time for the herring fishing. Archaeological evidence suggests that there has been an unbroken occupation of this village site for more than four thousand years.[23] Within that time span the Indians had developed a social organization that involved a finely tuned system of ranking, both of individuals and of groups, which was in turn founded on a very strict and comprehensive concept of the ownership of property. Also important in the Nootka culture was the elaborate ceremonial life. All of these features of the Indians' way of life were to have a bearing on their relations with Cook and, indeed, on Cook's relations with them. The Nootkan culture was not susceptible or brittle, and the Indians did not need to make major changes in their behaviour just because two boatloads of Europeans had suddenly arrived on their shore. Perhaps it was fortunate that the new arrivals came from the ocean, since for the maritime Nootka, the sea was the home of fewer malignant spirits than the dark inland forests. Certainly as soon as the expedition entered Nootka Sound the people of Yuquot approached the vessels in their canoes "without shewing the least mark of fear or distrust,"[24] receiving the visitors with traditional ceremonies of welcome.

One Nootkan characteristic that was deeply ingrained by the time of European contact was their great skill as traders. This keen ability, honed through years of intertribal trading, was instantly brought to bear on the Europeans. Trading relations were established as quickly as contact, and Cook's men were immediately impressed with the Nootkas' ability to drive a hard bargain. William Bayly expressed the general opinion when he wrote that the Indians "are very keen traders getting as much as they could for everything they had; always asking for more give them what you would."[25] Trading became virtually a daily routine, so commonplace that many daily log entries simply read, "Natives as before."[26] As the days passed the Indians were able to force up the price of their goods. Often they were able to achieve higher prices by sheer perseverence and determination.[27] This was not, as it has often been described, a trade in which the Indians acquired only worthless trifles.[28] From the first day of trading it was apparent that the Indians were not interested in beads or other trinkets, which, the sailors found to their chagrin, could not supplant the Nootkas' own ornaments.[29] Instead they traded for articles that were more useful. All of the journalists agreed that metal was the big demand item; particularly iron, but also copper and brass. Lead, pewter, and tin were traded initially, but soon fell into disrepute. Any crack or flaw in the iron diminished its value, leading one writer to correctly conclude that the Indians worked it cold.[30] The Nootka possessed iron prior to contact and were familiar with its properties and functions, especially when it had a cutting edge. The most valuable items that the seamen got in return were, of course, the pelts of the sea otter. Most crewmen had in mind the bitter cold that lay ahead in the northern latitudes when they purchased these furs, but some at least had an inkling of their possible value in China, having read accounts of the Russian fur trade with that country.[31] Although spring was often a lean season for the Nootka, the sailors also traded for food supplies, including a number of varieties of fish.

The Europeans praised the Indians' honesty in dealing with trade goods, although they also commented that they were as light-fingered as the Polynesians with other items. Evidently the Nootka made a clear distinction between the trade goods they were handed to inspect—which they were scrupulous about returning—and unprotected equipment, which they regarded as fair game. Among the Nootka, territorial ownership of either land or water included the right to salvage whatever drifted ashore, and it may well be that this concept was operating when goods were taken from the ships. Naturally the Englishmen called it stealing, but they were grudgingly impressed that the Indians were as purposeful in their stealing as they were in their trading. In contrast to the peoples of the south Pacific, who were indiscriminate thieves, the Nootka only took items that were useful to them. Again, it was various kinds of metal that were especially sought after.[32]

Another immediately apparent aspect of Nootkan culture, which invariably accompanied the frequent trading, was ceremonial. When the vessels first entered the sound the Indians from Yuquot paddled around them, throwing feathers and red ochre on the water. This ritual was a sign of their peaceful intentions, although to the inexperienced European it "might be as soon taken for a mark of enmity."[33] All subsequent encounters with the visiting seamen also included singing, dancing, and the display of wealth. The observers, not unexpectedly, missed much of the significance of these rituals. They saw them simply as buffoonery, and often described the leader of the ceremonies as a "Merry Andrew." Even the perceptive James King described individual dancers as exhibiting "little more than the Antick tricks of a Mountebank."[34] Not that he was completely wrong. Such performances were supposed to have entertainment value, but they also had a deeper meaning. The dances and songs were privately owned possessions among the Nootka and, by performing them before the Europeans, the Indians were displaying their wealth of privileges and, therefore, their power. The same is true of the masks that were frequently worn on these occasions. Often the lead dancer would put on a succession of masks representing animal or sometimes human figures. The Europeans assumed that these masks had either an ornamental or a utilitarian function, whereas once again valued, prestige-conferring possessions were being displayed to impress the visitors. In spite of, or perhaps because of, their value, these masks were sometimes offered as trade items, although the Indians usually seemed furtive about arranging such transactions.[35]

Many of the dances performed for the seamen were led by the same individual, and he emerges from the journals as a man of rank and authority among the Nootka. This one man stood out from the rest by his speech of welcome on the day the expedition arrived; on the following day he led the dancing and singing. He became a regular visitor to the ships and was often seen arranging and regulating relations with the Europeans.[36] In this way the Nootkan concept of rank was impinging on the outsiders. Probably the most tantalizing gap in the entire documentary record surviving from Cook's visit to Nootka Sound is his failure to name this Indian leader.[37] Many have subsequently assumed that the man was Maquinha, who was soon to become well known as a powerful Nootkan chief and fur trader. Perhaps the assumption is correct, although it must be said that there is no evidence to support it. But whatever this man's name, there was no doubt of his prestige and influence. The sailors "could easily perceive that he was a shrewd fellow & seemingly a Chief of some Consequence among his Countrymen, & for that reason was singled from among them by Captain Cook as a person more worthy of his Notice."[38] Just prior to Cook's departure the two leaders indicated their mutual regard for each other by an exchange of presents, but it was carried out according to the practice of the Nootkan chief rather than the British captain. When Cook gave the Nootka a small present, the chief was not to be outdone. He showed the generosity appropriate to his rank by giving Cook a sea-otter pelt of considerable value. When Cook added to his present, the chief gave him a sea-otter cloak of even greater worth, prompting Cook to reciprocate once again. Cook commented that he did not want the Nootkan to suffer by his generosity towards his visitor, but, of course, there was no danger of that. Having demonstrated his importance to the end, this sadly unnamed Indian leader was the last to leave Cook's ship.[39]

The expedition was not only subject to the influence of ranking individuals amongst the Nootka but also to the consequences of the intertribal power structure. Nowhere was this fact made clearer than in the way in which the "hosts" of Yuquot controlled the trade with the vessels. The pattern of things to come became apparent only five days after Cook's arrival. On 4 April the local Indians caused some alarm on board by arming themselves and congregating on one spot on the shore. It soon became obvious, however, that they did not intend to attack the ships but had received warning that another group of Indians was approaching the cove. When the strangers rounded the point, it looked for a while as if there might be a battle between the two groups, but the conflict was only verbal. There was much vocal and vigorous negotiating, the upshot of which was that the newcomers were prevented by the locals from trading with the Europeans. Cook and his men now realized that the Indians from Yuquot, who had first come to the vessels, were "determined to ingross us intirely to themselves."[40] They established a trading monopoly which other groups tried, without success, to break through. All outside visitors who traded with the seamen did so with the Yuquot people acting as brokers. There was at least one other group that apparently was not disposed to accept the trading monopoly, and it was concluded aboard the ships that they were either friends of the Yuquot or members of a tribe that was too powerful for them to subdue.[41] But even these, after lively negotiations, allowed Yuquot middlemen to act on their behalf. The Yuquot not only dominated the trade with the ships but also went off to gather furs from other groups to bring to the Europeans. In this way they ensured that their prices were not undercut and thus sustained a continual rate of inflation.[42] These trading tactics, first tried while Cook was at Nootka, were later to be used with even greater success when maritime fur traders began coming to the coast.

Observing the nature of this trade, Cook and his officers recognized the factionalism that existed among the Indian groups of the area. Indeed, they thought that the local Indians were very highhanded in their treatment of other groups. Some even saw the possibility that they would be drawn into quarrels between Indians.[43] But though they did not become involved in physical violence on the side of any one group, there is little doubt that the presence of the Europeans, and the Yuquot Indians' ability to manipulate it, greatly enhanced the wealth and power of the latter.

It is very difficult to sort out the precise nature of the intertribal divisions from the evidence provided by the journals. Obviously some of the new arrivals at the ships' side may simply have been Moachat families arriving at Yuquot for the summer fishing, or attracted by the presence of the Europeans. It is also likely that some of the visiting Indians were members of Muchalat groups. Their villages were located on the eastern side of Nootka Sound and up Muchalat Arm and they were longstanding rivals of the Moachat. Drucker's account of tribal boundaries actually puts Resolution Cove in Muchalat territory, although he is obviously describing a much later situation.[44] Clearly the Yuquot people were too powerful for any Muchalat group to sustain any rights, based on territorial ownership, to deal with the ships.

Whatever the situation within Nootka Sound, many of the visiting Indians undoubtedly came from without. News of the presence of the Europeans spread rapidly, and there is some evidence that even the group that came to Resolution Cove on 4 April, so soon after Cook's arrival, lived outside Nootka Sound.[45] Certainly some of the groups that came later did. On 12 April the ships were visited by what were described as a superior looking group of Indians who indicated, by pointing, that they came from the southeast. They were distinguished by a distinctive cut or scar across the bridge of the nose, perhaps indicating that they were Clayoquot. According to one of Drucker's informants, such incisions were sometimes made in the noses of Clayoquot infants when it was hoped that they would become great warriors.[46] This powerful group lived on Clayoquot Sound and were the uneasy allies of the Moachat. It was probably from these visitors that Cook acquired some carved wooden heads, which have been described as "among the most exciting and interesting pieces in the collections of the eighteenth century." In spite of the clear indication that these people came from the south, and the evidence that possibly they were Clayoquot, Gunther concludes that the masks were brought by the Kwakiutl from the north.[47] It was from another group of Indians, who also indicated that they came from the south, that the Europeans acquired two silver spoons which Clerke thought were Spanish. Some historians, missing the point that these spoons came from outside the sound, have cited them as evidence that Pérez must have been at Nootka. Indeed, one has even gone so far as to claim, quite wrongly, that Cook himself "mentioned in his journal that he regarded them as proof that the Spanish had been at or near the place."[48]

From their hosts' reaction to the other Indian groups, it was clear to the Europeans that they were regarded as the "exclusive property" of the Yuquot people, and "no people" in the experience of the voyagers "had higher ideas of exclusive property." This fact about the Nootka is echoed equally emphatically in the ethnographies. As Drucker puts it, "the Nootkans carried the concept of ownership to an incredible extreme."[49] If this attitude was evident when outsiders visited Resolution Cove, it was made absolutely clear when Cook visited Yuquot. While he was there he ordered some crew members to cut grass for the livestock, only to find that the Indians demanded payment. Apparently they had earlier asked for similar recompense for the wood and water taken at Bligh Island, but in the absence of Cook, his men had ignored the request. Perhaps their claim to the area around Resolution Cove was not strong enough for the Yuquot people to press the demand there, so they made a virtue out of providing these things without payment, saying that they did it out of friendship. But at their own village they were not

FIGURE 3.   Indian village at Yuquot, Nootka Sound. John Webber watercolour, British Museum, London.

to be denied. Cook discovered that "there was not a blade of grass that had not a seperated owner" and that each one demanded payment.[50]

In comparison with the situation at the ships, differing, although no less Indian, notions of hospitality applied during visits to the villages. Cook and his men were made welcome at Yuquot, and while they were guests there were no attempts to take any of their property.[51] The artist John Webber was obliged to make a payment before he could draw the large carved figures located inside a house at the back wall,[52] but apart from this restriction, the visitors were permitted to inspect the village and its environs without hindrance. From Yuquot, Cook travelled up the western side of the sound, where he was given a similar reception at other Moachat villages. When he landed at a village on the eastern shore, however, the welcome was somewhat less than enthusiastic. Here he was constantly asked to leave and was forbidden from entering the houses.[53] Yet even this atypical hostility can be explained in Indian terms. If it is correct to assume that the villages on the east side of the sound were Muchalat and that they had been frozen out of trade at Resolution Cove by the Yuquot, then it is not surprising that Cook

FIGURE 4.   Inside a House at Yuquot, Nootka Sound. Engraving after drawing by John Webber.

should have received a rather surly reception. Perhaps by now even the Muchalat saw the visiting vessels as Moachat property.

There was only one area where the Indians' hospitality was somewhat less than the sailors had perhaps hoped for. Having become accustomed to the ready availability of women at the Polynesian Islands, there are a number of rather wistful remarks in the crews' journals about the modesty of Nootkan women. Perhaps the two are connected, but the seamen also found these women less attractive. Despite reluctance on both sides, some Nootkan women did spend nights in the cabins and one, at least, was aboard for ten days. Cook was, of course, anxious to avoid the spread of venereal disease and it seems quite likely that sexual contact was confined to the *Discovery*. Certainly it is Clerke and his men, rather than the crew of Cook's *Resolution*, who provide the accounts of these liaisons.[54]

The women of Nootka proved more expensive than those at any other Pacific port of call, and it seems likely that only slave girls were made available. Women were brought aboard when there were items that male traders wanted and could not obtain by any other means. When the goods ran out, the women did not return. Such arrangements were made by Indian men, and the dejected, submissive demeanour of the women

MAP 10.   Sketch map of Nootka (King George's) Sound showing Indian "towns." From the journal of James Burney, Public Record Office, London.

involved led some to surmise that they were slaves, probably captured from other groups during wars. The Nootka later claimed that prostitution was not a part of their traditional culture and particularly that men did not prostitute their wives or kinswomen. Sexual restraint was expected, although not necessarily practised, especially among those of high rank; promiscuity was certainly not condoned. William Bayly was one who investigated these matters closely. Less constrained by notions of propriety, his was the only vocabulary to contain the Nootka words for the male and female genitals as well as another word which he translated as meaning "to Roger." So Bayly's claim that prostitution "was practised only among the lower class" whereas the "better sort would not hear any thing of the kind" was probably in accord with Nootkan norms of behaviour.[55]

Amorous contacts were limited at Nootka, but then so too was overt hostility. In a situation where mutual misunderstanding could easily have led to violence it was, perhaps surprisingly, kept to a minimum. There was one incident when an Indian caught stealing was fired on with buckshot, and there were a few minor tussles between sailors and Indians. But, apart from these few altercations, Cook's visit to Nootka Sound is remarkable for the lack of conflict between the two groups.

The location at Resolution Cove had the fortuitous, and fortunate, effect of limiting interracial violence. In contrast to Tahiti or Hawaii, the *Resolution* and the *Discovery* were not anchored close to a major village or at a place which invited long periods of time ashore. Contact between the two races was thus limited, hindering the gathering of ethnographic information, but at the same time reducing the possibility of conflict. The tight control that the Yuquot people exercised over the trade had the same effect. The number of Indians in daily contact with the ships was limited and much of the time the same individuals were involved. The nature of the contact probably reduced tension, and certainly facilitated the development of understanding.

But it was not just the situation that limited violence; both groups also made positive efforts to ensure the establishment and continuation of amicable relations. Ever since Poverty Bay in New Zealand, Cook—though he was not always successful—had tried to avoid conflict with the various peoples that he visited. It is true that his control was slipping on the third voyage, but this development was not apparent at Nootka. At other places, stealing by natives frequently prompted Cook to take reprisals, but amongst the Nootka he responded with equanimity. It was better, thought Clerke, echoing the views of his commander, to "put up with the loss of some trifles, than bring matters to a serious decision." In more general terms, King wrote that "in all our intercourse with Indians, we never gave so great latitude to insolent behaviour as we did to these." The independent spirit of the Nootka claimed the voyagers' admiration at the same time as they realized that the factional nature of Indian society precluded any united action against the vessels.[56] So once gain, Nootka was exceptional. Certainly Cook was not, as has been suggested, in the midst of a run of constantly escalating violence which was to culminate at Kealakekua Bay.[57]

Some crewmen, of course, relied on the implicit belief in the superiority of European weapons to bolster their sense of control over the Indians. Lieutenant Williamson, who, unlike Cook, believed that "barbarians must be first quelled by force," put a musket ball through a Nootkan war tunic and assumed that he had impressed the Indians with his power.[58] We are entitled to have our doubts. Like the Hawaiians, the Nootka did not necessarily share this assumption, and—according to one observer—never betrayed "the least fear of us or our fire Arms."[59] Others were impressed with the Indians' ability with their own weapons: so much so that Nathaniel Portlock believed that with their traditional arms they "would stand the test with an equal number of any men under heaven,"[60] a point that he kept in mind when he later returned to the coast as the leader of a fur trading expedition.

The Nootka seemed to be equally anxious to avoid bloodshed. During the incident on 4 April, when an attack on the ships seemed imminent, an Indian leader came aboard to explain the true nature of the situation, assuring Cook that the conflict was intertribal rather than interracial.[61] The Nootka considered physical violence, outside of warfare, to be a deplorable breakdown in human relations and therefore something to be avoided. War parties took time to organize and motivate and, in any case, the European visitors provided none of the traditional reasons for a full-scale attack. For the people of Yuquot, at least, they posed no economic threat and offered no affront to their prestige of the kind that might demand revenge.[62]

In the absence of violence, a considerable degree of mutual trust and confidence developed between Cook's men and the Nootka. The Indians sold many of their weapons in trade, and the Europeans went ashore unarmed. Admittedly, the sailors thought that they could be adequately protected from the ships, an erroneous assumption that had already cost a number of lives on the northwest coast.[63] But not at Nootka in April of 1778. There the voyagers considered themselves "on an exceeding good footing with the natives" and were glad that "the greatest harmony and friendship reigned among us during the time we stayed with them."[64]

There were aspects of Nootka Sound that the Europeans found uncongenial. In contrast to the exuberant luxuriance of tropical Polynesia,

the natural environment at Nootka seemed cold, austere, and impene
trable. Certainly no sailor that we know of wanted to desert his ship for a
life on the northwest coast. In spite of Dr. Johnson's famous opinion
that "one set of savages is like another," the people of Nootka also
proved to be rather different from those of Polynesia. Without deference
or submission, they immediately turned the presence of the Europeans
to their own purposes. The explorers, although hypercritical of some of
the Indians' ways, also admired their assurance and independence. "In
short," wrote one crew member in retrospect, "a more open and com
municative people does not live under the sun."[65]

For their part, the Yuquot people observed the departure of the
vessels with due ceremony. Even if only for economic reasons, they
seemed sorry to see the Europeans leave, and expressed a desire for them
to revisit Nootka. Cook was in no doubt of their sincerity when they
promised to lay in a good stock of furs against the voyagers' return.[66]

Cook's visit to Nootka Sound produced reverberations in both cultures. It played a part in stimulating Britain to assert claims to the area
against those of Spain, the publication of the *Voyage* revealed the
Indians and aspects of their way of life to the European mind, and,
perhaps most significant, some enterprising individuals saw the possibility of a profitable trade in sea-otter pelts between the northwest coast
and China. The Indians were on the threshold of an immutable process
of cultural change begun and sustained by European contact. Much
later this process would affect their lives more profoundly, but in the
years immediately after Cook they continued to be independent and
buoyant. To the extent that the word implies a one-way process, Cook's
arrival at Nootka did not herald the immediate "impact" of one culture
on another, and certainly the experience was not fatal for the Indians.
Cook's presence was a beginning, not the end of something. To the surprise of the Europeans, the Nootka controlled the maritime fur trade
just as readily as they had manipulated Cook's presence.[67] It has been
said that Cook's third voyage was one of "remarkable and unexpected
consequences."[68] The experience at Nootka was one of these. Like New
Zealand, "It was something different, something / Nobody counted on."

# The Spanish Reaction to Cook's Third Voyage

## Christon I. Archer

THE voyage of Captain James Cook to the Pacific beginning in 1776 galvanized the attention of the world and focussed international concern upon one of the few remaining major lacunae on the world ocean map. The fabled Northwest Passage, the possibility of untapped resources, and the prospect of learning about societies that had escaped the touch of European civilization—as well as purely scientific curiosity—heightened the hunger for solid information. The publication of the official account of Cook's voyage in 1784 lifted the mystery to some extent and convinced many that the North Pacific littoral contained great riches as well as the possibility of grand adventure. Cook tantalized his readers with leads; whether they were merchants, scientists, or pure adventurers, the Pacific islands, the northwest coast, and the continuing dream of an easily navigated passage through the continent led them on. There could be no turning back of the clock once there was solid evidence of potential. Cook's voyage, then, became the beginning as far as almost all observers were concerned. Before Cook, there had been apocryphal accounts and legendary figures. Few realized that Spanish mariners had preceded the English navigator and that they had written their own accounts on north Pacific exploration. Indeed, so pervasive was Cook's reputation that even today the authoritative *Enciclopedia universal ilustrada* of Spain reports that he, and not a Spaniard, discovered Nootka Sound.[1]

For Spain, Cook's voyage was a source of danger and acute embarrassment. Although Mexico offered excellent bases from which to dispatch scientific voyages or commercial ventures, few Spaniards recognized the importance of published accounts. Spain was slow to grasp the full impact of the Enlightenment, and there were numerous traditions and old ideas to overcome. Secrecy rather than publication had served in the past. Spaniards had long believed that other Europeans misrepresented and disparaged their efforts anyway and to give them new data would only add to the problem.[2] It would take some time for observers in Madrid to understand the advantages of launching expeditions similar to that of Cook. Since Spain claimed the entire Pacific rim of North America, there seemed to be no pressing reason for what Alexander von Humboldt described as "puerile ceremonies" of possession-taking that never consulted the native inhabitants.[3] Besides, with immense territories to populate from California to Texas, there was little immediate need or motivation to risk ventures into the unknown.

Even before Cook arrived in the north Pacific, however, Spain had been compelled to abandon its dependence upon isolation. Information obtained from St. Petersburg indicated that the Russians had established several fur-trading posts in northern North America and that new expeditions were projected to consolidate and expand commercial activities. Details on Russian explorations were scanty, but the Spanish minister obtained reports of expansion from Kamchatka.[4] Alarmed by the possibilities of further moves into regions of greater interest to Spain, the Minister of the Indies ordered the Viceroy of New Spain, Antonio María Bucareli y Ursúa, to despatch expeditions designed to ascertain the level of Russian penetration and to make formal claims to the entire coast.[5]

The Spanish expeditions of 1774 and 1775 predated Cook, and that of 1779 took place without any information on the English discoveries. Indeed, had Spain published the journals of the first expeditions instead of locking them away in archives, Cook may not have devoted so much attention to the northwest coast. As it was, even successive Spanish navigators lacked the complete record. Like others interested in the north Pacific, they would turn to Cook for much of their information.

From the beginning, the Spaniards approached the problems of exploration and scientific observation differently than did the English. True to their own traditions, they were much more interested in carrying the Catholic faith to the Indians and in gathering accurate ethnological data to facilitate this end. In some respects, they were less tempted to fantasize or to paint an idealized European picture of what they saw. After three centuries of intimate contact with the Amerindian populations, the shocks and misinterpretations resulting from first contacts would not be as great. While naturalism or inquiry based upon direct observation and reason was a product of the Enlightenment, similar data was a prerequisite to pacification, conversion, and settlement. The regime knew what it wanted to accomplish, the friars felt that they had the methodology required to convert the most primitive societies, and both the soldiers and seamen who accompanied the expeditions had experience with governing Indians. Many carried Indian blood themselves and looked quite similar to the indigenous population.

At the same time, however, the Spanish explorations were not launched with the same precision and planning that went into truly scientific expeditions. Viceroy Bucareli had few seasoned naval officers available, let alone botanists, mathematicians, artists, and others. He selected Pilot Juan Pérez, an experienced journeyman seaman and exponent of exploration, to lead the first expedition.[6] From the isolated naval station of San Blas, Pérez encountered considerable difficulties in fulfilling his orders to prepare a vessel, accumulate supplies, and hire a volunteer crew capable of dealing with a diversity of climates and other hardships.[7] There were few seagoing ships on the Mexican coast other than those needed to supply the posts of Alta and Baja California. Pérez ordered a survey of the frigate *Principe*, but the carpenters and caulkers declared it to be in need of a major refit to replace rotten works, a task that would take at least three or four months.[8] Beginning what would be a constant refrain for the period from 1773 to 1800, Pérez deplored the lack of intelligent tradesmen and artisans needed to maintain a naval base. Although the harsh climate was a definite factor, Pérez attached most of the blame to negligence and incompetence.[9] Unable to find a vessel suitable for exploration, he had to make do with a 225-ton frigate, the *Santiago*, a ship that would prove to be too large and unwieldly for accurate coastal reconnaissance.

These difficulties would hinder much of the Spanish exploration in the north Pacific and make some types of scientific observation difficult; nonetheless the viceroy anticipated important results. The major purpose of Pérez's expedition was to verify the existence of Russian bases and lay claim to the coast, but the secret instructions of Viceroy Bucareli were clear in their intentions to stimulate ethnological study and religious conversion. Article one of Pérez's instructions stated that the voyage was for new discovery and "... to attract the numerous Indians to the desirable vassalage of His Majesty, to spread the light of the gospel, to bring the spiritual conquest that may remove them from the

*Yndia e Yndio, Gefes de Nutca.*

FIGURE 5.  Indian man and woman of Nootka Sound. Museo de América, Madrid.

shadows of idolatry, and to teach them the road to eternal salvation."[10] To fulfill these pious intentions, Bucareli ordered Pérez to learn as much as possible about Indian customs, life style, numbers, interrelations, religion, and government. He was to determine how Indian societies functioned: if they had kings, or if they governed themselves through republics or clans. In the area of religion, he was to see what idols they adored and what sacrifices they performed, and to report on their ceremonies.[11] Under no circumstances was there to be any removal of the Indians' property without their express approval. The officers were given explicit instructions to prevent incidents, so that the Indians would welcome settlers in the future. Finally, the Spaniards were not to engage in hostilities even if provoked.[12]

Pérez would rather have had more frontier soldiers instead of missionaries and high-minded principles, but his arguments were rejected. The *Santiago* sailed on 25 January 1774; with delays at San Diego and Monterey, it was not until 18 July that the crew sighted land on the northwest coast. By 20 July, they were at approximately 55° latitude and in contact with the Haida Indians, who paddled out to the Spanish ship to trade. At one point, Pérez counted twenty-one canoes carrying men, women, and children.[13] This was the first real opportunity to observe the Indians and to speculate about the nature of their society. Although the labret worn by the women was described as "a very ugly thing," both Pérez and his second officer, Esteban José Martínez, formed a good impression of their visitors. Martínez described the northwest coast Indians in glowing terms: "These people are very docile since they give away their skins even before they are paid. They are robust, white as the best Spaniard, and the women I saw were the same."[14] The Spaniards were surprised to see that the Indians possessed bits of iron, and even more so when they produced half a bayonet that had been shaped into a knife. Martínez concluded that the metal must have come from the Russian expedition of Vitus Bering which in 1741 had lost a launch from the vessel commanded by Aleksei Chirikov.[15]

Strong winds, currents, and fog as well as the poor sailing capacities of the *Santiago* prevented Pérez from touching land during the entire voyage. Perhaps a more audacious commander would have been more willing to take risks, Pérez feared losing the ship in some uncharted harbour, and his caution limited observation. The Indians invited him to land on many occasions, but fear of treachery and complete ignorance of coastal waters kept Pérez from a step that would have ensured his fame in northwest coast history. Approaching Nootka Sound, he ordered his launch put into the water to locate a protected anchorage. Again, however, fate played its hand, for a strong west wind blew up, threatening to drive the *Santiago* onto the rocky coast. Pérez gave up the idea of landing, but the Indians came out to trade, offering sea-otter pelts and fish in exchange for California abalone shells. Both Pérez and Martínez described the exchanges in some detail, failing to grasp the commercial potential of their discovery. During this visit, the Indians may have obtained possession of two small silver spoons that would later be found by Cook and play an important role in the tangled diplomacy of Nootka Sound.[16] As important from the historical standpoint, Martínez became a strong exponent of the potential he saw in the northwest coast. In his view: "It is certain that if with time this land is conquered and populated and some ports are discovered in it, our Catholic Monarch will be able to say, 'I have another world of Spaniards and of land as rich and luxuriant as Spain, since thousands of ships and perhaps even more can be constructed.'"[17]

Viceroy Bucareli sympathized with the difficulties encountered by Pérez, but he could not determine the extent of Russian penetration from the 1774 expedition. Pérez had not made formal claims to the northwest coast, and, while his observations of the Indians were surprisingly detailed, he had not fulfilled many of the obligations outlined in his instructions.[18] In the following year, Bucareli dispatched a new expedition designed to complete the work begun by Pérez. By this time, there were six young naval officers from Spain who had been stationed at San Blas to facilitate explorations. Of these, Bruno de Hezeta and Juan Francisco de la Bodega y Quadra were destined for fame.

Bucareli ordered Hezeta to lead an expedition of two vessels, the *Santiago* and a small escort schooner, the *Sonora*, thus reducing the danger of sending one vessel into unknown waters and permitting vital inshore reconnaissance and charting. Departing from San Blas on 16 March 1775, the expedition soon became an epic which tested the true mettle of the Spanish navigators. Bodega y Quadra succeeded to command of the *Sonora* when the captain of a California supply ship accompanying the explorers became insane. Despite the small size of the schooner, it was difficult to handle, and even under full sail it lagged behind its larger consort. It rolled in calm seas and wallowed through waves, soaking the crew and everything on board. The men were miserable, and each time Bodega ordered more canvas set, they grumbled that the vessel would founder.[19] Scurvy had become a serious problem on both ships when, near present-day Point Grenville on the Washington coast, seven seamen were massacred by the Indians as they landed in heavy surf to obtain water.[20] Although Bodega opened fire when they attacked the schooner, a junta of officers decided that an attempt to seek vengeance would break their instructions. Besides, there was real danger of losing additional men and thus endangering the whole mission.[21]

Even before the massacre, Hezeta had lost his taste for exploration. Poor weather, scurvy, and the lateness of the season caused him to seek support amongst his officers for a return to San Blas. Bodega, however, was much more determined to fulfill Bucareli's instructions. The vessels became separated at the end of July 1775, allowing both captains to decide their future. Hezeta sailed north to approximately 49° latitude before turning south and sighting the Columbia River on his voyage home. Bodega reduced rations and continued north, landing at 57°2' latitude, where he took possession for Spain within sight of today's Mount Edgecombe.[22] Continuing to Kruzoff Island, he came into contact with Indians who once again demonstrated warlike characteristics and a very strong sense of sovereignty. They let the Spaniards know that payment was expected for water, wood, and masts taken from their lands. Bodega handed them some trinkets, but this seemed only to annoy and insult them. They menaced the Spaniards with long spears and other weapons before Bodega convinced them not to take up arms. He was able to continue to Bucareli Bay and to conduct quite detailed explorations until scurvy and shortages of provisions forced a return to the south.[23]

Despite the limitations upon Spain's scientific capabilities in the north Pacific, these voyages accomplished much of what Cook would attain, without the essential publicity and publication. Instead of basking in the glow of their own pioneer efforts, the Spaniards soon found themselves on the defensive. In 1776, Bucareli learned about the English intention to send Cook into the Pacific and, of most immediate concern, to the coast of California, ". . . to trace the commerce with New Mexico and endeavour to discover the famous Northwest Passage, and to win the prize offered by the House of Commons."[24] The commandants of California posts were given orders to exercise vigilance and if possible to foil the English without resorting to force. Bucareli studied French translations of previous English expeditions into Hudson Bay. From reading in the journals of Hezeta and Bodega that the coast extended westward, the viceroy thought it obvious that there could be no passage through the continent. Although in recent times Admiral George Anson had doubled Cape Horn and explored the coast as far north as Acapulco, there were great obstacles before anyone who wished to duplicate his feats, let alone sail farther north. The history of the Spanish voyages and even the chronic difficulties supplying the California posts underlined the hardships that would face Captain Cook.[25]

At the same time, Bucareli doubted that Spanish forces could resist Cook, and asked for information on exactly what strength the English planned to send into the Pacific. He was not at all convinced that a scientific expedition posed a serious danger and, as a result, he was not inclined to waste funds and energy upon measures to oppose Cook. When the Minister of the Indies, José de Gálvez, ordered a new expedition to the northwest coast in 1776, Bucareli delayed, arguing that the ships available were needed to supply the California posts.[26] This inactivity irritated Gálvez, who had decided in favour of a strong response to the foreign intrusion. Cook was to be stopped and imprisoned if he arrived at a Mexican port.[27] Gálvez ordered Bucareli to enforce the Spanish "Laws of the Indies" prohibiting foreign vessels from entering the Pacific Ocean.

While the Mexican officials procrastinated, Cook departed from Tahiti and headed towards the north Pacific. He possessed some information on the Spanish voyages from documents that had reached London, but not enough to dampen his exhilarating conviction that he was entering territory unseen by any Europeans. At Nootka Sound, where the English expedition stayed from 30 March to 26 April 1778, Cook discovered that the Indians possessed some copper, brass, and iron, and were anxious to obtain more.[28] He concluded that the small amounts of metal, including the two silver spoons purchased from an Indian who had been wearing them as jewellery, had arrived at the coast by way of trade with distant tribes across the continent or northwards from the Spanish settlements.[29] The spoons had no marks to identify their origins, but Captain Charles Clerke wrote in his journal that they were probably of Spanish manufacture similar to others he had seen while visiting a ship at Rio de Janeiro.[30] The evidence might have been used to suggest signs of previous visitors, but national interests and possibly Cook's own vanity led him to play down the facts. Of course, the language barrier prevented any meaningful communications with the Indians, and those contacted at Friendly Cove could have been from different bands than the ones Pérez had seen.

The English had completed their explorations on the northwest coast before Bucareli managed to act upon his orders. The third expedition, commanded by Ignacio Arteaga on the frigate *Princesa* and with Bodega y Quadra on the frigate *Favorita*, sailed from San Blas on 11 February 1779. Arriving at Bucareli Bay just after the beginning of May, Arteaga and his officers began the most thorough Spanish reconnaissance to date. All of the officers prepared detailed geographical and ethnological descriptions, reflecting Bucareli's displeasure at some of the skimpy reports submitted after the previous expeditions.[31] Arteaga was highly impressed by the port capacities, which he announced were "... capable of offering secure anchorage to all the vessels that in the present day plow the seas in the four quarters of the world without any one disturbing another."[32] Longboats were despatched to survey and chart the full extent of the port, an operation that took almost a month and was filled with incidents.

The Indians, who manifested great pleasure at being visited, did not take long to change their minds. Both the patience and good will of the Spaniards received some major tests. Bodega stated that it was difficult to set up instruments on shore without causing some provocation to the Indians, who coveted iron more than gold or silver.[33] They stole anything possible and visited the ships with the sole motive of stealing barrel hoops, latches, nails, and spoons from cauldrons. Arteaga was shocked when they offered to sell their children and ripped down a cross put up by the friars simply to extract the iron nails.[34] The officers made every effort to prevent vengeance, but with the purchased children warning of planned surprise attacks, and the numbers of Indians around the vessels much outnumbering the 205 Spaniards, incidents were unavoidable. By 10 June, Bodega counted eighty-six canoes with more than a thousand warriors, and there were many others on shore. Fearful of a sudden assault to overwhelm the vessels, Arteaga ordered the cannon mounted and maximum vigilance maintained.[35]

In these circumstances, it was exceptionally difficult for Arteaga and

Bodega to enforce the enlightened principles with which Bucareli intended to govern Spanish exploration. The use of blanks fired from cannon frightened the Indians for a short while, until they realized that no physical harm resulted. They soon joked about cannon and muskets—pointing to their own daggers and spears, which had a more terrible effect. During the expedition conducted by the launches, some Indians fired random arrows towards the seamen. Tempted to return a round of grapeshot to really chastise them, the Spaniards restrained their anger and put on displays of firepower against empty canoes and wooden tubs. Cannon balls fired into the woods or near occupied canoes shocked the Indians, but did not end their determination to possess European goods and metal. Sails, awnings, and clothing disappeared from the shore, driving the seamen to near desperation and increasing the level of violence. When some stolen items were returned in pieces, they whipped one Indian, confiscated a canoe, and fired into other empty canoes.[36]

On 13 June, when two sailors disappeared from a washing detail ashore, Arteaga decided to capture as many hostages as possible. The next morning, a flotilla of canoes surrounded the vessels and the prisoners were brought within sight of their comrades. They struggled to escape, but were restrained roughly, covered with mats, and taken back to the village. Arteaga ordered both ships to open fire to frighten the Indians—accomplishing rather more than he bargained for with his plan. The shock of massed fire terrified the Indians, even though the shot was not directed into their midst. Several canoes overturned, and nineteen prisoners were taken from the water by the ship's boats. One warrior died after being struck by an errant musket ball, but this was a definite error. Each of the prisoners was given gifts of cloth and trinkets rather than the horrible death they anticipated. At the same time, seventy-two sailors were sent ashore to recover the two hostages, but they found the Indians massed for battle. Armed with long lances, fully armoured, and angry, they fired showers of arrows towards the launches. In a two-hour standoff, the Spaniards kept out of range and did not return the fire. Finally, however, the two sailors were returned. They had gone with the Indians voluntarily—an impetuous act that cost them dearly. Each received a hundred strokes and a period confined in irons.[37]

In their two-month visit to Bucareli Bay, the Spaniards examined

Indian society closely and prepared some excellent descriptions and ethnologies. All observers were impressed by the strength of the men and the pleasing appearance of the women. The disfiguring labret was, of course, the one exception. By the end of their stay, the Spaniards knew a great deal about Indian weapons, dress, diet, and attitudes towards a wide range of situations. They had collected numerous carvings, utensils, and samples of Indian handicrafts. They had observed fishing techniques, maritime skills, and other customs, describing everything in great detail in their journals. There was less success with theoretical subjects, but despite the language barriers, efforts were made to comment on marriage, family relationships, systems of government, religion, and burial practices.[38] The seven Indian children who had been purchased— most of whom were sickly or of disagreeable physical appearance—were taken back to Mexico to become translators or converts who would be useful when new voyages took place.

Since Arteaga found no sign of Cook's presence or of any other European competitors, there appeared to be no immediate strategic reason for a return to the north. During the War of the American Revolution, defensive priorities drew Bodega and other officers away from the San Blas naval base. Within the Spanish empire as a whole, great reform efforts and administrative changes channelled energies away from north Pacific exploration. Spanish scientists and intellectuals joined their colleagues elsewhere in applauding the publication of the account of Cook's voyage in 1784, but they neglected to predict the commercial impact of the work. The high prices paid for sea-otter skins in China, combined with the Indian desire to obtain metals and other items, presented a blueprint for potential profits. While the Spaniards concerned them-selves with other affairs, the northwest coast was thrown open to commercial exploitation and the very real possibility of foreign takeover.

The development of the maritime fur trade in the 1780s escaped the attention of both Madrid and Mexico City. As far as Spain was concerned, Russia remained the major threat to northwest coast sovereignty. The scientific expedition of Jean François Galaup, Comte de la Pérouse, caused some comment when it visited Spanish California and Alaska in 1786, but the impetus for new voyages came only with reports of Russian expansion as far south as Nootka Sound.[39] It was not until 8 March 1788 that the first Spanish expedition since 1779 sailed for the north Pacific. This might be said to have been the first Iberian voyage in the post-Cook era, since Arteaga had not known anything about his English competition.

Viceroy Manuel Antonio Flórez selected none other than Esteban José Martínez, who had the necessary experience—if not the personality of a diplomat—to lead the expedition. Not only was Martínez one of the few real exponents of Spanish expansion into the north Pacific area but also he had been in contact with la Pérouse and had formulated some solid ideas about Spain's role on the northwest coast.[40] Unlike many of his contemporaries, he had read and digested the account of Cook's expedition as well as other foreign publications. Although his unfortunate character and the circumstances surrounding the arrest of British fur traders in 1789 caused him to receive the worst possible press, no one on the Spanish side was more active in trying to use the information of Cook and of the previous Spanish expeditions for the advancement of national interests.[41] Martínez's role in the occupation of Nootka Sound makes him a pivotal figure.

The 1788 expedition brought the Spaniards into contact for the first time with the Russian Alaska posts and gave Martínez indications about the level of English commercial activity in the north Pacific. Martínez, who seemed to get along better with the Russians than with some of his own subordinates, gathered a great deal of data, including the information that English traders had been moving into Nootka Sound and Bucareli Bay and opening a most lucrative trade in sea-otter pelts with China. If this was not sufficient cause for concern, the Russians claimed to be poised for a move to establish a garrison at Nootka Sound in 1789.[42]

Flórez ordered a new expedition for 1789 to safeguard Spanish claims to the northwest coast. Martínez would occupy Nootka Sound and counter what appeared to be a multinational challenge. The Russians could not be permitted to extend their activities southward. The Americans were also known to be sending expeditions into the Pacific, a fact that made Flórez's blood run cold. In his view, they were the enemy who in the long run might attempt to form colonies on the western coastline of the continent.[43] If they arrived at Nootka Sound, they were to be expelled with even more firmness than the British. Finally, the British, whom Martínez feared and respected, were to be shown the section of Cook's published journal that mentioned the silver spoons. Although

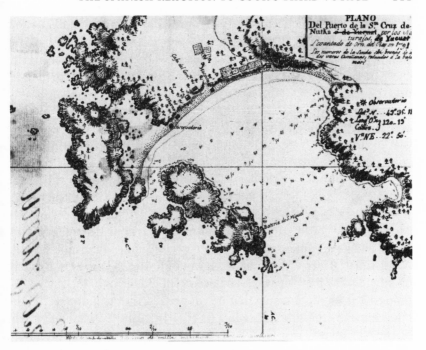

MAP 11. Spanish map of Friendly Cove (Yuquot), 1791. Museo Naval, Madrid.

neither Pérez nor Martínez had mentioned the spoons in 1774, they were to be used as solid proof that Spanish claims predated those of Captain Cook.[44]

Although the events of the Nootka Sound Controversy are too well known to require repetition in this study,[45] it is important to understand just how much Martínez was influenced by Cook as well as by the Spanish experience. One of the first things he did at Nootka Sound was to consolidate the rather flimsy evidence of the spoons by collecting testimony from the Indians who recalled the Pérez visit. He used the American fur traders as his witnesses, declining to follow Flórez's fear of them as potential enemies. Since Martínez lacked knowledge of the Nootka language, it was essential to befriend one or another of the trading groups to accomplish this end. The result, though unfortunate in some respects, as will be seen, did serve to bolster Spanish arguments.[46] According to Martínez's journal, Chief Maquinna, the principal leader at Nootka Sound, recalled the 1774 visit, when Martínez had thrown a conch shell into a canoe and by mistake injured one of the chief's brothers.[47] The Americans, likely concerned by the arrest of the British lest they should suffer a similar fate, announced that though they had believed Nootka Sound to have been English dating from Cook's visit, they now agreed with Martínez that Spanish claims predated all others.[48]

Establishing Spanish precedence was just the first part of the grand scenario Martínez planned. In July 1789, he informed Viceroy Flórez that during the 1774 expedition, he had sighted a large opening in the coast about forty leagues to the south of Nootka Sound. Since Pérez had not wished to approach the coast, Martínez claimed to have withheld the information from his own journal. Now, he decided to despatch pilot José Narvaez down the coast to ascertain the veracity of his previous observations. According to rumour, this was the strait through the continent and its terminus was very near New Orleans and the mouth of the Mississippi River. Martínez saw himself as God's instrument in opening up the passage which had been kept hidden until this date.[49] Although it is highly unlikely that he suppressed information in 1774, he knew enough from the fur traders to put in a claim for what just might be the Northwest Passage. Whatever the real source of the information, there were results in Mexico City. The viceroy commissioned a full report on French and British explorations of the continent, mentioning Samuel Hearne's discoveries and attempting to put Martínez's revelations into the general picture.[50]

This was only the first part of Martínez's north Pacific strategy. He drew Viceroy Conde de Revillagigedo's attention to a much more ambitious plan for the permanent occupation of the northwest coast and the Hawaiian Islands, and for the development of a trans-Pacific commercial system based upon the sea-otter fur trade. From Cook's journal and from reports received from fur traders, Martínez projected the formation of a Hawaiian victualling base to supply Spanish commerce and to deny the islands to foreigners.[51] On the northwest coast, he recommended the creation of a fur-trading company, similar to the Russian model, that would be granted a fifty-year monopoly over trade. The company would serve to reduce the financial burden upon the imperial treasury, since it would establish four military presidios of one hundred men each and sixteen missions. Nootka and Clayoquot Sounds were to be settled and used as shipbuilding centres and as the main defence against foreign competitors. In Martínez's view, the company would encourage Mexican industry and production as well as to secure a vital Spanish coastline. Because there were many other potential sources of wealth—lumber and metals, for example—he asked Viceroy Revillagigedo to give the matter his most urgent attention.[52]

Unfortunately for the future of Spanish interests, the viceroy did not share Martínez's unbounded enthusiasm for the north Pacific. The Russian example seemed worthy of consideration, but the mechanisms to create a company of that sort would require years of planning and consultation with Madrid. If, for example, the company received the right to import Chinese goods in exchange for furs, it would compete with existing Spanish monopolies and the interests of the Philippine Islands. Instead, Revillagigedo proposed the utilization of the existing commercial structures and the yearly Acapulco-to-Manila galleons.[53] As for the plan to create posts in the Hawaiian Islands, the viceroy believed that the disadvantages outnumbered the advantages. One or even several missions or presidios might not be sufficient to control the untrustworthy Hawaiians. The final misfortune experienced there by Captain Cook appeared to confirm the perfidy of the inhabitants. A similar disaster suffered by Spain might result in considerable embarrassment and heavy military expenditure.[54]

Unlike the English and American merchants, who recognized the potential of the sea-otter fur trade, those in the Spanish world were not eager to enter a business where the risks and profit margins were unknown.[55] If the Spaniards were to follow their competitors, it would have to be through state intervention rather than private enterprise. Since there was the possibility of opening an exchange of furs for quicksilver needed in the Mexican silver mining industry, Revillagigedo ordered experiments conducted to gauge the real worth of the fur trade. In 1790, Lieutenant Francisco Eliza carried ten cases of copper sheets to Nootka Sound with instructions to exchange them for pelts and to keep accurate records of his negotiations.[56] Profits were made in marketing furs in Canton, but the results were rather inconclusive; the xenophobia of the Chinese and a decline of prices for sea-otter pelts did nothing to stimulate the interest of Mexican merchants.[57] Indeed, the most persuasive arguments fell upon sterile ground in the Mexican merchant guild. Bodega y Quadra tried to interest them in free trade rather than in the creation of a monopoly; he saw no reason why Mexican-produced textiles and copper should not be able to drive out the foreign traders who had to import goods from Europe or Asia.[58] The Spanish explorer Alejandro Malaspina lent his support to this proposal and wrote to the Mexican merchants in an effort to arouse their attention.[59] Despite all of this pressure and advice, the business community did not respond. Martínez, one of the most outstanding advocates, was discredited for his defence of Spanish sovereignty at Nootka Sound, and no arguments of those who supported his commercial plans attracted merchant attention.[60] Spain was ill equipped to compete with the enterprising British or American traders, and one can see why Spaniards did not benefit from Cook's information.

This was not to be the case with regard to scientific investigation and ethnological studies. As we have seen earlier, the Spaniards made every effort to collect data on Indian cultures, religion, and attitudes, in anticipation of a spiritual conquest of the northwest coast societies. Aware, after the publication of Cook's journal, of just how important scientific expeditions could be in enhancing the international status of the Spanish nation, the imperial government commissioned Alejandro Malaspina to duplicate and even surpass the achievements of Cook and la Pérouse. But whereas Malaspina played an important role in extending Spanish exploration during the time of the Nootka Sound settlement, he was by no means the only advocate of scientific methodology. Viceroy Revillagigedo, himself a member of the enlightened regalist faction surrounding the court of Carlos III, was careful to stress the ethnological and scientific aspects of exploration. Each instruction issued to the commanders departing from San Blas for the north Pacific demanded far more than good seamanship; they were to make full scientific examinations of flora and fauna, meteorological conditions, and mineral deposits, with collections tabulated for submission to Mexico City. The spirit, character, and behaviour of the Indians were to be noted and their numbers estimated. Most important, however, each navigator was given explicit instructions to cultivate friendship with the Indians.[61]

When minor incidents did occur to mar Spanish-Indian relations,[62] Revillagigedo became even more specific in outlining his principles. In his orders to Dionisio Alcala Galiano and Cayetano Valdés who were sent to explore the Strait of Juan de Fuca, he stated: "Good treatment and harmony with the Indians are of primary consideration both in order to establish a solid friendship with them and so that our visits may not seem to them as dismal as those of other voyagers with detriment to humanity and the national credit."[63] Firearms were to be used only for self-defence, and even then: "it must be kept in mind that this is the last resort since their use is directly opposed to humanity and can only be excused by the necessity of self-preservation."[64] This policy accurately reflected the outlook of the imperial government. When one Spanish commander opened fire on a canoe, killing several Indians as a reprisal for the murder of an officer, the matter went right to the imperial cabinet and King Carlos IV.[65]

With attitudes such as these, it was little wonder that the Spaniards were able to add a great deal to the material that Captain Cook had collected. Revillagigedo harassed his officers unmercifully if he felt that they were neglecting their duty to present detailed reports on the Indians and other subjects.[66] Many officers consulted the French edition of Cook's journal and made efforts to utilize his vocabularies.[67] Since they spent far more time on the coast, they were able either to teach Spanish to the Indians or to study the Indian languages. Although in some cases the fur traders were even more fluent in Indian languages, their business interests and movements prevented them from making the same contributions. By the time of the Malaspina expedition, which arrived on the northwest coast in 1791, much of the groundwork had been done. Scientists such as José Mariano Moziño were able to collect data from numerous sources and to check some of Cook's statements. Without the post at Friendly Cove in Nootka Sound, much of this work could not have been accomplished.[68]

One negative result of the use of Cook's journal by both the Spaniards and the fur traders was that they became inordinately concerned with the topic of cannibalism. For scientific reasons as well as plain curiosity, Cook's men had shown great interest in the subject. On the first voyage, Charles Clerke purchased a human head during the visit to New Zealand. He cooked some of the flesh, and then offered it to an islander, who consumed it with great glee.[69] When human skulls, hands, and other parts appeared as items of trade on the northwest coast, Cook suggested that the Indians were cannibals. The fact that some of his subordinates were unconvinced by the lack of evidence did not influence the matter, since their journals were not published.[70] While none of the Spanish accounts before Cook made any reference to cannibalism, almost no observer after the publication of Cook's journal until the Malaspina expedition questioned the evidence.

In fact, the Spaniards obtained all of their information on cannibalism from Cook and the fur traders rather than from any authenticated reports or observations. The American, Joseph Ingraham, merely repeated Cook's impressions and added his own experiences that he too had been offered bones and severed hands.[71] Martínez repeated this information in his journal, adding a gratuitous remark about chiefs who ate human flesh when there was a shortage of fish. He was convinced that Indian children offered for sale might be destined for cannibal feasts, but on a number of occasions the Indians questioned him as to whether the Spaniards ate those they purchased.[72] John Kendrick, captain of the American vessel *Columbia*, described the butchering of children prisoners-of-war and his own horror at being offered a piece of loin and the hand of a four-year-old child. Although his tales shocked and impressed the more gullible Spanish observers, he was not entirely trustworthy. Quite likely his intention was to keep the Spaniards and Indians from developing close ties which would be detrimental to his business concerns.[73] Kendrick, like Ingraham, provided Martínez with detail on Indian cannibalism and advised the Spaniards to purchase children to save them from a terrible fate.[74] John Meares, whose published account was widely circulated in the Spanish world, presented even more grisly details of Maquinna's alleged cannibal ceremonies. Lack of evidence did not deter him from concocting wild tales which, if nothing else, would interest his readers.[75] Even the English seamen detained by Martínez in 1789 described ceremonies in which the chiefs crushed the skulls of children with clubs and then ate their flesh raw.[76]

Given the Spanish concern for the spiritual lives of the Indians, one might anticipate that the Franciscan friars would have undertaken research to either shatter or prove these myths. Despite the wealth of ethnological data and the compilation of vocabularies by the explorers, the friars were at a complete loss on how to approach the northwest coast Indians. According to their training, missions had to be established where there was good agricultural land available and where the Indians could be permanently congregated in order to be converted.[77] Like the mariners, the friars read Cook's accounts and then collected secondhand stories from the foreign fur traders. Unable to leave the Spanish post, they grumbled about the migrations of the Indians from village site to village site, cursed the rocky and sterile land, and satisfied themselves that by purchasing children they were saving them from a horrible

FIGURE 6.    Indian dance on the beach at Friendly Cove. Museo Naval, Madrid.

end.[78] As many as one hundred fifty to two hundred women and children were purchased to be sent to San Blas for education and conversion. This was part of the highly moralistic tone of the Spanish presence, but some expressed doubts about the traffic southward in human beings, believing that there was more involved than a desire to save children. Malaspina was especially critical of the traffic, since he rejected the theories about Indian cannibalism. Viceroy Marqués de Branciforte was suspicious about just what happened to the Indians who were sent to Mexico; he commissioned an inquiry to make sure that none were being held in bondage.[79]

As a part of the moral responsibility felt by the Spaniards, all of the expeditions maintained a high level of discipline that kept the mariners and soldiers from molesting Indians, and particularly Indian women. If Cook's men conducted an "amorous conquest" of the Pacific peoples, the Spaniards did everything possible to maintain a detached position and to protect native societies. Indeed, Cook's men had been highly critical of the "flesh-subduing Dons"[80] who did not accept the sexual advances of the Tahitian women. There could be no David Samwell aboard a Spanish vessel looking for new conquests of the "Dear Girls" at each new landfall.[81] While the military discipline may have been resented by the Spanish seamen and the soldiers garrisoned at Friendly Cove, it permitted the development of good relations with the Indians.

In many respects, the Spanish reaction to Cook's third voyage was a blending of the old and the new. Their concern for conversion, capabilities at ethnological observation, and realistic view of Indian societies came from their own past experience in the Americas. Cook gave them a growing awareness of the full importance of applying the Enlightenment and of publicizing the national scientific exploits. Spain could not have gained from the commercial lessons and entered the sea-otter fur trade with China, but the Spanish expeditions sent to the northwest coast can be said to have continued the very best traditions begun by Cook. The apogee was attained between 1791 and 1793, beginning with the arrival of Malaspina. His vessels were specially constructed for exploration, provided with the most advanced instruments, and manned by scientists and artists. The problem was that it was too late either to give previous Spanish navigators their full due or to place Malaspina in the category of Captain Cook. Because Malaspina became hopelessly entangled in the political intrigues surrounding the court of Carlos IV, his excellent journal was not published until 1885. It was not until 1802 that the imperial government rejected its past secrecy and published the account of Dionisio Alcala Galiano and Cayetano Valdés, who in 1792 had circumnavigated Vancouver Island.[82] Spain withdrew from the north Pacific in 1795, and the Age of Revolution ended any possiblity that there would be new explorations or settlements. The journals and ethnologies relating to the northwest coast in the period of first major contacts with Europeans were to remain unseen until well into the twentieth century.

# Cook's Reputation in Russia

## Terence Armstrong

WHILE Russians were of course aware of James Cook's first two major voyages of discovery either during their course or after their completion, it was the third voyage which made a greater impact upon Russian consciousness, for towards its end the *Resolution* and the *Discovery* met Russian seamen and visited Russian territory. In August 1778 the two ships made contact with Russians in the Aleutians, and in 1779 they spent some months in close contact with other Russians at the harbour of Petropavlovsk in Kamchatka: from April to June on their way north, and from August to October on their way south. Cook himself had died before the voyage that reached Kamchatka, but his men had very friendly relations with the Russian governor and his people. First-Major Magnus Behm (Bem in transliteration from cyrillic), the governor on their first visit, was particularly helpful, and George Vancouver, a midshipman aboard the *Discovery*, later recorded his sense of obligation by naming a channel in southeast Alaska Behm's Canal. Furthermore, Captain Charles Clerke, Cook's second-in-command, himself died as the ships approached Kamchatka for the second time, and there was a moving scene as he was buried by the local Russian priest.[1]

But if relations were friendly enough, there was a rather strong undercurrent of suspicion. For one thing, in 1771 there had been a notable incident in Kamchatka when a Polish or Hungarian exile, Maurice Benyowsky, had murdered the local Russian commander at Bol'sheretsk, seized a ship, and sailed successfully to freedom.[2] Benyowsky in the end reached France, and his return with French naval suport was constantly feared, a fact which led to various precautionary actions on the part of the authorities.[3] There was also some very reasonable apprehension that the appearance of major European powers in the north

Pacific might upset the strongly claimed but weakly held Russian position there. So friendliness in the harbour at Kamchatka did not necessarily imply friendliness farther up the chain of command.

However, the usefulness of the work Cook was doing quickly became apparent. The expedition confided its records to First-Major Behm for onward transmission to the British ambassador in St. Petersburg, and information contained in them was incorporated in a map compiled by Major M. Tatarinov in Irkutsk in 1779, a year before the ships returned to England.[4] An ethnographic collection relating to Pacific peoples likewise found its way to the Kunstkammer in St. Petersburg, where it is still preserved. Furthermore, detailed accounts of the voyages started to become available in Russia in 1780 (see Appendix, page 128). Thus Cook's reputation grew steadily.

There followed a period of Anglo-Russian naval co-operation, and a quite extensive exchange of personnel between the two navies. This development certainly helped to publicize Cook's work. At least two of his men on the last voyage went on to serve in the Russian navy. The most interesting case was that of Joseph Billings, an able seaman on the *Discovery*, who enlisted in St. Petersburg as a midshipman in 1783. Known to be a "companion of Cook," Billings soon found himself in command of a major Russian expedition—the Northeastern Geographical and Astronomical Marine Expedition—which spent nine years (1785-94) exploring Chukotka and the northwest Pacific, not with very spectacular results but with commendable devotion to duty. There is irony in the fact that Billings, the shipmate of Cook, was sent out by the Russian government to explore the far northeast, the need for doing which was a direct result of the supposed threat caused by Cook's third voyage. Billings was well respected in his adoptive country, and his work surely enhanced Cook's reputation.[5] The second case was a little later. In 1787 James Trevenen, a midshipman on the *Resolution*, entered the Russian service, and although he was expecting to command a north Pacific voyage of discovery, he was diverted to active service in the war with Sweden and was killed in action in 1790, having attained the rank of captain.

In the early nineteenth century the Russian navy started to show its paces in the Pacific. The creation of the Russian-American Company in 1799 established a formal Russian claim to what is now Alaska, and the need arose to secure the lines of communication. A painstaking analysis of the Russian attempt to do this has recently been made by James Gibson.[6] Russian seamen, with Cook's charts in their hands, were now able to appreciate his work through firsthand experience. One of the earliest to do so was A.J. von Krusenstern (I.F. Kruzenshtern), who made a round-the-world voyage in 1803-06 in the *Nadezhda*. Krusenstern held the highest opinion of Cook ("the great Cook," he calls him), chiefly for his navigational skill. Determinations of position by Cook could be accepted as totally reliable, Krusenstern thought, and he set his chronometers by them. The chart of the Bay of Avacha, on which Petropavlovsk stands, ascribed by Krusenstern to Cook but in fact made after his death, was found to be "perfectly correct." Krusenstern erected a monument at Petropavlovsk to Captain Clerke.[7]

The *Nadezhda* was accompanied for much of the voyage by the *Neva*, commanded by Yu. F. Lisyanskiy. This officer, too, was an admirer of Cook, referring to him in his own account of the voyage as "this truly great man" and "Europe's most celebrated navigator."[8] But he was perhaps not quite as prepared as Krusenstern to accept Cook's determinations of position, expressing some puzzlement about Cook's co-ordinates for Easter Island and some real doubt about his estimate of the island's population.[9] On this last point, however, one must note that Lisyanskiy's own estimates were sometimes far from exact, as when he declared Mount Edgecumbe in Alaska to be over 8,000 feet high [10] and it was subsequently found to be only 3,271 feet.

Aboard the *Nadezhda* were the young officers Otto von Kotzebue (O.Ye. Kotsebu) and F.G. von Bellingshausen (F.F. Bellinsgauzen). Krusenstern's enthusiasms must have infected them, for they too greatly revered Cook. Kotzebue commanded round-the-world voyages in his turn, in 1815-18 and again in 1823-26. In his narrative of the first, there are many references to Cook. A typical one: "My calculation of the longitude of the Pallisers agreed with that of Cook, within three minutes. Between our latitude and Cook's there was no difference; I therefore had no reason to complain of my time-keepers."[11] To that narrative Krusenstern contributed an introduction; there, not only does he praise "the immortal Cook" on the very first page but also two pages later he postulates his supremacy in rather extravagant terms: "that which was impossible to Cook could hardly be possible for another." Bellingshausen likewise often mentions Cook in his narrative, always with great respect.[12] Bellingshausen's voyage, a circumnavigation of the antarctic, was to a greater extent than any of the others a conscious attempt to amplify and complement (but not compete with) Cook's findings. M.P. Lazarev, Bellingshausen's second-in-command, certainly shared his opinion of Cook. Lazarev took copies of Cook's books on his own later round-the-world voyage in the *Kreyser* in 1822-25.[13]

If Krusenstern seems to have been the father of this pro-Cook sentiment among officers of the Russian navy, one should add that he participated in the other half of the naval exchange, and served in the Royal Navy for a period from 1793. He became and remained a good friend of Sir John Ross and Sir John Barrow. Lisyanskiy likewise was sailing with the British from 1793 to 1799, seeing active service in North America, the West Indies, India, and South Africa. Lazarev also was in the Royal Navy from 1803 to 1808. If that experience led them to admire Cook, the same may have been true of their fellow officer V.M. Golovnin, who served under Nelson, Cornwallis, and Collingwood between 1803 and 1806. In Golovnin's account of his Pacific voyage in the *Diana* in 1807-11 we find again the attitude that if his determinations of position agree with Cook's then he must be right.[14] It is true that Golovnin also criticizes Cook on several counts. He notes, on a later round-the-world voyage in the *Kamchatka* in 1817-19, that Cook made several mistaken identifications and gave new names to features already discovered by Russians, particularly in the Gulf of Alaska. But he also acknowledges that in the case of giving new names, Cook could scarcely act otherwise, as the Russian names were not published, and even if they had been, a foreign expedition could do a useful job fixing their positions with greater accuracy than Russians were equipped to do.[15] Whether these four—Krusenstern, Lisyanskiy, Lazarev, and Golovnin—actually rubbed shoulders with any of Cook's men is not known, but it would have been quite possible.

All these officers were very familiar with Cook's published work, which was circulating in Russian translation at the time. The very first material of this kind to appear in Russia was an account of the health measures taken by Cook on the second voyage,[16] indicating the early technical interest in problems of long voyages. An interesting point arises here. The translator and editor of the first Russian account of both the second and third voyages was L.I. Golenishchev-Kutuzov, who became an admiral and president of the Admiralty College. His admiration for Cook was great, as might be expected in a translator, but he was also in a position of authority. It is known that he made himself responsible for editing Bellingshausen's account of his antarctic voyage, and the accusation has recently been made that he suppressed in that account anything which might have been interpreted as denigrating or in anyway contradicting Cook.[17] Although the evidence that he did so is entirely circumstantial, and the case is by no means made, the accusation must be admitted to be plausible. We have noted in Krusenstern the attitude that Cook cannot be bettered, and this is but one step further. Many nations venerate their heroes to excess. In the case of Britain, it is possible to show that our national respect for the ideas and actions of a Nelson or a Florence Nightingale becomes, after a few decades, a very real brake on further progress. In the Russian case, the oddity here is that the hero is not Russian. But there were, in Russia, precedents for that also. At this very time Lord Byron was exciting Russian admiration of a different sort, and in a wider circle; today, the example is Karl Marx.

The pendulum, of course, had to swing. Even in the early days one can discern the beginnings of another view of Cook in Russia. The first points to attract criticism were Cook's treatment of the natives and his failure to prevent misbehaviour towards them by his crews. Even on Krusenstern's voyage of 1803-06, M.I. Ratmanov, one of his officers, tempers his regard for Cook with a reminder of his harsh attitude towards some natives.[18] A little later, Kotzebue expresses the same views in the narrative of his second round-the-world voyage.[19] Much later still, these primarily moral strictures were expanded to include the political accusation that Cook was pursuing British imperialist aims and was an agent of the East India Company.[20] In Soviet times there was, of course, strong emphasis on these political themes, but this is entirely to be expected and need not be documented in detail. However, a further critical point was made: that Cook overstated his finding on the second voyage that a southern continent did not exist. This assertion requires closer examination.

In 1949 the Soviet Union became anxious about the future of Antarctica. A carve-up by countries with a history of antarctic exploration (and some without) seemed to be in train, and the Soviet Union wished either to prevent this or to be included in it. There had at that time been just one Russian expedition to the region, and that was Bellingshausen's in 1819-21. This was, as it happened, both a very good expedition and a very useful piece of history to be able to quote. Bellingshausen, as we have noted, was chiefly anxious to complement Cook's work. But the Soviet interest demanded that Cook should be shown to be wrong and Bellingshausen right, in order to buttress the claim that Bellingshausen discovered Antarctica. Now most historians of geographical discovery would probably agree that continents are discovered piecemeal: successive expeditions contribute pieces of evidence, the cumulative effect of which is to demonstrate the existence of a continent. Such a demonstration for Antarctica could not have come before the middle of the nineteenth century. Cook's contribution was largely negative, in that he showed that any southern continent would be much smaller than hitherto supposed. Bellingshausen further narrowed down the area within which a continent might lie, and on one, perhaps two, occasions, sighted ice of a kind and at a point which we now know must mark the edge of the continent. He could not tell it to be such, and had he tried to make the point, he would have been going beyond his evidence.[21] But the "official" Soviet view now is that Bellingshausen's first sighting (on 27 January 1820, new style) constituted continental discovery; and scorn is poured on Cook's statement, "I had now made the circuit of the Southern Ocean in a high Latitude and traversed it in such a manner as to leave not the least room for the possibility of there being a continent, unless near the Pole and out of the reach of Navigation."[22] In fact, Cook's further remarks make it quite clear that he did think there was a continent, "and it is probable that we have seen a part of it." The politics of the twentieth century have intruded upon the interpretation of the history of the eighteenth.

It would seem, therefore, that Cook's reputation in Russia reached its nadir around 1950. Examination of the big reference works confirms this view. The nineteenth-century encyclopaedia *Entsiklopedicheskiy Slovar'* (Brockhaus and Yefron) has an entry for Cook published in 1895 and written by Yu. M. Shokal'skiy, a leading Russian marine scientist. The entry calls him "the famous English seaman" and is straightforward and factual, expressing neither praise nor blame. The second edition, known as the *Novyy Entsiklopedicheskiy Slovar'* (c. 1914) has a slightly abbreviated version of the same entry, and the *Entsiklopedicheskiy Slovar' Granat*, of the same date, follows a very similar line. The first edition of the *Bol'shava Sovetskaya Entsiklopediya* (1937) still calls him "the famous English seaman" and is complimentary without voicing special praise. It may have been written by V.N. Vladimirov, who had recently published a very fair and useful life of Cook[23] in which both the imperialist issue and the attitude to natives are sensibly faced and Cook himself largely exonerated from blame. The second edition (1953) terms him "the well-known English seaman," and the unsigned entry is not friendly in tone. Most emphasis is placed on his imperialist mission, his "discovery" of lands already known and named by others, and his inferiority to Bellingshausen. This view is reflected in later popular works on Pacific exploration. Finally, the third edition (1973), categorizing him simply as "the English seaman," returns to a factual account, with no special praise or blame. It is by I.P. Magidovich, the author of a general history of exploration in the second edition[24] of which he devotes fifteen pages to Cook and treats him fairly, if a little more critically than Vladimirov.

If the pendulum has started, since the 1950s, to swing back again, the credit for this must be given to the Soviet scholar Ya.M. Svet. Svet has been the leading figure in bringing out Russian translations of J.C. Beaglehole's new edition of Cook's journals.[25] He has written, sometimes in collaboration with others, an introduction and notes to each voyage narrative. In his introduction to the second voyage he writes unequivocally: "Without hesitation one can recognize this voyage as the most important event in the history of geographical discoveries and investigations of the second half of the eighteenth century."[26] On antarctic discovery he takes an eminently sensible line: "Thus the statements of Lomonosov, the conclusions of Cook, and the discoveries of Bellingshausen, all connected with the existence of Antarctica, could be fully appreciated only in our time, when the veil of secrecy and ignorance surrounding the expanses of the Antarctic had disappeared."[27] The availability of these new editions, two of which were translated into Russian by Svet, contributes at least as much to keeping Cook's reputation bright as do the editorial notes. The number of copies printed in these editions, it may be added, is of the order of tens of thousands—very considerably larger than that of Beaglehole's originals.

In summary, then, whereas Cook's third voyage caused some suspicion in Russia (partly for reasons quite unconnected with Cook), his reputation soon grew, thanks in part to Anglo-Russian naval co-operation at the relevant time. A stage was even reached at which no wrong could be imputed to Cook. Later, however, his star waned, and deficiencies—moral, political, and geographical—were discerned. Soviet nationalism, fanned by an anxiety over the future of Antarctica, was a partial cause. But in the last twenty years the appearance of a new Russian edition of the voyages, with annotations by a discerning and experienced scholar, has presented a balanced view of Cook's achievements to the Soviet public, and the result must surely be favourable to his reputation.

## Appendix:
## Publication of the narratives of Cook's voyages in Russian

### FIRST VOYAGE

*Opisaniye puteshestviya okolo zemnago shara... v 1768 do 1771*, ed. G. Kampe (Moscow, 1798). (Translated from German.)

*Pervoye krugosvetnoye plavaniye kapitana Dzhemsa Kuka. Plavaniye na "Indevre" v 1768-1771 gg.*, trans. A.V. Shalygina, ed. Ya. M. Svet and N.G. Morozovskiy (Moscow, 1960).

### SECOND VOYAGE

*Puteshestviye k yuzhnomu polyusu* (St Petersburg, 1780). New abridged trans. by Ya. M. Svet (Moscow, 1948).

*Puteshestviye v yuzhnoy polovine zemnogo shara i vokrug onogo... v 1772-1775*, trans. and ed. L.I. Golenishchev-Kutuzov (St Petersburg, 1796-1800). (Translated from French.)

*Vtoroye krugosvetnoye plavaniye kapitana Dzhemsa Kuka. Plavaniye k yuzhnomu polyusu i vokrug sveta v 1772-1775 gg.*, trans. Ya.M. Svet, ed. V.L. Lebedev, N.G. Morozovskiy, and Ya. M. Svet (Moscow, 1964).

### THIRD VOYAGE

H. Zimmermann, *Posledneye puteshestviye okolo sveta kap. Kuka* (St Petersburg, 1786, repr. 1788 and 1792).

*Puteshestviye v Severnyy Tikhiy Okean... s 1776 po 1780 god* (St Peters-burg, 1805-10), trans. L.I. Golenishchev-Kutuzov. (Translated from English.)

*Tret'ye plavaniye kapitana Dzhemsa Kuka. Plavaniye v Tikhom okeane v 1776-1780 gg.*, trans. and ed. Ya. M. Svet (Moscow, 1971).

### GENERAL

A. Kippis, *Podrobnoye i dostovernoye opisaniye zhizni i vsekh puteshestviy angliyskogo morekhodtsa kapitana Kuka*, trans. T.I. Mozhayskiy (St Petersburg, 1790).

# Medical Aspects and Consequences of Cook's Voyages

## Sir James Watt

STEWART Henderson, in the first number of *The Medical and Physical Journal* of 1799, expressed a popular view of Cook's achievement in preserving health at sea. "That great and celebrated circumnavigator," he wrote, "proved to the world the possibility of carrying a ship's crew through a variety of climates, for the space of near four years, without losing one man by disease; a circumstance which added more to his fame, and is supposed to have given a more useful lesson to maritime nations, than all the discoveries he ever made."[1]

That view was first advanced by Sir John Pringle, president of the Royal Society, on the occasion of the award of the Copley medal in 1776, and rests upon Cook's own claim that the record of the *Resolution* during her second voyage vindicated the health measures he had introduced.[2] They included a clean, dry, well-ventilated and fumigated ship, scrupulous cleanliness of the persons, hammocks and bedding of his men, clean warm clothing, a three-watch system to ensure adequate rest, and an antiscorbutic diet. Priority was given to fresh vegetables, and to certain articles Cook believed antiscorbutic which could be used as preventives at sea, chiefly "wort" or inspissated juice of malt, sauerkraut, and portable soup. The "rob" or concentrated juices of lemons and oranges was one of a number of therapeutic articles, including carrot marmalade, mustard and elixir of vitriol, dispensed by the surgeon to actual scurvy sufferers.

In examining Cook's claim, Henderson asks us to bear in mind that Cook's vessel enjoyed peculiar advantages over other men-of-war in terms of accommodation, antiscorbutics, clothing, a selected and volunteer crew, and the opportunity of avoiding unhealthy harbours. Fletcher, equally cautionary, contrasts the leisurely progress of the *Resolution* and the *Adventure* with the tight schedules of despatch vessels, which were prohibited from calling at ports where fresh provisions might be obtained.[3] To add to our difficulties the official medical records have been lost, and the surgeons' documents that remain have little medical content, so that we are obliged to rely upon lay opinion which precludes any statistical or qualitative analysis for comparison with the carefully documented data of men like Robertson or Blane.

Since Cook's reputation for preserving health at sea rests largely upon the record of the second voyage, it is convenient to consider it first. It has the additional advantage of permitting comparison of the health records of the *Resolution* and the *Adventure,* victualled to the same standard and experiencing the same environmental conditions.

Outward bound, the *Resolution* lost a carpenter's mate overboard shortly after leaving St. Jago, in August 1772. The *Adventure* had an outbreak of fever which cost the lives of two midshipmen attributed to bathing and making "too free with water" from a dirty well.[4] At Capetown, the *Adventure's* first lieutenant, Shank, was surveyed and invalided to England because of gout and chronic illness. The 10,980 miles from Capetown to New Zealand took 117 days. A month after leaving the Cape, Cook, in the *Resolution,* made wort from malt for "such People as had symptoms of Scurvy" and "one was highly scorbutic" despite the use of the rob of lemons. Sparrman confirms this outbreak and was one of the victims.[5] On 10 January 1773, he noted several with "swollen jugular glands" which he attributed to "drinking ice water,"[6] more probably to sucking ice. Philipp has suggested throat infections through lowered physical resistance,[7] but the more likely explanation is swelling of the parotid glands resulting from oedema and destruction of the duct orifices within the mouth as part of the general oral inflammation.[8] The ships separated on 8 February and, on 10 March, Henry Fenton was killed by a fall from the rigging. On the arrival of the *Resolution* in Dusky Bay, New Zealand, on 27 March, Cook refers to "scorbutic people" but to only one man who could have been called ill and two or three on the sick list. Marmalade of carrots was beneficial in one case, but sweet wort and carrot marmalade were also given "to such as were of scorbutic habit."[9] Sparrman, however, found spruce beer "refreshing to our tired bodies tainted with scurvy,"[10] which implies that there were more cases than Cook allowed, and scurvy was certainly advanced in the sheep and goats, despite the assumption that such animals synthesize adequate amounts of ascorbic acid.[11] Moreover, the fact that Cook was prepared to spend six weeks at Dusky Bay before making his rendezvous with Furneaux suggests that not only had he been worried about the outbreak of scurvy but also the crew were much longer convalescing than he had anticipated.

He finally reached Queen Charlotte Sound on 19 May, the *Adventure* under Furneaux having arrived on 7 April. They sailed together for the first tropical sweep on 2 June, and on the 23rd Sparrman notes an outbreak of veneral disease among the *Adventure*'s company,[12] a legacy of Furneaux's days of indolence before Cook joined him. James Scott, the *Adventure*'s lieutenant of marines, was posing a psychiatric problem. His persecution complex may well have been induced by drink and drugs, since he was an intimate friend of the surgeon's first mate, John Kent. On 23 July, Furneaux's first entry relating to illness reports the death from scurvy of Mortimer Mahoney, the *Adventure*'s dirty and indolent cook. By 28 July, the *Adventure* had twenty men sick with scurvy and flux.[13] Meanwhile, scurvy had reappeared in the *Resolution* and Mitchel brewed wort for scurvy patients, who were again given carrot marmalade.[14] The following day, however, Cook reported only one man sick, suffering from chronic dropsy. It illustrates the difficulty of estimating morbidity from Cook's own statements. Sparrman, who tacitly admits some scurvy in the *Resolution*, attributes the difference between the two ships to the *Resolution*'s longer stay in Dusky Bay and the greater use of greenstuffs and wort at the first sign of sickness, a view which Cook shared. Sparrman also refers to use of malt as an external application, presumably for scorbutic ulcers, with rather less benefit, one would imagine, than the orange juice used "avec un succès merveilleux" by Labat in 1696 or Armstrong's lemon juice in 1840.[15]

At this point, Cook assumed responsibility for the *Adventure*, sent over a cook, gave Furneaux precise instructions regarding the collection and use of local greens, antiscorbutics, and other health measures and altered his plans in order to call at Tahiti for refreshments. He observed significantly that effective antiscorbutic measures required "the authority and example of the commander," making the very pertinent observation that "it would be proper to examine the Surgeon of the *Adventure*'s journal to know when and in what quantity the wort was given to these Scorbutic people, for if it was properly applyed, we have a proof that it alone will neither cure nor prevent the Sea Scurvy."[16] By

6 August the flux had ceased and scurvy was arrested, but four days later, Cooper mentions twenty-eight on the *Adventure's* sick list. On arrival at Tahiti there were "thirty men on the Sick List but few others without scorbutic complaints." Again, Cook assumed responsibility and sent her surgeon's first mate ashore with them each morning. In the *Resolution*, Isaac Taylor died from consumption.

At Tahiti, both crews picked up a venereal disease which appears to have been gonorrhoea, but few were affected.[17] Evidently one of the surgeons, either Patten or Anderson, drew Cook's attention to an indigenous venereal-like disorder which we now know was yaws, and this convinced Cook that venereal disease in the Society Islands was pre-European. Cook also made observations upon "the sickness of Pepe" communicated by the Spanish ship *Aquila* eight months previously, which appears to have been an acute virus infection.

When the ships finally parted company on 30 October, the *Adventure* sailed to New Zealand, where a boat's crew of eight was murdered by Maoris. These were the only deaths sustained by the *Adventure* during the rest of her voyage. Meanwhile, during the second ice-edge search, a "gloomy and melancholy air" pervaded the *Resolution* because of mouldy bread, loathsome salted meat, and reduced rations—restored after a complaint by the first lieutenant.[18] Cook was not well. He had been vomiting, although he appeared to recover as the ship proceeded south, but on 27 February, vomiting recurred and he developed intestinal obstruction which almost cost him his life. He slowly recovered, although he was still off duty on 18 March.

Meanwhile, scurvy had appeared again. Forster, who was a casualty himself, reports that "a number crawled about the deck too weak ... to take enough wort," and Wales explains they had then been without fresh vegetables for fourteen weeks. Sparrman had mentioned scurvy as early as January and now speaks of a further outbreak "kept in bounds by a diet of sauerkraut and wort." At Easter Island on 12 March, Cook had recovered sufficiently to search for refreshments but succeeded in finding only a few roots which restored the appetite. Three days later many of the crew were "more or less affected with scurvy," yet Cook boasted on his arrival at the Marquesas that, after nineteen weeks at sea, there was not a sick man in the ship and only two or three with the least complaint.[19] But what were the criteria for health? One searches in vain for any reference to health screening like that practised by Rollin, surgeon to la Pérouse, which disclosed scurvy in men who had not reported sick.[20]

Beaglehole suggests that it was Cook's intention to complete his huge second tropical sweep by sailing from the Friendly Islands to Tierra del Fuego, and Forster believed he had been dissuaded by Patten, whose recent experiences must have led him to doubt the stamina of the ship's company for a passage of such length.[21] Off the New Hebrides, some were stricken by an allergic reaction after eating a large red fish, and Anderson sent Pringle detailed case histories.[22] It was a week before they recovered. Similar symptoms appeared after eating a species of tetraodon off New Caledonia.

After rounding Cape Horn during the third ice-edge search, even Cook was heartily sick of salt provisions. Deteriorating victuals and general dissatisfaction therefore decided him to steer for the Cape of Good Hope. The tensions which had developed over the quality of provisions during the days prior to arrival at the Cape appear in a revealing entry by Clerke for 16 March, when three officers entered the galley with drawn swords to threaten the cook![23] Sparrman, however, is more explicit: "It was now of... the greatest consequence to us, to enter the harbour, as several of our crew were attacked with the scurvy."[24] He goes on to paint a melancholy picture of the state of the provisions: mouldy bread alive with grubs, and soup swarming with maggots; pepper, vinegar, coffee and sugar long gone; tough salt meat, dried and shrunken after three years on board. As Milton-Thompson points out, sea rations of that period provided approximately 4,450 calories per day even after the deduction of the begrudged purser's eighth, ample for energy requirements, but nutritionally disastrous.[25] Cook spent over a month at the Cape and, his crew refreshed and the ship reprovisioned, he sailed for England on 26 April via St. Helena, arriving in Plymouth in July with a healthy ship's company.

In terms of mortality, the *Resolution* lost four men, one from consumption and three from accident. The *Adventure* lost eleven, but if we exclude the eight members of the boat's crew murdered by the Maoris on the homeward passage, her mortality rate compares favourably with that of the *Resolution*: three died, one from scurvy and two from fever. Morbidity rates, however, are impossible to determine, for though we know that the *Adventure* had one serious outbreak of scurvy with thirty cases on the sick list and many more of the crew

TABLE 1
Incidence of Sickness and Mortality on the Second Voyage, 1772-1775

| The *Resolution* | | The *Adventure* | |
|---|---|---|---|
| **Sickness** | | | |
| Scurvy | 5 | Scurvy | 2 |
| Salivary Adenitis | 1 | Salivary Adenitis | 1 |
| Allergic Reactions | 2 | Dysentery | 1 |
| Venereal Disease | 1 + | Veneral Disease | 2 + |
| **Mortality** | | | |
| Consumption | 1 | Scurvy | 1 |
| Accident | 3 | "Fever" | 2 |
| | | Murdered | 8 |
| Total | 4 | | 11 |

affected, we have no idea how many men were ill in the *Resolution* either from scurvy or any other illness. There is ample documentary evidence of at least four outbreaks of scurvy in the *Resolution* during this epoch-making voyage which, for two centuries, has been identified with the conquest of scurvy by Cook (table 1).

What is clear is that the outbreak in the *Adventure* during the first tropical sweep was much more serious than that in the *Resolution*. Cook must not be denied the credit for this nor for the arrest of scurvy in the *Adventure* after he had taken charge. There were, however, other factors. The *Resolution* was particularly favoured in her surgeons and also had the benefit of a well qualified physician in the person of Anders Sparrman, the Swedish botanist, all of whom were, on Cook's testimony, serious and competent professional men. James Patten, the surgeon, was an excellent clinician and won high praise from Cook, Forster, and Sir John Pringle. After the voyage, he established a reputable surgical practice in Dublin. Cook thought so highly of the gifted and conscientious William Anderson, his surgeon's first mate, that he appointed him surgeon and naturalist for the third voyage, and he refers to the second mate, Benjamin Drawater, as "a steady clever man."

Here then was a team of educated medical men with the care of the ship's company at heart. What they lacked, however, was any idea of the experimental methodology which characterized the work of Lind, Robertson, Blane, and Armstrong. This led to a blunderbuss approach to antiscorbutic treatment which confused the issue by failing to differentiate true antiscorbutics from the empirical remedies of longstanding tradition. It misled both Cook and Pringle into endorsing malt wort, which thus came to be accepted—without a scrap of scientific evidence—as the treatment for sea scurvy to the exclusion of lemon juice. Lemon juice was finally delivered the coup de grace by Cook himself in a letter to Pringle on his return: "The dearness of the rob of lemons and oranges will hinder them from being furnished in large quantities, but I do not think this so necessary; for, though they may assist other things, I have no great opinion of them alone...."[26]

The *Adventure* was by no means so fortunate in her surgeons. Thomas Andrews was a boisterous, hard-drinking type. When he incorrectly diagnosed the fever picked up at St. Jago, he prescribed Dr. James's powders, and two midshipmen died. Trotter describes an identical incident at St. Jago followed by malaria and dysentery and treated successfully with quinine.[27] John Kent, the surgeon's first mate, certainly had odd friends, and we know nothing about the second mate, John Young. It is little wonder that, in these hands, scurvy made rapid progress in the *Adventure*, where antiscorbutics were on the surgeon's prescription. Nevertheless, whereas Cook rightly emphasized the overriding importance of fresh provisions and would row many miles a day in search of likely antiscorbutics, Furneaux was complacent and appears to have placed his confidence in cider. Furneaux was a Devon man and probably took advice from Dr. John Huxham, a Plymouth physician who, in 1747, had written to the *General Evening Post* on his experiences of twelve hundred cases of scurvy in Admiral Martin's fleet. That same year, he published *A Method for Preserving the Health of Seamen in Long Cruises*, recommending apples, oranges, lemons and rough cider for the prevention and cure of scurvy. Unfortunately, he was later persuaded that Devonshire colic was due to "too great a Use of the very acid Juice of Lemons" and in his *Observations on the Air and Epidemic Diseases* (1759), advocated apples and cider only.[28] Huxham's views on scurvy are those quoted by Pringle in his *Diseases of the Army*. This advice, and an incompetent medical staff, no doubt deprived the *Adventure*'s scorbutic patients of lemon juice and goes some way towards explaining the differing experiences of the two ships.

The other factor, as Trotter demonstrated, was Cook's superior officership.[29] However, the association of scurvy with flux is of special interest in the light of a recent report on tropical sprue in Puerto Ricans by Klipstein and Corcino, which established a relationship between the onset of intestinal symptoms and overindulgence in cooked hog's flesh and foods cooked in pork dripping. They showed that the oxidation resulting from prolonged exposure of hog's fat to warm temperatures and, in particular, to frequent reheating, causes the fat to become rancid. Long-chain, unsaturated fatty acids are formed which influence bacterial colonization of the intestine, causing diarrhoea and malabsorption of food nutrients.[30] It will be obvious that under conditions of low vitamin C intake and high utilization, scurvy would rapidly appear.

Before Cook joined him prior to the first tropical sweep, Furneaux had spent six weeks of indulgence in Queen Charlotte Sound without, however, acquiring antiscorbutic plants for the diet of his men. Scurvy affected the crews of both ships, but that in the *Adventure* was severe and associated with flux. It is therefore tempting to ascribe this outbreak to tropical sprue, the result of excess consumption of rancid animal fat at Queen Charlotte Sound. It also provides belated scientific evidence to support the views of Palliser, Hutchinson (Wallis's surgeon), and Cook himself that consumption of fat skimmings from the coppers in which salt meat was boiled was deleterious, and thus confirms that Cook was right in strictly forbidding its use.

Cook's dependence upon the quality of his surgeons is again demonstrated by the health record of his voyage in the *Endeavour* from 1768 to 1771. The surgeon was William Brougham Monkhouse. His journal reveals him to be an intelligent and perceptive observer, but with the eye of the tourist rather than the clinician or naturalist.[31] Other journalists suggest a flamboyant, brash extrovert more at home in the company of gentlemen than of the sick, always among the first to land, his musket at the ready, and with a discerning eye for the belles of Tahiti. Perhaps the ship's company was fortunate in being left to the care of William Perry, the first mate, a conscientious young man of twenty-one whom Cook appears to have rated more highly than the surgeon.

Before the voyage, on 12 July, Monkhouse was interviewed by the Sick and Hurt Commissioners and instructed about the trial he was to carry out on portable soup and the rob of oranges and lemons prepared at Haslar hospital.[32] It is worth noting that one week later the commissioners felt it necessary to send written instructions to Cook.[33] Cook significantly received his instructions about a trial of malt wort direct from the Admiralty secretary, with whom MacBride, its protagonist, had corresponded, and not via the Sick and Hurt Board.[34] A Victualling Board minute, detailing the long list of provisions, included an instruction for "a fair Tryal to be made of the efficacy of the Sour Krout against the Scurvy."[35] There was thus laid upon the surgeon the obligation to undertake four separate trials, in two of which he had been personally instructed. Yet, after the death of Monkhouse at Batavia, Cook found he had left "no journal properly drawn up and attested by himself." On survey of the medical stores, which the surgeon himself was obliged to provide aided by a small annual allowance, Perry reported "a very great deficiency" and requested an advance of twenty pounds to cover the purchase of medicines urgently required for the increasing number of sick. Whether Monkhouse had been living beyond his means and had been unable to purchase enough medicines or had used the allowance for other purposes, we shall never know, but his journal does not suggest an absorbing clinical interest. It is perhaps noteworthy that Monkhouse was the only officer able to supply Cook with an eyewitness account of the arioi practices in Tahiti.

During the first voyage, Alexander Weir was drowned at Funchal on 14 September 1768, and Peter Flower at Rio on 2 December. The only other reference to health during the *Endeavour*'s long haul to Rio is Wilkinson's entry for 11 October that "the People began to be very Sickeley."[36] This is just about the time we would expect symptoms of scurvy to appear. Banks's two negro servants died from the combined effects of alcohol and exposure during an expedition on 17 January 1769 in Tierra del Fuego, where celery and cranberries checked scurvy.[37] In the south Pacific in March, William Greenslade committed suicide by jumping overboard. Banks developed his first symptoms of scurvy and turned to the lemon juice given into his charge by Nathaniel Hulme.[38] Both concentrated juice and the juice preserved with one-fifth part of brandy were in excellent condition. He began with the latter. Banks had eaten sauerkraut constantly, but preferred salted cabbage, and had drunk a pint or more of wort every evening, "but all this did not so intirely check the distemper as to prevent my feeling some small effects of it. About a fortnight ago my gums swelled and some small pimples rose in the inside of my mouth which threatned to become ulcers, I then flew to the lemon Juice...." He took six ounces a day. "The effect of this was surprizing, in less than a week my gums became as firm as ever...."[39] Here, then, is a factual statement that regular and adequate use of sauerkraut, salted cabbage, and wort failed to prevent the onset of scurvy which lemon juice speedily cured. It is at variance with Perry's ambiguous report of a trial of the wort in four cases of scurvy at this time when he was one of the sufferers. Although he attributed the cure to wort alone, lemon juice appears also to have been given.[40]

On arrival at Tahiti, on 13 April, Cook reported few men on the sick list and with "slite complaints" only, a health record which he attributed to sauerkraut, portable soup, and malt. They had not been there more than five days before the "venereal disease" then prevalent in Tahiti appeared in the ships and soon affected twenty-four seamen and nine marines. Since Wallis's crew had escaped, Cook naturally attributed the contagion to the French under Bougainville who had visited the islands in the interval. Cook informs us that by the time they sailed, the ship's company "from hard duty... and the too free use of women were in a worse state of hilth than they were on our arrival for by this time full half of them had got Venereal disease."[41] It appears to have caused him to cruise among the Society Islands in order to give his crew the chance to recuperate before proceeding to New Zealand.

Apart from the death of John Reardon from an alcoholic debauch on 28 August, there is no further mention of sickness until Banks, on 29 March 1770, describes a short-lived epidemic of violent headache and vomiting followed by fever which was probably dengue or sandfly fever.[42] Forby Sutherland died of consumption at Botany Bay on 1 May, and eight or nine sick were sent ashore on 19 June at Endeavour River "with different disorders." Cook does not mention scurvy, but Banks reveals that both Tupia and Green had symptoms. Perry's report to Cook at the end of the voyage described four cases of scurvy in the south Pacific in addition to "3 in a port in New Holland and 2 previously off the New Zealand coast." The rob of lemons appears to have been the determining factor in their cure.

The shadow over this first voyage, however, fell at Batavia, where Cook's immediate concern was for the ship. Again we have difficulty in interpreting statements on health, for—though Banks refers to the jeers of the Endeavour's rosy-cheeked sailors at the spectres of Batavia Dutch-

men and Cook claims there was not a man on the sick list on arrival—
Hicks, Green, and Tupia were sick enough: Hicks from consumption
and Green and Tupia from scurvy. It is clear that there had been health
problems. Off New Guinea on 3 September and again off Timor on the
16th, Cook had been pressed strongly by his officers to acquire
refreshments, and on 17 September at Savu had himself referred to
those who were in "a very indifferent state to health and ... mind."[43]
The latter was ascribed to "nostalgia" by Banks, to whom we are
indebted for the important information that the second lieutenant called
on the *Radja*, explaining that "we were an English man-of-war who had
been long at sea and had many sick on board, for whom we wanted to
purchase such refreshments as the island afforded."[44] On this evidence
and our knowledge of the empty medicine chest, the ship's company was
ill prepared for events at Batavia, an unhealthy city intersected by canals
carrying the town's sewage and surrounded by a swamp caused by the
earthquake of 1699, an ideal breeding ground for malaria-carrying
anopheles mosquitoes.

Those living on shore were the first to be attacked by malaria,
Monkhouse himself dying of violent fever. Banks put Tupia under canvas on Cooper's Island to benefit from the cooling breeze, and here tents
were erected for the ship's company who fell daily sick with dysentery.
It was a low, unhealthy location and a bad choice. After two days in
Tupia's tents, Banks was smitten with a tertian fever. It was the mon-
soon season, and Banks found mosquitoes "breeding in every splash of
water."[45] Tayeto fell ill with a fever and a lung condition and both he
and Tupia died. By 9 November not more than twenty were fit for duty.
Banks makes it thirteen or fourteen and says Cook was ill on board. On
18 December, the ship repaired and reprovisioned and his weak and
sickly crew back on board, Cook sailed for England, having buried five
men in Batavia.

The ravages of dysentery and malaria were now to be experienced in
full. By 26 December, there were forty on the sick list and the remainder
were weak and ill. On 6 January 1771, Cook called at Prince's Island to
take on rather suspect water and presumably rest his crew, but the un-
cleared island merely increased the risk of malaria. Banks, who had
cured himself with a private supply of cinchona bark, fell ill again after
an expedition ashore and once more found the bark effective.[46] Unrecog-
nized, however, mosquitoes had been spreading malaria since the ship

left Batavia, for on 1 January Banks writes: "I have been unaccountably troubled with Musquitos ever since we left Batavia, and still imagin'd that they increased instead of decreasing, although my opinion was universally thought improbable; today, however, the mystery was discovered, for on getting up water today, Dr. Solander who happned to stand near the scuttle cask observed an infinite number of them in their water state in it, who as soon as the sun had a little effect upon the water began to come out in real Effective mosquetos incredibly fast"[47]—an important observation which, had it been pursued, might have linked the mosquito with the spread of malaria one hundred years earlier.

The log from Prince's Island to the Cape is punctuated by a depressing list of deaths, twenty-two in all, which included Spöring, Parkinson, Green, and Jonathan Monkhouse. Cook may have been right in attributing the first signs of amelioration to the trade winds, which at least got rid of the mosquitoes.

The *Endeavour* anchored in Table Bay on 14 March, and on this occasion, Cook's first priority was the health of his men. Fresh provisions were obtained and the sick sent ashore. In spite of every care, three more died and many were in very poor health when they returned on board before sailing for England on 15 April. They were not the last; Robert Molyneux died from complications the following day, probably from a liver disorder if Cook's reference to his intemperance is relevant.[48] Hicks died from consumption on 26 May and, on 1 July, John Still died. The *Endeavour* anchored at the Downs on 13 July, and Wilkinson succumbed shortly afterwards.

It was not an impressive health record. In addition to three drownings, thirty-eight out of a ship's company of ninety-eight had died: three from consumption, three from alcohol—hastened in two cases by exposure—one from epilepsy, and thirty-one from malaria and dysentery. There were three recorded outbreaks of scurvy and a very suggestive history on two other occasions. Eight died before Batavia; five at Batavia (Cook makes it seven); twenty-two between Batavia and the Cape; three at the Cape; and three on passage to England. One died immediately afterwards (table 2).

The malaria appears to have been a mixed vivax and falciparum infection, either causing tertian attacks or pursuing an atypical course with pulmonary and cerebral manifestations. Tayeto, for instance, had acute pulmonary complications, and Green neurological signs. Dysentery

TABLE 2
Incidence of Sickness and Mortality on the First Voyage, 1768-1771

| The *Endeavor* | | | |
|---|---|---|---|
| Sickness | | | |
| Scurvy | 5 | "Dysentery" | 1 |
| Dengue | 1 | Venereal Disease | 1+ |
| Malaria | 1 | | |
| Mortality, by cause and location | | | |
| Consumption | 3 | Pre-Batavia | 8 |
| Alcoholic Excess | 3 | Batavia | 5 |
| Epilepsy | 1 | Batavia - Cape | 22 |
| Drowning | 3 | Cape | 3 |
| Malaria & "Dysentery" | 31 | Cape - England | 3 |
| Total | 41* | | 41* |

*Plus one following arrival in England

either co-existed or confused the diagnosis in cases with gastrointestinal symptoms.

Bontius, the great Dutch physician of seventeenth-century Batavia, attributes the high mortality rate from dysentery to an "inflammatory liquor" the Chinese made from rice and the holothuria, or sea slug, an echinoderm. He distinguishes the "quallen" from arrack made in the proper manner and observes: "Happy were it for our sailors that they drank more moderately of this liquor, the Plains of India would not then be protuberant with the innumerable graves of the dead." He adds: "When the intoxicated drinkers are all a-glowing with the pernicious draught, they throw down immense quantities of water into their stomachs to extinguish the heat, then lye along the ground like beasts, or stretched on the decks of the ships.... By which means they received into their bodies the noxious vapours arising from the earth."[49]

Thus we have an explanation both of the dysentery and the malaria. The sea slug is a filthy animal feeding on excreta and refuse. Even allowing for the antiseptic properties of spirit, the consumption of large quantities of contaminated local water is sufficient to account for the dysentery, while lying exposed to the night air invited attack by mosquitoes.

But what was the nature of the dysentery? It appears to have had a comparatively long incubation period with serious and late complications following a stormy and protracted course and eventually affecting most people to some degree. Banks again provides a clue. On 22 January, the epidemic was at its height with almost all the ship's company ill "with either fluxes or purgings." On the 25th, he "endured the pains of the Damnd" and "at night, they became fixed at a point in my bowels."[50] Taken together, we have a picture of typhoid fever rather than bacilliary or amoebic dysentery. Cook mentions an unusually high sickness rate in the Indies for that year and considers his mortality rate favourable compared with that of the Indiamen, but omits to mention their greater complements of up to 350, excluding passengers, in Dutch ships and between 100 and 135 in English ships.[51] The *Endeavour*'s mortality rate of forty-three per cent must be considered high by any standards. One of the reasons may have been Perry's reluctance to use quinine at the onset of malaria. Banks cured himself from a private supply; this suggests Perry was not using it. If so, it again highlights the influence of Pringle and the Edinburgh School upon the Cook voyages, for in the Galen and Boerhaave tradition which it followed, repeated bleedings, purging, and sweating were employed in fevers; quinine was withheld until complete intermission occurred. Pringle himself warned against its premature exhibition.[52] The naval physician Lind, on the other hand, prescribed the bark freely, not only as a remedy but also as a preventive, and laid down strict precautions to be taken in fever-ridden areas. They included anchoring well away from shore, closing the shore-side ports, clearing the upper deck of men at night, vigorous ventilation and frequent fumigation of the ship, and strict antimalarial discipline for working parties on shore, including locating camping sites on high ground.[53]

John Millar, drawing upon the experiences of East India Company ships, later inveighed against those who followed Boerhaave's doctrines and gave too little bark too late.[54] It is therefore scarcely surprising to find him, in a letter to Viscount Melville, commending Patten for the success of the second voyage and castigating Monkhouse for the Batavia debacle, whilst exonerating Cook: "How hard would it have been to have rendered Captain Cook responsible for the sickness and mortality of the *Endeavour* and has not the merit of Mr. Patten on board the *Resolution* been too much overlooked? Might not the surgeon of the *Endeavour* have been justly tried by a Court Martial, and required to show cause why he should not have been lyable to such punishment as might have been judged adequate to his neglect or incapacity?"[55]

But was Cook quite as blameless as Millar suggests? His preoccupation with the ship at Batavia rather than with the men is evident from his journal. The men were kept hanging around the ship although there was little work for them and there was a possibility of finding health on high ground.[56] It is conceivable, however, that Cook's indulgent attitude towards the drinking habits of his crew may have been the critical factor. Wallis, who had called at Batavia three years previously, took a much tougher line and followed Lind's precepts, stopped shore leave and prohibited alcohol from being brought on board. In spite of these precautions, malaria and flux put forty men on the sick list, and he makes the important observation that all who attended the sick were quickly taken ill. He kept the sick on board, made a large sick berth, purified all drinking water and sterilized it with red-hot iron, while his surgeon, John Hutchinson, was "indefatiguable."[57] He also called at Prince's Island and only three lives were lost, but it must be conceded that he intentionally limited his call at Batavia to seven days.

In a letter to the Victualling Board at the end of the voyage, Cook attributed the *Endeavour*'s freedom from scurvy largely to sauerkraut, observing in his report to the Admiralty that the surgeon had found malt "indifferent" as an antiscorbutic. In order to utilize the malt advantageously, Cook had boiled it with wheat for breakfast; this food had appeared beneficial, though he admitted supplies had run out in the latter part of the voyage. He enclosed an extraordinarily ambivalent report from Perry which included an account of Cook's antiscorbutic measures. Understandably, he observed that "It is impossible for me to say what was most conducive to our preservation from Scurvy so many being the preventives used." The only trial he specifically mentions relates to malt wort, but his results are invalidated by the use of the rob which, he claims, was attended by success. A letter from the Sick and Hurt Board to the Admiralty secretary discloses that the surgeon's journal contained no information about the robs, but the commissioners had learned from him and others in the *Endeavour* that the robs had been useful.[58] Perry declares that little opportunity had occurred for a trial of wort, in spite of his own and Cook's reference to this, yet he reaches the astonishing and damaging conclusion that "from what I have seen the wort perform, from it's mode of operation, from Mr. MacBride's reasoning I shall not hesitate a moment to declare my opinion, viz that the Malt is the best medicine I know, the inspissated Orange & Lemon juices not even excepted."[59] Perry was a well educated young man who had read MacBride's works and resented his derogatory remarks about sea surgeons. He was therefore on the defensive, aware of the wrath that would descend upon his head if he gave an adverse report. That appears to explain his ambivalence. Such is the influence of status and patronage upon the young!

Patronage is also relevant to the story of malt wort, for the consequences of this report on the health of seamen were even more tragic than Pringle's strictures on the use of quinine in malaria. James Lind had initiated the concept of the controlled clinical trial in 1747 on board HMS *Salisbury*. It demonstrated conclusively the power of orange and lemon juice over other popular remedies to cure scurvy in matched scorbutic cases on a scorbutic diet.[62] His three major works provide a compendium of naval preventive medicine argued from sound principles and containing those measures practised with such resolution and effect by Cook and elaborated by him in his paper to the Royal Society on 3 March 1776. They included all Lind's proposals, probably passed on by Sir Hugh Palliser, Cook's own patron, who is reported to have consulted Lind when in command of the *Sheerness* in 1748.[61] The emphasis, however, was upon malt, not lemon juice, owing to the extraordinary arrogance and persistence of David MacBride, a former naval surgeon whose brother, a naval captain, enjoyed the patronage of Palliser and Sandwich. MacBride was a Dublin physician in search of a reputation which, in the scientific milieu of eighteenth-century England, had to be founded upon experiment. He claimed to have discovered a means of releasing, by fermentation of malt, the fixed air (carbon dioxide) which he believed "essential to the digestion and absorption of nutrients" from the intestine.[62] His *Experimental Essays* not only plagiarized Lind but rather too obviously are based upon the methodology of Pringle, whose attention he sought to attract. He had his *Essay on Scurvy* forwarded through George Cleghorn, a Dublin anatomist, to John Hunter, the London surgeon, and Henry Tom, a commissioner for the Sick and Hurt, and a trial was ordered at Plymouth and Portsmouth Naval Hospitals. The intervention of Captain Brett of the *Torbay*, who lost a good seaman through the trial, and adverse reports from the hospital physicians failed to deflect MacBride from obtaining a trial at sea.[63] In February 1763 Tom informed him that the navy surgeons had not reported. He therefore sought the help of Robert Adair, an influential

Army surgeon, friend of Pringle, and hero of the popular song, "Robin Adair."[64] The Admiralty ordered a sea trial. Meanwhile, he had succeeded in having a trial of sorts carried out in his brother's ship, HMS *Jason*, on her circumnavigation of the Falkland Islands from 1763 to 1765. The surgeon, Alexander Young, admitted that the only case of scurvy to have taken wort on the outward passage had been supplied with apples and oranges by the captain, and those who developed scurvy at Port Egmont had eaten wild celery. Yet as Lloyd and Coulter exclaim, on the strength of this prejudicial testimony, he claimed that wort was as powerful an antiscorbutic as fresh citrus fruit.[65] First Wallis, then Cook, were asked to experiment, and Carteret after "a fair and long tryal" reported that "we did not find it would cure the Scurvy."[66]

Baron Storsch of Berlin used his influence to achieve a trial of carrot marmalade during the second voyage. In his report, Cook equivocated, and his surgeons reported adversely. Pelham, one of the commissioners of victualling, also used his position to introduce the inspissated juice of malt and hops for brewing beer at sea, on the grounds that scurvy only developed after the beer was expended. The life of the beer supply was, of course, well within the time required for scurvy to appear. Beer contains no vitamin C.[67]

Lind enjoyed no such patronage. The Sick and Hurt Board therefore ignored his brilliant experiment with the citrus fruits and advised the Admiralty they did not consider the rob efficacious in scurvy.[68] Cook conducted no trial, yet lent his considerable authority to the promotion of malt as an effective antiscorbutic, a disastrous error which condemned many thousands of seamen to death until the patronage of Rodney and Gardner was extended to Gilbert Blane, one of Lind's disciples, who succeeded in obtaining its general issue to the fleet in 1796, one year after Lind's death. Only then was the chapter on malt wort, to which Cook had been principal contributor, finally closed.[69]

It was not the end of the story of lemon juice, however. Nathaniel Hulme, another Lind disciple, had provided Banks on the *Endeavour* voyage with three casks of lemon juice preserved by different methods. Banks appears to have made use of only one. It cured him of scurvy, but there was no trial. That had to await McClure's expedition of 1850, which led to the discovery of the Northwest Passage. Alexander Armstrong, the surgeon, obeying stringent experimental criteria, found that the antiscorbutic properties of pure inspissated lemon juice compared equally well with those of the juice in spirit, but the controversy remains.[70] Hughes has recently tested lemon juice which he claims was prepared to Lind's formula, and found that eighty-seven per cent of the vitamin C content was lost after twenty-eight days' storage.[71] Wyatt argued that the naval methods of storage excluded light and oxygen and thus prevented rapid deterioration.[72] However, the vitamin C content of the preserved juice was probably adequate to maintain body stores above the critical level until replenished by fresh vegetables in harbour, since the amount of vitamin C required to prevent scurvy has been found to be only about ten milligrams daily.[73] We have also Blane's evidence that, in less than two years after the general issue of lemon juice, scurvy became extinct, while Carré attributes British victories during the Revolutionary Wars to healthy, well trained crews, and Nelson's transformation of Sicily into a vast lemon juice factory.[74] That was fortunately before the parsimonious Admiralty Board substituted West Indian lime juice for Mediterranean lemon juice in the mid-nineteenth century and created the problems of scurvy all over again.

Nevertheless, Cook made two notable contributions to the prevention of scurvy, since its onset is determined by the size of the body pool of vitamin C and its rate of utilization. The impressment of men for sea service after long voyages was uneconomic because, with vitamin C stores exhausted, they were among the first to suffer. Cook's policy of short sea passages and frequent calls for fresh food rich in the vitamin ensured saturation of the body pools which, under normal circumstances, appear to have a turnover rate of about forty days.[75] Acting on the advice of Wallis, Cook also reduced the rate of vitamin C utilization by providing his men with dry, warm clothes and putting them into three watches, thus significantly reducing stress, which increases requirements. It is therefore to be regretted that among the excellent hygienic and dietary measures Cook introduced, lemon juice, the only sea-transportable antiscorbutic, was dismissed in favour of malt, which has no vitamin C content whatever.

The introduction of malt, however, may not have been an unmixed curse, for malt is a potential source of the B complex of vitamins also deficient in the seaman's diet, although its potency would obviously depend upon conditions of storage and there are several references by the journalists to its deterioration. Overt symptoms of deficiency included weakness and paralysis of the limbs or swelling, and occasional sudden heart failure, often mistaken for scurvy. It explains why lemon juice alone occasionally failed to cure all scurvy cases, and why Cook met with success when lemon juice was combined with malt. Perhaps this is the reason why Cook ignored scurvy reported by others, in the belief that the absence of oedema, which we now know to be a symptom of vitamin B deficiency, meant absence of scurvy. When oedema was gross, it was called dropsy, and could also result from liver disease caused by syphilis, alcoholic excess, or protein deficiency. A further factor would be the high sodium content of salt meat tending to cause water retention within the body tissues.

More direct criticism of Cook may be made of his failure to exploit one of Lind's important innovations, the distillation of sea water. Its history is equally tortuous. Distillation appears first to have been undertaken in British vessels by Sir Richard Hawkins in 1593, and Netherlands East India Company ships regularly distilled water at sea during the seventeenth century, using it to wash the salted scurvy-grass they also carried. Lind laid his method before the Royal Society in 1762, and the second edition of his *Health of Seamen* showed how still heads could be fitted to ships' coppers, the distillate passing by means of a wormed tube surrounded by a cask of cooling water into a collecting vessel.[76] The idea seems to owe something to a book on distilling by Hieronymous Brunschwig in 1519.[77] Lind's idea was seized upon by Charles Irving, a British naval surgeon, who in 1772 received £5,000 from Parliament for the invention, and by Poissonière, a French naval physician, who was rewarded by the French government the same year. Lind, of course, received nothing, but his still was fitted to the *Dolphin* in 1766 and Hutchinson, the surgeon, obtained thirty-six gallons of fresh water in five hours from fifty-six gallons of sea water.[78] Bougainville used the Poissonière version to provide fresh water between the Magellan Straits and Tahiti in 1767, and Irving provided distilled water for Phipps.[79] It was Irving's less efficient apparatus which was installed in the *Resolution* and the *Adventure*. According to Pringle, Cook made little use of it, and he implied that a great opportunity had been lost to experiment both with the still and Hales's ventilator, with which the ships were also fitted. Nevertheless, Cook's influence in the field of hygiene was profound. For instance, Spencer Wells, a nineteenth-century naval surgeon who became president of the Royal College of Surgeons of England, significantly reduced his mortality rate by introducing naval standards of cleanliness and ventilation into his London operating theatre.[80]

The medical history of the third voyage in the *Resolution* and the *Discovery* was dominated by Cook's death. There were neither innovations nor experiments, and Anderson, quite the most intelligent, percipient, and scientifically orientated of the surgeons, was engaged almost exclusively upon natural history and his duties as interpreter. But he was a very sick man and died from consumption on 3 August 1778. John Law, surgeon of the *Discovery*, who succeeded him, seems to have been a plodding, unimaginative, but kindly and conscientious man who, in 1784, while surgeon of HMS *Trusty*, attended Captain King dying from consumption in Nice.[81] The fragment of his journal that remains tells us little.[82] David Samwell, first mate of the *Resolution* and later surgeon of the *Discovery*, was a passionate man and intelligent observer, but rather given to hyperbole. He provided the best account of Cook's death.[83] Unfortunately his Celtic romanticism, expressed so admirably in his poetry, extended uninhibited to his nymphs of the South Seas, and it is evident that both he and possibly other surgeons were actively engaged in the traffic Cook sought so desperately to control. William Ellis, second mate of the *Discovery*, wrote a more compassionate account of the voyage and was a competent water colourist.[84] Their journals tell us a great deal about the Polynesians, practically nothing about the ships' companies except their unbridled sexual appetite; and it is significant that when Bayly developed an "apsis" of the leg, Clerke, the captain, dressed it although Samwell was then the *Discovery*'s surgeon.[85] We know nothing about James Snagg, first mate of the *Discovery*, but when Robert Davies was promoted to first mate of the *Resolution*, Cook found it necessary to give him directions in writing on how to conduct himself.[86] With the exception of Anderson, it was not the sort of medical team to give the backing Cook needed to combat the spread of disease by and among the turbulent and rebellious ships' companies of the third voyage.

Fourteen men died. Four marines from the *Resolution* were killed with Cook at Kealakekua Bay. Two of the *Discovery*'s marines were drowned, and young McIntosh was killed when the mainstay gave way. All who died from disease were in the *Resolution*: Roberts from pneumonia complicating dropsy, old Watman from a cerebrovascular accident,

TABLE 3
Incidence of Sickness and Mortality on the Third Voyage, 1776-1780

| The *Resolution* | | The *Discovery* | |
|---|---|---|---|
| **Sickness** | | | |
| Scurvy | 1 | Manchineel Conjunctivitis | 1 |
| Venereal Disease | 4 | Jaundice | 1 |
| | | Venereal Disease | 4 |
| **Mortality** | | | |
| Killed at Hawaii | 5 | Drowned | 2 |
| Dropsy & Pneumonia | 1 | Accident on Board | 1 |
| Stroke | 1 | | |
| Dysentery | 1 | | |
| Consumption | 2 | | |
| Unknown Cause | 2 | | |
| Total | 12 | | 3 |

McIntosh from dysentery contracted at Hawaii, Gibson from a lingering illness, and Davis from an unknown cause. Clerke and Anderson died of consumption (table 3).

Spruce beer quickly removed any "seeds of scurvy" at Queen Charlotte Sound in February 1777, and it was not seen again.[87] Manchineel sap blinded wooders for several days at Tonga.[88] In September, at Tahiti, Cook developed sciatica which was cured by manipulation and massage from Tahitian women, but Bayly remarks that he was still "a little indisposed" at Huahine a month later when half the people were suffering from venereal disease and four or five men from "Yallow jaundice."[89] Jaundice had evidently reached epidemic proportions on arrival at Hawaii in January 1778, but quickly subsided.[90] It was probably a viral hepatitis contracted at Tahiti, but it is possible that an increasing number of sailors were being tattooed (Parkinson and others were tattooed on the first voyage and Trevenen on the third) and that the hepatitis was of "serum" type. If so, it is the first record of a serious complication of tattooing.

But the real problem of the third voyage was venereal disease. At Tonga, in May 1777, girls could be procured for a hatchet or a shirt a night.[91] Anderson made an attempt to differentiate between tertiary syphilis, which he attributed to the visit of the *Resolution* and the *Adventure* in 1773, from yaws, which he rightly judged indigenous. He may have been right, because Bontius differentiated Amboyna Pox (yaws) from syphilis on the same grounds.[92] What the men both gave and received at Tonga was gonorrhoea, but syphilis cannot be absolutely excluded. The story was repeated at Tahiti in August. Again, it seems plain it was gonorrhoea. According to Bayly, "few men catch'd it and those very slight"[93] and even men with active disease appear to have been accepted by the native women although, since primary manifestations of yaws and syphilis were similar, Tahitian women may have been more ready to disregard it than the evidences of gonorrhoea. Omai was a victim. King admired the discipline and self-control of the Spaniards who had visited in 1775 and claimed they had won Tahitian respect for their abstinence, but Samwell characteristically despised the "flesh-subduing dons" held in derision by his paramours.[94]

The spread of venereal disease was one of Cook's main preoccupations during the voyages, and on the third voyage it provided the occasion but not the cause of Cook's exasperation and changed attitude towards his men.

Venereal disease appeared in the *Endeavour* five days after her arrival in Tahiti, and half the ship's company was affected. This could only have been gonorrhoea and perhaps chancroid. Banks saw ulcerated and crusted skin lesions among natives which were obviously yaws,[95] but learned that Bougainville's ships, which visited Tahiti ten months previously, had left behind a virulent venereal disease associated with loss of hair and nails and acute intestinal disturbance; Williamson, who had sailed with Wallis, was surprised to find an "inveterate itch or yaws" he does not appear to have seen previously.[96] According to Bougainville, his men acquired every type of venereal disease.[97] It certainly included either chancroid or lymphogranuloma venereum, two non-syphilitic venereal disorders then common in Europe, and presumably gonorrhoea. There is no evidence that he saw active yaws. His visit was too short to allow the Tahitian women to acquire and retransmit other than gonorrhoea, but the incubation period he reports would be right for syphilis or lymphogranuloma venereum if it pre-existed in Tahiti. This evidence indicts Wallis. We have, however, to explain the acute post-Bougainville epidemic described by Banks,[98] for loss of hair was a frequent accompaniment of secondary syphilis in Europe until quite recently, and rotting flesh with the loss of nails suggests septicaemia. It is therefore possible to argue that Wallis left lymphogranuloma venereum at Tahiti which Bougainville's men picked up (and we have Robertson's word that "inveterate poxes and claps" affected three of Wallis's crew), while Bougainville brought syphilis, which he admits had been present in his ships, and discharged not only treponemeta but also plague-infested rats into the Tahitian community, giving rise to a virulent but short-lived epidemic.[99] This may also be the explanation of the Naples epidemic of 1494 which has been taken traditionally to signal the explosive spread of syphilis throughout Europe after it had been brought back from America by Columbus.[100] Either Wallis or Bougainville—or both—introduced gonorrhoea.

If yaws was present in Tahiti, although it was not mentioned by Wallis, the problem is complicated by the question of whether syphilis and yaws are two separate diseases or different manifestations of the same disease transmitted by different means, since the treponemes responsible for yaws and syphilis are morphologically and immunologically identical. The arguments are too specialized and complicated to rehearse here, but Van der Sluis and Smith, who take different viewpoints, have made notable contributions.[101] Hackett, in 1953, attempted to trace the evolution of syphilis from pinta, through yaws and endemic syphilis, as the result of mutations of a single organism in response to environmental influences over thousands of years.[102] This work led him to a study of bones from accurately dated burials throughout the world before the end of the fifteenth century. He published his preliminary findings in 1976 and they revealed, surprisingly, that fewer than 6 skulls of 4,500 pre-Columbian American Indians showed any evidence of yaws or syphilis, that only 1 of 450 Maori skulls showed suspicious changes, but that about 1 per cent of 4,500 Australian aboriginal skulls met the strict criteria he had established. He therefore concluded that only in Australia was there positive evidence of a pre-Columbian treponemal infection, which was probably yaws.[103] Studies of other Pacific communities have been carried out,[104] but the absence of internationally agreed criteria does not allow us to draw similar conclusions at the present time; the outcome of further research should determine whether yaws existed before Europeans arrived or whether their sexually transmitted treponemes were subsequently propagated through direct contact from the initial skin lesions of syphilis by treponemes able to survive under the critical conditions of temperature and humidity, i.e. temperatures of about 80°F. (27°C) and fifty inches (1.3m) rainfall occurring in certain areas of the Pacific.[105] If, however, yaws antedated Europeans, syphilitics in the ships would have been protected against yaws, but natives suffering from yaws may not have been immune to syphilis, since cross-immunity develops rapidly in syphilis but takes years to develop in yaws.[106]

During the second voyage, the *Adventure* acquired gonorrhoea on both her visits to New Zealand, presumably left by the *Endeavour* previously, and mixed venereal infections appeared in both ships at Tahiti, for Duncan, whose informant appears to have been Andrews, the *Adventure*'s surgeon, informs us that the majority of cases in the *Adventure* were due to gonorrhoea, implying that other venereal infections were also present.[107] James Colnett, midshipman in the *Resolution*, later declared he saw chancres and buboes.[108] Both may have been witnessing non-syphilitic lesions, for the perceptive Patten "made it his business to enquire" and could not confirm any cases of "pox."[109]

It was during the third voyage, however, that venereal disease was to bring such dire consequences. Cook knew only too well that the gonorrhoea his men acquired in the Friendly Islands had been left there by his own ships during the second voyage, and it is significant that it was here that "the cool discernment" Burney so much admired in his captain first began to crack. He punished his men by a reduced allowance, a discipline he had never before used, and ordered twelve lashes for the doubtful offence of "a quiet and good man." The father-figure of the second voyage who had shown his crews "every indulgence which was in my power to give them" and "the great and good man" whom the old Maori remembered patting his cheeks as a child, became the feared despot from whom his "mutinous and turbulent crew" could expect "not the least indulgence,"[110] while two to six dozen lashes became the norm for thieving natives, with mutilating wounds for good measure. What was even more extraordinary was Cook's behaviour at the initiation of the king's son. Normally cautious and sensitive to local feelings, Cook threw discretion to the winds and took great risks in breaking taboo to rub shoulders with the natives, to their embarrassment. Bared to the waist and with hair streaming, he was scarcely recognizable as the erstwhile commander of His Majesty's Ship *Endeavour* who, at Rio, was haughtily conscious of the dignity of his sovereign. Yet these exhibitions were but facets of a more subtle change in Cook's personality, his questing spirit unchallenged by news of Fiji and Samoa as he sailed without apparent purpose through the Tongan Archipelago.

The Society Islands contributed their quota of gonorrhoea, and by the time Raiatea was reached in October, there were scarcely enough hands to work the ship.[111] It was therefore hardly coincidental that October should also witness another of Cook's explosive outbursts as he rampaged across Moorea in search of a stolen goat, burning and destroying houses, canoes, hogs, and dogs. When the Sandwich group was discovered in January 1778, Cook, now thoroughly roused, was determined to prevent the communication of this European disorder to its disease-free population in whom Samwell saw signs neither of venereal disease nor of yaws.[112] Cook laid down stringent regulations. Again, they were circumvented. The men's recently contracted gonorrhoea, together with their own reactivated syphilis, were transmitted to the unsuspecting Hawaiians, and Cook was obliged to give William Bradeley two dozen lashes for having relations with women knowing he was infected.[113] The crews escaped to continue their wanton way at Nootka, undeterred by the filth of the natives. Samwell and Ellis both describe a ceremony of purification before the act which cost the gentlemen their pewter tableware.[114] Trevenen occasionally glimpsed rare relaxation of "the almost constant severity" which Cook now displayed, evidence of his increasing strain.[115] The gonorrhoea his men caught at Samgoonoodha was of Russian origin.

The Hawaiians were only too aware of the legacy they had inherited when the ships returned in November. King describes gonorrhoea and syphilis, chancroid or lymphogranuloma venereum. Many died and others suffered excruciating pain, clear proof of the syphilis which la Pérouse was to confirm on his visit to the Sandwich Islands in May 1786.[116] The natives made no secret of their infection, and their accusations stung an exasperated Cook into action. He threatened and punished with increasing severity, but to no avail. Ashore, occupants of the observatory broke taboo and encouraged the women to do so, losing the respect of the chiefs and therefore obliging Cook and Kalaniopu to meet daily to resolve differences.[117] King was in charge and there is evidence that by this time Cook, like Bligh, had seen through King's cultivated facade. Retribution was dispensed by the Hawaiians themselves, who returned their micro-organisms with interest.

Cook was defeated. Some of his officers were involved in the traffic. Law was no Patten, and some of his surgeons were among the chief offenders. Cook became increasingly morose and withdrawn. His legendary intuition and even his memory were beginning to desert him. Failing to restore the men's rations "in a land of plenty," he was the recipient of a mutinous letter. He lost his rapport with his men. The angry outbursts of a commander under stress were replaced by the detachment of a man no longer in charge of events. At the ceremony of presentation to the gods in 1779, Cook remained "quite passive and suffered Koah to do with him as he chose."[118] Later, Ledyard watched the daily decline of his prestige, to which Cook appeared quite insensible.[119] It may explain his desecration of the morai before sailing. There were therefore good reasons why, when misfortune compelled the ships to return, the native men, who had been the chief sufferers from sexually transmitted diseases, received them in sullen silence. Preoccupied with the problem of unseaworthy ships and unreasonable men, a dispirited Cook landed at Kealakekua Bay.

He had been ailing since the second voyage when, during the second ice-edge search in December 1773, Forster observed that Cook "looked pale and lean and laboured under a perpetual costiveness" accompanied by vomiting. In January 1774, Edgar described him as "close and secret," and on 8 February, Forster was writing that "the warm weather which was beneficial to" Forster Senior had "proved fatal to Captain Cook's constitution."[120] He never recovered his appetite and in 1779, at the ceremony before the gods in Hawaii, he could not bring himself to swallow even a morsel of hog's flesh and excused himself as soon as possible.[121] Although Cook appeared to improve in the cold of the ice-edge searches, on 27 February 1774, he developed serious gastrointestinal symptoms which he first concealed, treating himself by starvation until intestinal colic supervened. Purgatives merely increased the vomiting, and constipation became absolute and was associated with such violent hiccoughs that he almost died[122]—a classical picture of acute intestinal obstruction. Thrower believes Cook had an acute infection of the gallbladder with secondary paralytic ileus,[123] but it is more likely, since Cook was anything but fastidious about eating native foods, that this was a heavy ascaris (roundworm) infestation of the intestine, a condition that can cause acute obstruction and which Pringle found was often associated in the army with bilious fever, worms sometimes escaping by the patient's mouth. In autopsies, they were even found lying free in the abdominal cavity after perforating the intestinal wall.[124] Ascariasis was present in Tahiti.[125] Enemas having no effect, hot baths, plasters, and the tender care of the devoted Patten finally answered the purpose. Forster found Cook "far from being recovered" on 14 April and mentions the ill effects of the sun at Easter Island. It is also noteworthy that when, in September, Cook and his officers ate the tetraodon, Cook appears to have been the most severely affected of them all, with acute neurological symptoms.[126]

On the third voyage, Cook was a different man. At Tonga, his behaviour and violence were as uncharacteristic as his reluctance to make new discoveries. His fury at Moorea, his increasing severity and diminishing rapport with his men—were they the result of stress alone? His curious detachment at Hawaii, his passivity and his almost trance-like state and indecision were attested to by Harvey, Ellis, Bayly, Edgar, Ledyard, and Samwell, and led directly to his tragic death at Kealakekua Bay. Was there an explanation?

If we accept that Cook suffered from a parasitic infection of the intestine, probably of the lower ileum, and alternative diagnoses are unlikely in the light of his subsequent medical history, the parasites would cause inflammation of the wall of the intestine, allowing colonization by coliform bacteria which could interfere with the absorption of the B complex of vitamins and probably other nutrients. Gross effects are relatively easy to diagnose, but early symptoms arising from moderate malabsorption of niacin and thiamine are notoriously difficult[127] (table 4). They include prolonged ill health, fatigue, loss of appetite, stubborn constipation, loss of weight, digestive disturbances, loss of interest and initiative, irritability, depression, loss of concentration and memory, and change of personality—all symptoms exhibited by Cook during the third voyage and faithfully recorded by eyewitnesses. He also had an interesting episode of sciatica,[128] and there is not a shred of evidence that any of his symptoms were venereal in origin.

During the second voyage, Forster had observed that Cook was pale and lean; anaemia may also occur in this condition because of associated malabsorption of vitamin B12. Nevertheless, unlike the syphilitics, he

TABLE 4
Early Signs of Some Vitamin B Deficiencies

| Niacin | Thiamine |
|---|---|
| Progressive ill health | Leg pain and paraesthesia |
| Fatigue | Fatigue |
| Headache and insomnia | Headache and insomnia |
| Loss of appetite | Loss of appetite |
| Breathlessness | Breathlessness |
| Loss of weight | Irritability and depression |
| Painful mouth and tongue | Loss of interest and initiative |
| Digestive disturbances | Loss of concentration and memory |
| Constipation or diarrhoea | Psychoneurotic personality change |
| Sensitivity to sunlight | |

was better in cold, dark weather than in hot tropical conditions, and sensitivity to sunlight is a feature of niacin deficiency.

Finally, recent research suggests that in cereals such as maize, millet, and even wheat,[129] niacin may exist in a bound form which may prevent its utilization by some individuals; while certain greens, such as wild spinach and some of the cresses, may not be without their harmful properties. It is therefore possible to conclude that Cook fell victim to his own passionate conviction that health at sea was to be found only in the nutrients provided by fresh provisions. By concentrating on vitamin C deficiency, however, historians may have ignored for too long the serious effects on decision-making resulting from vitamin B deficiencies, which could help to explain some otherwise inexplicable actions of the great naval commanders.

There is one other factor in the saga. Only six deaths were attributed to tuberculosis during Cook's three voyages, but there may have been more. Green, Tupia, and Molyneaux all had chronic ill health in the *Endeavour*, and Tayeto's pulmonary condition might have been an acute miliary tuberculosis. Gibson, who made all three voyages, died of a lingering illness which must be suspect, and so must that of Still. King died of tuberculosis later. The incidence was highest amongst the officers and their associates, doubtless more susceptible to infection than the crewmen, who were likely to have developed immunity through frequent exposure during childhood. Hicks probably communicated it to Clerke during the first voyage; Clerke to Anderson during the second; and Anderson to King during the third. There can be little doubt that Cook felt Anderson's death keenly, and it is entirely a possibility that Cook, already suffering from nutritional deficiency and spending more and more time on the third voyage with Anderson, one of the few men of unquestioned rectitude whom he could wholly trust, had begun to recognize symptoms of tuberculosis in himself which his iron discipline suppressed.

Perhaps more than the *Resolution*'s foremast gave way on 8 February 1779.

# Cook's Posthumous Reputation

*Bernard Smith*

*Lives of great men all remind us*
*We can make our lives sublime,*
*And, departing, leave behind us*
*Footprints on the sands of time.*

The Reaper and the Flowers,
Henry Wadsworth Longfellow (1807–1882)

UNQUESTIONABLY, Cook possessed a considerable reputation prior to his death. At the age of thirty-four, six years before embarking on his first Pacific voyage, he was described by his superior officer, Lord Colville, as a man of "genius and capacity."[1] At the time of his death his achievements were famed throughout Europe. In the Pacific many thousands of the indigenous peoples had encountered him personally and knew good reasons why they should fear, cherish, and in some cases, detest his memory.

Cook's tragic death at Kealakekua Bay on 14 February 1779, however, propelled his memory far beyond the level of mere fame to those exalted realms of the human imagination where only saints, heroes, and martyrs dwell. This paper will provide an outline account of some of the channels by which Cook's posthumous reputation was moulded and transmitted to later generations. As there is much material relevant to this subject still to be investigated, this essay should be considered no more than a tentative foray into a fascinating field, an exercise in the ideology of reputation and, at least by implication, in the relation between the creation of reputation and the writing of history.

In embarking upon such an enquiry it is desirable to keep constantly in mind two distinguishable kinds of intention: the intention of those disposed to provide to the best of their ability an accurate account of what occurred at various times during Cook's remarkable life; and the intention of those who have concerned themselves with celebrating his life while using it, even if unwittingly, to support their own interests and concerns. Admittedly, an absolute distinction is impossible, since even the most careful observer is not neutral. John Beaglehole, the finest and most meticulous of Cook scholars, did not flinch on several occasions from describing Cook as "our Hero"; and if Beaglehole can be shown to possess an occasional blind spot, it will serve to remind us of our own. Indeed the problem is built into our discipline. Clio is a schizophrenic muse who insistently enjoins us to now praise famous men while telling the truth, the whole truth, and nothing but the truth.

*HISTORIOG*

After his death, Cook's life and achievements provided the material from which a new kind of hero, one admirably adapted to the needs of the new industrial society of Europe in its global expansion, was fashioned. Cook became the first and the most enduring hero of European expansion in the Pacific; or to put it bluntly, the prototypical hero of European imperialism.

The first men to assess Cook's character and achievement knew him and worked with him at close quarters. They ranged from some of the most significant figures in contemporary European science, such as Banks and the Forsters, to common seamen. All of them, though aware of his weaknesses, deeply cherished and fostered his memory. They were disposed towards making sober assessments of his character and achievement; as members of a scientific voyage that is what they had been trained to, and this was Cook's disposition also. "The public will, I hope," he wrote on one occasion, "consider me as a plain man, zealously exerting himself in the service of his country."[2] The tone is antiheroic, in keeping with his temperament and calling. Yet we must be careful about accepting such modesty entirely at face value. By the time he made it, Cook's disclaimer was already something of a literary *topos*. More than once he had occasion to point out that he had been bred to the sea, and that the sea was no school for fine writers.[3] Bougainville, whose works were essential reading for Cook, had already pointed out that it "was not in the forests of Canada nor on the breast of the sea, that one learns the art of writing."[4] And others before Bougainville had made the same point. Cook is not so much admitting a literary deficiency as maintaining the ideals of a new kind of rhetoric, that art of plain speaking which Thomas Sprat in his *History of the Royal Society* (1667) had sought from the society's fellows (and remember Cook was one from 1776): "a close, naked, natural way of speaking; positive expressions,

clear sense; a native easiness, bringing all things as near the mathemati-
cal plainness as they can; and preferring the language of Artisans,
Countrymen and Merchants before that of wits and scholars."[5] What
Diderot much later was to describe as "*la ton de la chose*";[6] a language,
that is to say, suited to the needs of the new sciences, and one that was
beginning, during Cook's lifetime, to affect the tone of literary discourse
also. About twenty years after Cook's death, Wordsworth, in the Preface
to the *Lyrical Ballads* (1798), recommended it as the language appropriate to poetry.[7]

It was not the new plain rhetoric, however, that provided the mould
within which Cook's heroic posthumous reputation first came to be
fashioned, although we must note in passing that the basic information
from which the reputation was constructed in the journals of Cook,
Banks, the Forsters, King, Samwell, and others was composed in the
plain style (indeed George Forster became a master of the style). Because
it carried the authority of those who were there and knew Cook it came
to exercise a sobering and transforming constraint upon the heroizing
process. It is a case of the plain style of the medium helping to determine
in the long run the tone and substance of the heroic message.

Shortly after his death, Cook's reputation was submitted quite consciously and deliberately to a heroizing process, not by his fellow voyagers but by academicians, poets, and artists whose imaginations had
been gripped by the magnitude of his achievement. Most of these people
had already embraced with considerable warmth the attitudes and values
of the Enlightenment. This is not surprising, for two reasons. Firstly,
Cook himself adopted many, though by no means all, of the attitudes of
the Enlightenment. Secondly, the initial phase in the construction of
this heroic reputation was completed during the ten intellectually high-
spirited years that elapsed between his death and the outbreak of the
French Revolution. In saying that Cook's first hero-builders embraced
the attitudes and values of the Enlightenment I mean, to quote Peter
Gay's admirable description, that they adopted "a programme of secu-
larism, humanity, cosmopolitanism, and freedom, above all, freedom in
its many forms—freedom from arbitrary power, freedom of speech,
freedom of trade, freedom to realize one's talents, freedom of aesthetic
response, freedom, in a word, of moral man to make his own way in the
world."[8]

The beginnings of the heroizing process may be studied in the eulogies to Cook delivered and published by Continental academicians during the 1780s and early 1790s. The work of the eighteenth-century literary academies has not been fully studied, but it is already clear that they and not the universities were the institutions in which the ideas and values of the Enlightenment were discussed and tried out on the educated public.[9] The eulogy or funeral oration was one of the main literary genres employed for this purpose, and one in which the literary devices of classical rhetoric were given full play. It had reached its apogee in the great funeral orations of Bossuet a century before the death of Cook, but in the 1780s was still very much alive, serving as a medium for the propagation of the values not of the Church but of the Enlightenment. Even so, its elaborate, forensic rhetoric was by the 1780s somewhat old-fashioned.

One of the earliest of the eulogies to Cook occurs as a section of the poem *Les Jardins* by Jacques Delille, published in Paris in 1782.[10] Delille had been admitted to the Académie Française in 1772 but his admission had been deferred because Louis XV suspected him of being an *encyclopédiste*. *Les Jardins*, which is modelled on Virgil's *Georgics*, is a dull poem, but it does provide some early pointers to the direction that the heroizing of Cook was to take. Cook is praised because he brought the agricultural arts of his country, instead of the roar of the cannon, to the Pacific. In fact, of course, he brought both; but the heroizing process required the selection of facts from a moral standpoint, and the setting of those facts as evidence of heroic behaviour against their antitheses, since heroes, in order to exist, require antagonists. War himself forgot his dire commands at the sight of Cook's ships: a reference to the French government's decision not to molest the *Resolution* and the *Adventure* following the outbreak of war with Spain in 1779. It is fitting, Delille observes, that such a universal hero should receive the laurel wreath from a foreign hand. He then proceeds to enquire, rather cheekily by way of concluding his eulogy, why it is that the fierce sons of Britain cannot be truly great like their own hero, instead of always seeking despotic sway over their equals. Already we may glimpse here a rift appearing between Cook's potential role as universal hero and as patriotic hero.

Delille's piece is but a fragment. What appears to be the first of the complete eulogies to Cook, that of Michelangiolo Gianetti, was published by the Royal Academy of Florence in 1785.[11] For Gianetti, as for

Delille, Cook's achievements were of the kind that greatly advanced the Enlightenment program. Our hero, he informs us, has banished terror from the seas, where not a shoal has been neglected, not a depth untried, and not a danger unexplored. Cook has subdued human terror also, embracing his prisoners and winning their affections with gifts and kindnesses. Gianetti contrasts unfavourably the deeds of the old military heroes—Alexander, Scipio, Cortez, Pizzaro—with those of this new man of peace whose excellences are not physical but mental and who has revealed the whole earth to us under a new form that is safe for navigation and commerce. Yet, Gianetti hastens to point out, Cook possessed the traditional virtues also. "An Enlightened Monarch, an Enlightened Society and an admiring people had commanded him: '... go to the Island of Otahiete... and there regulate the stars by your calculations; haste, examine, and make discoveries, bear the British name to New Zeland, rectify false opinion, improve Geography, discover new passages, and return with a glory worthy of your Country, and yourself.'"[12] And Cook, hearing the awful voice of his country which claims a hero for herself, took sorrowful leave, like Regulus, of his wife and went.

Gianetti's Cook is a blend of Enlightenment and patriotic hero. But he does select one aspect of Cook's life of special relevance to my theme. Cook is the self-made man. While hidden among the obscurity of the vulgar, he contemplated the stars and raised himself above his station in life by assiduous application to his studies. Now, the genesis of most of the technology that launched the industrial revolution was due mainly to the intense assiduity and resourcefulness of such self-made men, who possessed also a consuming interest in the application of science and mathematics to the practical problems of their trades and callings.

Gianetti's characterization of Cook, though couched in the elaborate rhetoric of the late-baroque eulogy, is pretty much on mark. Cook, we suspect, might well have seen himself like that, though he would have put it more modestly. Nevertheless it is a conventional tribute that does not enquire into the potential significance of Cook's work for future generations. For this we must turn to the finest of the academic eulogies, Pierre Lémontey's *Eloge de Jacques Cook*, which won a prize for eloquence awarded by the Academy of Marseilles on 25 August 1789—a few weeks after the fall of the Bastille.[13]

Lémontey is worthy of more attention than he has received hitherto from Cook historians. Born at Lyons in 1762 of a merchant family, he studied law and practised as a barrister up to and during the early part of the Revolution. He was a powerful advocate for the civil rights of Protestants, and played a leading part in organizing the petition from the Lyonnaise to Louis XVI for the recall of Neckar. Elected as a deputy from the Loire to the Legislative Assembly, he later became its president in December 1791. He aligned himself with the moderate minority and failed in his efforts to preserve the constitutional monarchy. After the insurrection of 10 August that captured the Tuileries and overthrew the monarchy, Lémontey found it prudent to leave France for Switzerland, where he lived until 1795, when he returned to Lyons. In later life he wrote several plays and some historical works. His *Eloge de Jacques Cook*, written when he was twenty-seven, was the first of his literary productions. The fact that it was written in the year of the Revolution or shortly before and published in Paris in 1792 at the height of the struggle for power may help to explain the fervently optimistic, almost millenarianist tone which prevails throughout.

The reputation of Captain Cook, Lémontey assures us, will not be subjected to the twists and turns of the goddess Fortune because the impact of his discoveries will increase from age to age, and mankind will confer upon him that kind of veneration which it reserves for those who bring universal benefits to mankind. Cook is the very personification of Europe. For him, movement was freedom. In movement he realized his innermost nature; to remain at home was, for him, to be a captive. Europe is like that; a geographical imperative impels it; it must be on the move or perish. Just consider the fanatical pilgrimages of the Crusades, the bloody brigands of Mexico and Peru, the tyrannous calculator of India (perhaps a reference to Warren Hastings, whose trial had just begun), and consider too the adventurers and philosophers of the South Seas. But Lémontey asks us, where can Europe possibly expand to now? It cannot go on Crusade again; we shall only hurt ourselves or starve in India; and since the Americans have won their freedom they are determined to bring European culture to the new continent themselves.

There is only one part of the world left: that made available by Cook, the harbours of the south (*les échelles du sud*). This is Lémontey's phrase for all the discoveries made, re-enlivened or promised by Cook, and it becomes the *leitmotif* of his eulogy. The merchant navies, he continues, are the prime movers of the European nations, they are changing the centres of gravity and the balance of power. Each nation strives for a larger mercantile marine, for the creation of which Europe is depopulating its forests. We shall have to reach out to the Isle of Pines and the forests of New Zealand to replenish our stores. And commerce grows with this growth of merchant navies; for commerce feeds on its own excess and impoverishes all that it does not swallow. But Cook has found new routes, new ports, new foods, and brought knowledge of them to existing ports in Indochina and the Philippines. The Sandwich Islands will become a new entrepôt for the colonies of Russia and England for the purchase of cloth, skins and furs, bows and arrows. All this is but further evidence of a continuing conspiracy between the inhabitants of the land against the inhabitants of the sea, of those periodic crusades when maritime peoples unite to make the sea a fertile field that nourishes the human race: for the sea itself is a school of vigour, skill, and courage. The fishermen of England, France, and Holland will unite and sail right up to the ice of the Southern Thule in search of those whales which long hunting is causing to desert the northern latitudes.

*1789*
*Enlarge*

Furthermore, with the growth of the *échelles du sud* population will increase and parochial prejudice dissolve in one great sphere of human activity. Although it is difficult, Lémontey concedes, to estimate the social effects of discoveries where chance and passion prevail, the promise of gold being mined abundantly and easily in New Caledonia may have the beneficial effect of the abandonment of those hellish caverns of America in which the Inca perished. How astonished, he adds with a flourish, the sun itself would be were the land to be returned to his own ancient admirers.

For Lémontey, *les échelles du sud* are of the first importance, for they hold out the promise of a new kind of commerce which will not involve the misery of indigenous tribes or black Africans. Their wealth will be based upon work that is free. Already England has planted a new colony at Botany Bay consisting of a frightful mixture of convicted and depraved men, but, like Rome of old, they will develop into a strong nation. Human manure in the hands of good cultivators can produce golden harvests and spreading vines. New Holland will become a meeting place of the world. China will deposit her surplus population, which is the cause of her present feebleness, there. The Japanese, now so isolated, will mix themselves there with the great human family where Europeans, Malays, Americans, and Asians will encounter one another with astonishment; and there too the plants and animals of the north and south will mingle and flourish to the advantage of all.

Lémontey, you will recall, came of a merchant family and successfully entered a prize piece to the Academy of a city which was, one might say, the great *échelle du sud* of France, with a proud mercantile history first as a Phoenecian, then as a Greek and Roman colony which prospered commercially and culturally as it extended its sway over the barbarous tribes of its hinterland. What, Lémontey, enquires of us, is the true grandeur of ancient nations? The ruins of Carthage, the ostentatious debris of Thebes and Palmyra? Of course not. It is rather the colonies that they spread in all regions: Gaul civilized, Lyons and Marseilles embellishing themselves from age to age. These are the true monuments of antiquity. Europe therefore, Lémontey concludes, must throw herself without relaxing into the new hemisphere. May the nations long dispute the honour of carrying into this new world Europe's force of life, order, and fecundity, which like a miracle produces dwellings, harvests, and cities.

The last eulogy to which I wish to refer is that by Pierre Louis Paris, published in 1790 and probably written, like Lémontey's eulogy, the year before.[14] Paris was a member of the Oratoire and several academies. Like Lémontey, he contrasts the earlier European voyages of exploration based upon rapine and slaughter with the peaceful, philosophic, and above all useful voyages of Cook. Paris was a religious, and his text is clustered with christological *topoi*. While the nations compete with one another, each in its own domain studying science, a great event is prepared in the heavens, and Cook is charged with taking English scientists to the Pacific to watch the transit of Venus. The wise are jealous of this young man who was not educated in the right schools, but he confounds them and instructs them in the true geography. Paris, like Lémontey, presents Cook as the new hero of free and civilized trading. Whereas Columbus sought gold, Cook respected the rights of humanity. Indeed, if one possessed the genius of Cook, it might be possible to trace the ascent of man from the state of the lowest savages of Tierra del Fuego up to that of those Europeans who could give birth to a genius like Cook himself.

This brief outline of the substance of some of the eulogies will already have provided an impression of the literary techniques involved in the heroizing process. For example, no mention is made of any of Cook's associates by name; if given a corporate mention they function only in the capacity of assistants or disciples. On one occasion when he found it necessary to mention Banks, Paris apologized in advance to his hero for mixing the praise of a stranger with his own. It was a strict convention of the eulogy to keep the spotlight of fame fixed on the hero. Again, as I mentioned briefly earlier, the treatment of facts and events differ greatly from their treatment in logs and journals. In the latter case, facts were collected and set down to provide new information for a growing number of new sciences; but in the eulogy, facts are selected to illustrate the virtues of the hero and to edify the audience. Further, the sequence of events may be altered for aesthetic reasons. For example, Paris had the *Endeavour* breach its hull on a coral shoal in the Tasman Sea between New Zealand and Australia, not in the Coral Sea, doubtless in order to provide a dramatic turn to events at a point in the story where it was felt to be needed.

The hero of the eulogies is a blend of the new and the old. By a continuous use of classical and biblical *topoi*, Cook's legitimate descent from the heroes of the past is traced. Although he discovers in Tahiti an Arcadia as alluring as Circe's grotto, he alone among his company resists the seductions of the sorceresses and, again like Ulysses, guides his little company through the Scylla and Charybdis of the coral shoals; and in the underworld of Antarctica faces the terrors of the deep: hideous marine monsters, frightening waterspouts, mountains of ice. Like Christ, he comes of humble human origins but confounds wise men and comes bringing a new message—free trading and civilized behaviour—to the gentiles of the south. Like Christ, too, he identifies with all humanity, treating all men as his brothers, rebuking them, as Peter was rebuked, from acts of violence against the native peoples. "The life of one man," Paris asserts unequivocally "was more precious in the eyes of Cook than the knowledge of a continent."[15] In discovering new lands, he comes into his own kingdom; everything new reminds him of home and he names the unknown rivers and seas, headlands, and islands after his friends and benefactors, claiming them all in the name of his sovereign king. In my father's house there are many islands. And in the final episode of his life he is likened in Anna Seward's *Elegy on Captain Cook* (1780) to Orpheus, torn limb from limb by the very savages to whom he had carried the arts of civilization.

Yet Cook is also a new kind of hero for a new time. His wisdom is based upon his command of the new technologies which he uses to practical advantage, such as the maintenance of the health of his crew. Unlike the old navigators, he publishes his voyages: freedom of trade is dependent upon freedom of knowledge. He upgrades a whole range of homely virtues neglected by the old military and naval heroes but essential for achievement in the coming industrial age: professionalism, competence, prudence, thoroughness, stubborness, patience, a constrained pride in achievement. The old-style genius had been a man inspired by the gods and guarded by a tutelary benefactor. Cook did not depend much upon God; he kept his powder dry, mentioned Providence rarely, and performed the Sunday naval service intermittently; but he was perfectly willing to play god himself, as he did at Hawaii, if the cultivation of peaceful cultural relations depended on it. Almost a century before, Carlyle defined this new kind of self-dependent genius that the times had need of as "the transcendent capacity for taking trouble."[16] Cook had already demonstrated the new type in the Pacific.

I propose now to turn to a brief consideration of the part played by the visual arts in the heroizing process. Like the logs and journals kept by Cook and his companions, the visual records executed on the voyages had as their object a complete and accurate documentation of the peoples, places, and things encountered. And even when such works were further developed as art works destined for the Royal Academy and other such prestigious places, they were still—despite their aesthetic modifications—directed towards the new visual rhetoric of naturalism which sought to tell, within the limitations of painting, truths about geography and environment, light and weather. The application of painting to the heroizing process, while also providing a truthful account of events, constituted a problem. For the process demands the selection of a series of crucial incidents linked in temporal succession: the humble birth, the illuminating call to the mission, the embarkation and fulfillment of the mission, and finally the heroic death. But as Lessing, who was Cook's exact contemporary pointed out, painting does not lend itself to heroizing in the way that verbal narration does. The painter must respect the non-temporal character of his medium and choose a crucial moment in the hero's life, and by concentrating on the expressive potential of that one moment reveal within it the events preceding and the events succeeding. In the case of Cook, as for most martyr-heroes, the crucial moment for the painter was obviously the moment of death or that immediately preceding death.

Let us examine some of the paintings of the death of Cook that appeared (like the eulogies) during the 1780s and early 1790s. In doing so, we may observe in the heroizing process two modes paralleling those of the corresponding verbal rhetoric: a plain style that keeps close to the eyewitness accounts of Cook's death; a grand style that elevates and allegorizes the events.

The first paintings of Cook's death were composed to illustrate faithfully the event as recorded in the official account of the third voyage by Captain James King. John Webber, the only artist who might possibly have witnessed Cook's death (though we have no evidence that he did) follows King's account closely: the two boats offshore, with the marines firing from the more distant, and a couple struggling in the water to gain the boats (figure 7); Lieutenant Phillips, fallen to the ground, firing at his assailant; Cook about to be stabbed in the back by a huge native as he turns and gestures towards the launch. The gesture is key to the emotional tone of the painting, and is enigmatic. Is Cook waving to Williamson to stop firing and pull in so that he can escape, or is he commanding him to stop firing at the natives? The ambiguity is sufficiently strong to support a reading of Cook as martyr-hero willing to sacrifice his life rather than command the death of his native friends. John Cleveley's painting—which was based, it is alleged, (probably erroneously) on a drawing by his brother James, who was carpenter on the *Resolution*— also focusses the action upon a similar enigmatic gesture, and makes use of a puff of musket fire to provide a halo for the hero (figure 8). Significantly, these two paintings provided the basic material for those innumerable illustrations of Cook's death which appeared in books recounting his life and voyages. Those which chose moments in the death struggle less central to the tragedy were, predictably, used less. George Carter, for example, depicts Cook in a fit of desperation going for his assailant with the butt of his rifle (figure 9). It may well have occurred;[17] but that is not at all the way a prospective hero should behave. D.P. Dodd also portrayed Cook in an unheroic position, at the moment when he had fallen face downwards and was being either pushed into or pulled out of the water by his attackers (figure 10). It is significant that neither Carter's nor Dodd's paintings were much copied or adapted by later illustrators of Cook's death.

FIGURE 7.   John Webber, *The Death of Cook*. Figures engraved by F. Bartolozzi; landscape by W. Byrne.

FIGURE 8.   Aquatint by Francis Jukes after John Cleveley, *View of Owhyhee one of the Sandwich Islands*. Published 5 July 1788 by Thomas Martyn.

FIGURE 9.   George Carter, *Death of Captain Cook*, oil, 76 × 91 cm. Carter Collection, Bishop Museum Library, Honolulu, Hawaii.

FIGURE 10.   D.P. Dodd, *The Death of Captain James Cook, F.R.S. at Owhyhee in MDCCLXXIX*. Engraved by T. Cook. Published 20 November 1784 by J. Fielding and others.

FIGURE 11.   *Death of Cook*, lithograph illustration in *Narrative of Captain James Cook's Voyages around the World* (London, 1839).

It is possible to trace the descent of the image of Cook as hero-martyr from the Webber and Cleveley paintings from their day to ours, as they came to be interpreted in the light of their own interests: by men imbued with the values of the Enlightenment, then by schoolteachers and evangelists; by philosophical beachcombers, colonial nationalists, and novelists in search of a good adventure story for boys. Two examples will have to suffice. Firstly, an attractive primitive lithograph which appeared in a collection of Cook's *Voyages* published in 1839 (figure 11). It depicts Cook completely disarmed, passively awaiting the coup de grace from one native who looks like an English village blacksmith, and another like Edmund Kean playing a typical villain role at Drury Lane. Secondly, the illustration by Gordon Browne, which appeared in Low's edition of the *Collected Voyages*, published in 1895[18]. A general feature of these illustrations of the later nineteenth and early twentieth centuries is the tendency to emphasize the bestiality of Cook's assailants; they are sometimes portrayed to look, as in an illustration by Will Robinson, remarkably like monkeys[19].

The life of Cook came to exercise a profound effect upon the younger sons of those large Victorian families in all parts of the United Kingdom

FIGURE 12. Frontispiece to William Fordyce Mavor, *The British Nepos; or Mirror of Youth, Consisting of Select Lives of Illustrious Britons* (London, 1798). Drawn by John Thurston, engraved by W. Taylor.

who found it necessary to leave home in order to better themselves. One of the first writers to present Cook as a British worthy and model for schoolboys to emulate was William Fordyce Mavor, the schoolmaster of Woodstock, who included a life of Cook in his *British Nepos or Mirror of Youth Consisting of Selected Lives of Illustrious Britons* (1798). The frontispiece depicts the "genius of biography directing British Youth to the Temple of Honour in the path of Industry" (figure 12).

When a martyr dies, he is received into glory. Complementing the martyr-victim images of Cook, we have those which apotheosize him. The Greek practice of transforming heroes into gods was revived in the seventeenth century in the baroque ceiling paintings of Italy and central Europe, from whence it spread to book illustration. Despite the religious implications, the apotheosis became a popular visual trope by which the Enlightenment sought to venerate famous men. For though they questioned immortality, the Philosophers were great promoters (by way of compensation, perhaps) of secular fame.

Johann Ramberg, a German historical painter and illustrator who is said to have studied under Reynolds and Bartolozzi, depicted Cook being received into glory for the frontispiece of Reverend Thomas Bankes's *New System of Geography* (1787) (figure 13). Cook is depicted, looking uncomfortable, in an uncharacteristic pose midway between that of the Apollo Belvedere and the strut of a rococo dancing master. He stands on a rock that is changing into a cloud though it is still solid enough for a sceptical astronomer to stand on. Fame trumpets his arrival, while Neptune introduces him to History (it may be Clio's research assistant), who has started to take down from Cook's personal dictation the heavenly edition of the *Voyages*. Below, and this is central to my thesis, Britannia receives tribute from the four continents, personified in that most typical of baroque motifs, as four typically dressed young matrons of generous proportion. To the right, the *Resolution* and the *Adventure* sail into port with new treasure from the southern seas.

Phillip James De Loutherbourg's *Apotheosis of Captain Cook*, published as an engraving in 1794, is more dramatic and less utilitarian than Ramberg's (figure 14). Below, we see the tragic attack at Kealakekua Bay in progress; above, Cook is depicted ascending into the clouds clutching his sextant in one hand while he endeavours to fend off with the other the rapidly advancing buttocks of Universal Fame, only to fall into the welcoming lap of Britannia. The women of heaven, he seems to be thinking, are rather like those of Tahiti.

The neo-baroque style, like the rhetoric of the eulogies, was rather old-fashioned by the time these apotheoses were executed. It was left to Johann Zoffany, who might have joined the second voyage had Banks got his way, to paint a death of Cook in the more contemporary neoclassical manner (figure 15). Here, as Charles Mitchell has indicated,[20] contemporary history is re-created on a timeless and ideal plane. Cook is presented to us as a hero-victim in the pose of the Dying Gladiator, while his huge antagonist is posed with equal dignity in the manner of the Discobolos; and Cook reveals no emotion upon his face, only that "fixed expression of suffering" which characterizes the antique tragic mask. The tragedy is thus elevated into a realm of timeless ideality.

The death of the hero was one of the central themes of neoclassical painting and sculpture. Cook's death was but one of the many deaths of contemporary famous men for which heroic parallels with antiquity were sought, the best known and one of the first in the field being Benjamin West's death of Wolfe (1771).[21] Although it is rightly famed beyond any painting associated with Cook and became enormously popular with the British public after its highly successful engraving by Woollett, it was Cook, it seems to me, the quiet man whose effective charting of the St. Lawrence helped make Wolfe's victory possible, who was endowed with an heroic status more potent and durable than Wolfe's. For Wolfe was an old-fashioned military hero, not a man for a new time. And this might also be said of that other great hero of Empire, Horatio Nelson. Intrepidity, skill, courage: Nelson's virtues had all been demonstrated, and in many cases demonstrated better, by the heroes of antiquity. Dallying with Emma Hamilton on shore leave and kissing Hardy as he expired may well have been engaging and typical foibles in a British sailor-lad, but they were not—Trafalgar Square notwithstanding—the sort of qualities that make a modern hero durable. Cook, I would argue, grew in stature as an imperial hero because his life story was better fitted to the ideological belief—however distant from the true state of affairs—in a world-wide empire dedicated to the arts of peace (a *Pax Britannica*), not one based upon war. Perhaps it was the vision that haunted the men of the Enlightenment of a *Pax Universitas* that inspired the French sculptor Lucien Le Vieux, in 1790 at the height of the Revolution, to model a bust of Cook in the idealized image of the young Augustus Caesar, the creator of the *Pax Romana*.[22]

This universal peace, however, was to be erected upon the principles of free trade, and Cook was to become the hero, as Napoleon once put it in a state of irritation, "of a nation of shopkeepers." For Cook, the realist, was well aware that the survival of his company depended upon his capacity to establish and maintain markets with the native people encountered at each of his major landfalls. These markets were established by means of a subtle combination of gift giving, friendliness, and, where necessary, a show of force. Tools and toys (I use the word in its eighteenth-century sense) from Matthew Boulton of Birmingham were exchanged, as Cook himself put it, for "refreshments": that is to say, fresh food and the rights to fuel and water essential to the life and health of his company. In the process of establishing these markets, Cook developed a technique of culture contact with primitive peoples that proved to be highly successful. By means of friendliness and force, the conventions essential to the maintenance of a free market (such as the

FIGURE 13. Johann Ramberg. Engraved frontispiece to Rev. Thomas Banke's *New System of Geography* (London, 1787).

FIGURE 14. *The Apotheosis of Captain Cook, from a design by P. J. de Loutherbourg R.A.* "The view of Karakakooa Bay is from a drawing by John Webber, R.A. (the last he made) in the Collection of Mr. G. Baker." Published 20 January 1794.

FIGURE 15. Johann Zoffany, *The Death of Cook*, canvas, 137 × 185 cm. National Maritime Museum, Greenwich.

European conception of private property) were impressed upon the native mind. Cook must have been the first European to *practise* successfully on a global scale the use of tolerance for the purpose of domination, an administrative technique that came to play a vital role in the European colonization of the world during the nineteenth century.[23]

On such matters the parallel between Cook and Adam Smith is interesting. Smith was born five years before and died eleven years after Cook. In the lectures which Smith delivered in Edinburgh during 1748-49 he became an effective and influential champion of the new rhetoric which insisted upon a plain style, non-artistic arguments, and direct proofs;[24] a style that Cook adhered to firmly in writing up his daily transactions. This is not to say that Cook was influenced by Smith's ideas on rhetoric but that he belonged linguistically and temperamentally to the same intellectual movement. Smith's great work, *Wealth of Nations*, appeared in March 1776 when Cook was taking on provisions prior to departing on his last voyage, the official account of which was placed in the hands of Strachan and Cadell, who were also the publishers of *Wealth of Nations*.

Cook was in a sense Smith's global agent, for he developed markets and spread the notion of enlightened self-interest, bringing to prehistoric cultures the disguised checks and balances of a market economy regulated by what Smith described as a "hidden hand"—though Cook had to reveal that hand from time to time, when natives made off with the boats or the chronometers, in order to instruct them in the rules of the new game.

Seen in this light, Cook emerges as a Promethean hero who brings metallurgy and its related forms of culture to primitive man. He achieved this great task by displaying a range of virtues—patience, tolerance, fortitude, perseverence, stubbornness, attention to detail, professionalism, and so forth—about which Beaglehole and others have written eloquently. But this array of virtues, we may remind ourselves, is precisely that by which men seek to attain the efficiency of machines. Although Cook possessed in considerable measure what we might describe for the purposes of our discussion as the pre-industrial virtues—physical courage, loyalty, devotion, humility, faith, hope and charity—he was admittedly weak on some of them, and all them were less relevant to the performance of his task. Yet there is little reason to doubt that Cook on any reading was a man of great virtue; my point is rather that we should recognize the sociality, the timeliness of his array of virtues, his inborn capacity to exercise an ethics of situation. To say this is not to accuse him of expedience but rather to stress that, when he was most himself, he was most in harmony with the new, secular, industrial order that was emerging as the new world order during his lifetime: his array of virtues made it possible for him to rediscover the Golden Age in the Pacific and to bring to it the values of the Iron Age so long in preparation in Europe.

To identify the spread of a British empire based upon industry and free trade with the universal progress of human culture was the theme that the Royal Society of Arts and Manufactures chose to adorn the great hall of their new building by Robert Adam in the Adelphi in 1783. It was an appropriate theme, for the society was one of the earliest, and has continued to be one of the most effective, institutions dedicated to the progress of the agricultural and industrial arts. Painted by James Barry and entitled "The Progress of Human Culture," it set out to depict the stages of man's development, beginning with "Orpheus Reclaiming Mankind from a Savage State" and culminating with "Navigation or the Triumph of the Thames," which depicted, to quote Joseph Burke's fitting description, "the expansion and sharing of benefits under the new Olympians, the British (plate 10). Among the Tritons and Nereids swim Sebastian Cabot, Raleigh, Drake, "the late Captain Cook of amiable memory," and Barry's friend the musical historian, Dr. Charles Burney."[25] It puzzled many to find Burney there—though his son did travel with Cook twice. Barry, however, insisted that he wished to introduce "the personification of music" into "this scene of triumph and joy."[26] Nevertheless Burney's inclusion did create discussion. "It irks one to see my good friend Dr. Burney," an indignant dowager of the time remarked on seeing the painting, "paddling in a horse pond with a bevy of naked wenches."[27] But to describe that ample allegorical ocean as a horse pond was quite unfair to Barry, and the enormous Pharos, supported by a giant whose hand alone, as Professor Burke has noted, is far larger than the ship below; all this is very much in the spirit of that commercial utopia of the échelles du sud which Lémontey was to describe in his eulogy five years after Barry had completed his painting.

There are other paths along which Cook's heroic image was transmitted to later generations and maintained: for example, the editorial processes by which the original accounts of the voyages were transformed into books of edification and adventure for children, inspiring

FIGURE 16.   James Barry, *Navigation, or the Triumph of the Thames*, oil on canvas, 3.35 × 4.62 m: 1777-83, Royal Society of Arts, London.

them to go out and do likewise as missionaries, explorers, colonial administrators, or even as beachcombers—those pioneering drop-outs from industrial society of whom Cook would not have approved. There is the process by which the hero-image of Cook has developed, like a multi-facial Indian god, its own avatars: not only the posthumous history of Cook as a manifestation of the god Lono in Hawaii[28] but also that manifestation by which the hero is transformed into a founding father, or historical Adam, for the new nations of the Pacific. As founding father he performs the primal historical act, that of taking possession in the name of the British sovereign.[29] This act had been commemorated continuously in the striking of medals and the issue of postage stamps upon suitable occasions; in the execution of historical paintings and the preservation of Cook relics in the national libraries and museums of Australia, New Zealand, and elsewhere; in the erection of obelisks, memorial tablets, and statues at almost every beach in the Pacific Ocean where he is known to have stepped ashore; and in the re-enactment in such sacro-secular groves at periodic intervals, determined by the movement of those stars which Cook studied with such scientific detachment, of appropriate rites to celebrate his memory. Finally, we might consider that topic so close to our discipline which Arnold Toynbee once described as the "inspiration of historians." In this case it would be the relationship that subsists between the funding of celebrations commemorating Cook and the historical investigations supported by them. It might help to throw a little more light on Clio's mental problem: the role of history in the manufacture of fame, and history as critical enquiry.

A true hero invariably possesses a worthy antagonist who becomes the agent of the hero's death. That is the moral of Zoffany's painting. But the antagonist is only an agent; the hero dies because the charisma of the gods deserts him. Cook based his relations with native peoples largely upon his own personal courage and peaceful temperament, and a careful appraisal of the situation, going up to them alone with gifts in his hand and a welcome on his face. It was only as a last resort that he made use, as he once put it, of "the smart of our fire" from the small line of marines held in support behind. At Hawaii, however, the device of looking them in the eye, the well-tried procedures of peaceful domination, failed; and Cook died, struck down from behind, his body hacked to pieces by daggers fashioned from iron spikes[30] that were quite probably manufactured in Matthew Boulton's Soho factory in Birmingham. They had been brought out, as Cook had put it in his requisition order to the Admiralty, "to be distributed to them in presents towards obtaining their friendship."[31]

Like his celebrants, Cook's antagonists have continued to be active long after his death. I have not studied the activities of the anti-Cook party in detail and I shall only suggest some pointers towards further research that should repay detailed examination.

The base for the criticism of Cook and his achievements originates in those aspects of Enlightenment thought which placed greater emphasis upon the natural rights of men to decide their own moral destiny than upon the growth of free trade and the progress of civilization. The criticism, in fact, appears prior to Cook in Diderot's *Supplément au voyage de Bougainville*, written in 1772 but not published until 1796, a book due in part to Diderot's misreading of Rousseau on the nobility of savages.

But it was George Forster, the only man to travel with Cook who embraced the whole critical program of the Enlightenment, and probably the most intelligent and farsighted of them all, who first voiced concern at the likely outcome of Cook's voyages. In a much quoted passage in his *Voyage*, he wrote: "If the knowledge of a few individuals can only be acquired at such a price as the happiness of nations, it were better for the discoverers and the discovered, that the South Seas had still remained unknown to Europe and its restless inhabitants."[32]

Forster's apprehensions and concerns were taken up, as we know, by the satirists and more seriously by moralists like Gerald Fitzgerald. In his poem "The Injured Islanders" (1779),[33] Fitzgerald expressed grave concern about the effects which the introduction of European commerce and European diseases would have upon the Polynesians. "The imaginary value annexed to European toys and Manufactures and the Ravages of a particular disorder, have already injured their morals and their peace; even the instruments of iron, which must facilitate the ordinary Operations of Industry have been used as weapons of Destruction, or perverted to the purposes of Ambition and Revenge."

Even the French academic eulogists of Cook had to take note of such criticism. At one point in his *Eulogy*, Lémontey breaks off from his paean of praise to Cook and puts in a word for the other side. "An arm arrests me," he announced oratorically:

Cease imprudent orator, usurper of the language of posterity, or be impartial as it is. Dare you judge without understanding the law? Are not the benefits of Cook rather mixed? When a victor marched to the Capitol the curses of the Parthians and the Numidians mingled with the cheers of the Roman people. The hero of the Tiber was only a brigand on the banks of the Danube. Praise yourselves, civilized peoples, wise nations, exalt those discoveries which flatter your pride, increase your wealth, perfect your knowledge; it is not you who pays for them with your happiness. But the ignorance of how many innocent tribes have you not violated by your barbarous curiosity and enflamed their passions by the fatal presence of your vices and your needs? The Eulogy of Cook is only a reckoning, a catalogue of egoism, and its laurels will perish on the theatre of its glory.[34]

Lémontey was aware of the anti-Cook case, but it was not his case. He introduced it only to destroy it. Introducing arguments drawn from Montesquieu and others based on geographical determinism and the role of Europe in civilizing the world, he set out to demolish it.

I suspect that through most of the nineteenth century the anti-Cook case remained a kind of prehistoric and sub-literate resentment among the indigenous peoples of the Pacific that rarely surfaced. When it did take a written form, it came from Europeans who were disposed to discredit Cook in order to advance their own interests. John Stokes has shown that the strong anti-Cook sentiment which prevailed in Hawaii from the later 1830s up till quite recent times was largely the result of the work of the Reverend Sheldon Dibble, an American missionary and schoolteacher who encouraged his pupils to interview old Hawaiians to provide material for a local history. The memories of these old people conflated Cook's activities with that of subsequent early visitors. Then Dibble himself edited the interviews and wrote up the history to the discredit of Cook. Stokes argues convincingly that there was little anti-Cook sentiment in the island prior to Dibble's history, which was used as a text in schools.[35] This is an interesting example of the creation of an anti-Cook ideology. As a missionary, Dibble was antipathetic to Cook's secular pragmatism in accepting the impersonation of Lono that was largely thrust upon him, and as an American he was strongly influenced by the anti-British sentiment engendered by the war of 1812 and still present in Hawaii in the 1840s as a significant factor in island politics. Nevertheless, I do not think we can take Stoke's account of the growth of anti-Cook feeling entirely at its face value. It is doubtful whether Hawaiian opinion about Cook is best assessed from the written accounts of what Hawaiians were prepared to tell missionaries and visiting voyagers in the days before Dibble, even though they venerated Cook as a god prior to their conversion to Christianity. We should remind ourselves that on the first occasion, when they venerated him as a god, they also killed him. Furthermore, Dibble's spurious history found a receptive soil to flourish in through the nineteenth century. My point is this: though it may satisfy a European mind to distribute praise and blame among individuals in the precise way that Stokes does, the conflation of Cook's acts with those of his less high-minded successors exemplifies the process by which heroic legend is constructed and then countervailed. It will always be difficult for the native historians of the indigenous peoples of the Pacific as they come increasingly to write their histories to draw a fine line between Cook the individual and the culture their ancestors inherited in the wake of his vessels. Cook is not their culture hero, nor was he regarded as a culture hero by the republican circles that sprang up in the Australian colonies in the 1880s.[36]

Although the tone of this paper may in places have given that impression, I want to emphasize that it has not been part of my intention to discredit the achievements of Cook. My intention has been to suggest that it is timely that they be placed in a new perspective. Amidst the collapse of the European colonial empires, amidst mounting criticism of the cultural consequences of high technology, it seems desirable that Cook and his achievements be interpreted in a less Europocentric fashion than they have been in the past. We might have to admit, for example, that he discovered little in the way of new lands; that wherever he came there were usually people who had been settled for centuries. They provided, through trading, the provisions so crucial for the successful prosecution of his ventures. The discovery of the world is really a subject for prehistorians. Cook was not a discoverer of new lands in any fundamental sense of the word. He was the highly successful leader of three well-balanced, scientific research teams; a communications man, who was instrumental in bringing a mixed bag of goods, ironware and syphilis, written language and centralized government, and much more to the Pacific. It could be said of Cook more than of any other person that he helped to make the world one world; not an harmonious world, as the men of the Enlightenment had so rashly hoped, but an increasingly interdependent one. His ships began the process of making the world a global village.

# The Artistic Bequest of Captain Cook's Voyages—Popular Imagery in European Costume Books of the Late Eighteenth and Early Nineteenth Centuries

*Rüdiger Joppien*

THE voyages of Captain Cook produced an enormous number of works of art in paintings, drawings, and engravings. These works include the output of Cook's artists themselves, and artists who were working in England at the time and who became concerned with Pacific subject matter.[1] They are precious material to all Cook scholars of our time—be they natural scientists, anthropologists, geographers, or art historians—and are becoming increasingly better known as documents of exploration.[2] However, another group of works, made subsequent to Cook's voyages, has been almost totally neglected and yet is worth study for what it can tell us of Cook's impact and reception in Europe.

The medium of print, above all, popularized the figure of Cook and the event of the voyages. During the post-Cook era, a flood of engravings, etchings, woodcuts, and aquatints were produced; they were pirated from illustrations of Cook's narratives and often altered and badly distorted in the process of transmission. "Until the 1830s," writes Bernard Smith, "these engravings held the field virtually unchallenged for the illustration of editions of Cook, and they had become the chief source of information concerning the Pacific in all kinds of publications —travel books, geography texts, missionary tracts, and articles on the Pacific in journals and newspapers."[3] They served mostly as book illustrations, but were also published individually. Their purpose, beyond the point of embellishment, was to inform and to instruct. In an age in which geographical discoveries had reached the level of public interest and suspense, demand for these illustrations was flourishing.

When, between 1773 and 1784, the original engravings from Cook's voyages were published in London, they made known a good number of nations of the Pacific and illustrated their appearance. The representations which had been drawn by Cook's artists immediately inspired considerable interest, as they enlarged the vision of the family of man and invited comparison with other races of the world. In 1784 the German philosopher Johann Gottfried Herder, an early champion of anthropology, strongly called for a pictorial history of man, a gallery of nations, and proposed that all representations that could be proved authentic should be collected in order to lay "the foundation of a perspicuous natural philosophy and physiognomy of man... art, could not easily be employed in a more philosophical pursuit."[4]

Herder's ideas of a comparative study of man, assisted by the graphic arts, were very much in the air. During the next few decades some ambitious publications were issued which treated man on a global scale; their illustrations depict his physical features and discuss his customs and spiritual ideas. In an attempt to spread out and to propagate all knowledge available about people living in different quarters of the globe, their scale became truly encyclopaedic. Reporting not only on man's appearance and guise, but also on societal aspects such as religion, warfare, or arts and crafts, their concept was decisively moralistic in that they meant to contribute to universal recognition and understanding. It was upon this type of book, which in the idiom of the period was often called "costume book" or "gallery of nations," that the plates illustrating Cook's voyages exercised a powerful influence. Of all the popular imagery which was produced in the wake of Cook's voyages, the plates illustrating "costume books" are the most interesting from the standpoint of disseminating human knowledge. Artistically they are also the most relevant.

Before looking at some of these illustrations from the 1780s onwards, it is useful to refer to an early engraving by Page, after a drawing by Richard Samuel, and published in London in 1778. Titled "Persons and Dresses of the Inhabitants of the South Sea Islands," it was issued to illustrate the printed travel account of *New Discoveries concerning the world and its inhabitants* published by J. Johnson[5] (figure 17). It reflects keen interest in the population of the Pacific as it was known after Cook's second voyage and is among the first prints of this kind. Instead of treating all figures in individual plates, the artist has conceived them

FIGURE 17. "Persons and dresses of the inhabitants of the South Sea Islands," engraving by Page after a drawing by Samuel, London 1778.

in a "group picture" set against the foil of a generalized south sea land-scape. Each figure and the striking features of the landscape are given letters which are explained in a key underneath the print (missing from the reproduction).[6] Arranged in a lively, frieze-like composition, each figure has been given room to be shown naturally and to advantage. On the right, the most dominant figure is the chief mourner of Tahiti in his dress of ceremony. Next to him, as if to assist in a ceremonial scene, are a priest, a woman dancer, and two musicians from the Society Islands. The impression of an actual scene is maintained by the couple of the Marque-sas Islands, with the woman holding a branch of the breadfruit tree while her companion seems to be addressing the chief mourner. Farther left, natives of New Zealand, Tahiti, Mallicolo, Australia, and New Caledonia, some of them holding weapons, form a loosely connected queue; detached from it is a native family from Easter Island sitting underneath a tree. A kangaroo serves as the only representative from the animal kingdom. The print, which borrowed greatly from the engravings illustrating the editions of Captain Cook's first and second voyages,[7] is a clever example of recasting and rearranging earlier images provided by Cook's artists. Several of the engravings in Cook's accounts showed a head-and-shoulder portrait and thus required the draftsman of this composition to make up some of the full-length figures himself. With no adequate models at hand, these are by no means correct, but it is commendable that they refrain from spectacular fiction. In true con-cern for detail (also expressed in the boats, huts, and other elements of landscape in the back), the print is a concise summary of various anthro-pological and geographical information which had been published in Cook's narratives but had not yet reached the level of popular education.

In 1784 the official account of Cook's third voyage appeared and contained the largest number of illustrations of native people to date. At about the same time Europe saw the publication of two works which rank among the most interesting "costume books" of the period: Teodoro Viero's *Raccolta di... Stampe, che rappresentano figure ed abiti di varie nazioni* (Venice 1783, 1791), and Jacques Grasset de St.-Sauveur's *Costumes civils actuels de tous les peuples connus* (Paris 1784).[8]

Viero is the earliest of the important publishers to be considered here. He had just missed the publication of the third voyage but makes good use of the plates of the second. Out of 360 hand-coloured illustrations in three parts, 17 are devoted to nations of the south Pacific, and these reflect his intensive examination of the print material that was available. If one compares Hodges's portrait of a "Man of Christmas Sound"[9] with Viero's elegant, partly draped figure entitled "Uomo del Canale de Noel,"[10] one is struck by the redevelopment and elaboration of the original source (figure 18). Cook had reported on the inhabitants of Tierra del Fuego: "they are a little ugly half starved beardless Race; ... They were almost Naked; their cloathing was a Seal skin; some had two or three sew'd together, so as to make a cloak which reach'd to the knee, the most of them had only one skin hardly large enough to cover their shoulders, and all their lower parts were quite naked."[11] Viero's figure is far from that description, and with little regard for physical and economic conditions of the natives. But probably in his eyes there was no qualitative difference between one nation and another, a race like the Fuegans or a people who represented higher cultural standards such as the Tahitians. Viero's print of "Potatow Capo dei Tahiti"[12]—based upon Hodges's portrait of Potatow in the engraving of J. Hall[13]—is invested with mannerist elegance; the gestures of the figure are of decorative theatricality but were certainly meant as an expression of a free and natural way of life. In the National Library of Australia is kept a crayon drawing of that print by an anonymous artist[14] which, owing to some minor difference with the print, could be regarded as a model for the former rather than as a copy (figure 19).

Except for one, all of Viero's prints of south sea islanders are indebted to prints after Hodges which were published in the account of the second voyage.[15] They all represent full-length figures, whereas the majority of their models are confined to head-and-shoulder. Viero very deliberately reworked and re-elaborated Hodges's earlier records, aiming at an idealized effect. In his book there are no passages quoted from Cook; thus no verbal evidence is given to accompany his prints. To this extent Viero may be seen as emulating earlier European costume books of the baroque tradition which often emphasized entertaining variation rather than sound instruction. On the other hand, it must be admitted that Viero follows the visual sources where they are available.

A representation which is based more faithfully upon the engravings provided in Cook's account is Viero's "Donna della nuova Caledonia"[16] (figure 20). This is an interesting composite depiction; the woman's head and shoulders are borrowed from Hodges's portrait print of the same title,[17] while the rest of her body leans upon a figure in Byrne's

FIGURE 19. "Potatow Capo dei Tahiti," crayon drawing by an un-known artist for Viero's *Raccolta di ... Stampe* (1783-91), National Library of Australia, Canberra.

FIGURE 18. "Uomo del Canale de Noel," engraving from Teodoro Viero's *Raccolta di ... Stampe* (Venice 1783-91).

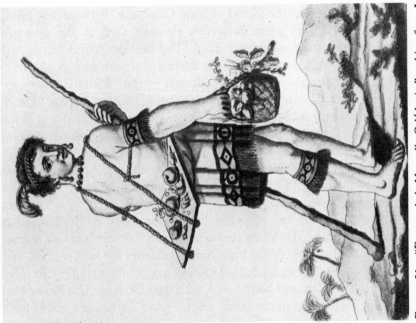

FIGURE 21. "Femme de la Nouvelle Calédonie," etching from J. Grasset de Sauveur, *Encyclopédie des voyages* (Paris 1795-96).

FIGURE 20. "Donna della nuova Caledonia," engraving from Viero's *Raccolta di... Stampe* (1783-91).

engraving "View in the Island of New Caledonia."[18] From that print, Viero also borrows some decorative elements such as the woman's petticoat and the flask in her hand. The beehive-shaped hut in the background with its characteristic narrow door, as well as the foreground bird, are also supplied by Hodges's print. Where it proves applicable, Viero is keen to introduce elements of native culture or of landscape in order to add to the local flavour. Having only the plates of the second voyage at his disposal, he inevitably had limited possibilities for copying, and thus had to make additions and inventions.

Imaginative as Viero's illustrations occasionally are, they seem modest when compared with illustrations by St.-Sauveur, the second publisher of costume books of the period. The difference between Viero's woman of New Caledonia and the same figure interpreted by St.-Sauveur is revealing[19] (figure 21). Where the Italian largely follows his model, leaving the woman half naked, the Frenchman decorates her with a dress, earrings, and a feather in her hair. The flask has been replaced by the more gentle device of a small hand basket with fruit. St.-Sauveur's illustration is from his later costume book, Encyclopédie des voyages (see below), but it is symptomatic of the author's general approach. The first publication in which St.-Sauveur represented natives of the south seas is the Costumes civils, published in four volumes of which the first appeared in 1784. It is adorned by 305 etched and hand-coloured illustrations, executed probably after St.-Sauveur's own designs.

St.-Sauveur was born in Montreal in 1757, was educated in Paris, and travelled widely in southeast Europe and the Middle East.[20] He began to publish his work at the age of twenty-seven. In the preface to the first volume of the Costumes civils, he states that after the Costumes religieux & dignitaires (appearently an earlier costume book of his, of which, however, I know no edition), the present work is much needed. An anthology of civil costumes of the world, comprising all nations and classes of society, in his eyes serves as a history of man and thus appeals to a wide circle of readers. He claims that because of its documentary and comparative approach his work is as valuable for posterity as it is for the present age. It permits the philosophical voyager (le voyageur philosophe) to study all nations and, in St.-Sauveur's view, it is indispensable to foster universal brotherhood. Adults and children of both sexes benefit from it, and so do women, who are enabled to discuss their fashions all over the globe. Last but not least, the author wishes the theatre to make good use of it, since inaccuracies, he assures his readers, in matters of theatrical costume are longstanding.[21]

In order to satisfy all groups of readers, St.-Sauveur maintains that all costumes are correctly drawn and coloured after nature.[22] This he vouchsafes by his own experience as a traveller, as well as by referring to the works of illustrious voyagers and their illustrations.

Though the work does not fulfill its promises, it is all the same one of the most noteworthy costume books of its time. The plates are grouped by nation and each plate is accompanied by explanatory texts concerning native laws and customs. Nations of Europe are freely mixed with those from other continents in the same volume without order. This and the lack of pagination suggest that the work was first published in subscribed installments and only later bound.

The third volume of the *Costumes civils* was issued some time after 1784 and contains twenty-two plates of natives whose figures had first been published in the edition of Cook's third voyage; surprisingly there are no illustrations which hark back to the plates of the edition of the second voyage. Though the relation between St.-Sauveur's plates and those published in the Cook edition is very close, the figures are not strictly copied but altered with picturesque embellishment. It is instructive to compare, for example, St.-Sauveur's "Pirogue Sandwich"[23] (figure 22) with Webber's famous "Man of the Sandwich Islands in a Mask,"[24] showing the same gourd helmet. As Viero had done, St.-Sauveur uses a portrait and gives it a body which is partly based on an actual source and partly on his own invention. Thus, of the figure itself, only the pubity girdle can claim to have been borrowed from Webber's composition of a "Man of the Sandwich Islands Dancing."[25] When compared with Viero, St.-Sauveur emphasizes muscular strength and energy over elegance and artful adjustment of the members. He is not concerned with a proper background for his figures, and neglects all information that might be drawn from the original engravings. He places his Hawaiian paddler against an empty sky and upon a low terrain socle with only an indifferent landscape behind.

Another illustration by St.-Sauveur is the "Insulaire d'Owhyhee."[26] Deviating from normal practice, this is based on none of the plates in the edition of Cook's third voyage, but on Bartolozzi's and Byrne's line engraving of "The Death of Captain Cook" after Webber's oil painting of the same title,[27] published in 1784 and 1785[28] and probably also well known in France. The model chosen for it is the warrior in the right foreground of the composition seen in an attacking position with a spear in his hands. Although the plate shows the figure laterally inverted, a drawing perhaps by St.-Sauveur himself which is now in the National Library of Australia reveals a close relationship between the model and the copy[29] (figure 24). Apparently the figure was singled out for its striking costume of a feather cape with a geometrical pattern on the back. By comparison, the scene of the murder of Cook has been diminished in importance; limited to just three figures, it has been pushed into the back, where it serves as an allusion to the warlike spirit of the central figure.

In 1795–96 St.-Sauveur published his second costume book under the title *Encyclopédie des voyages*.[30] It is a revised and enlarged version of the first, in five volumes, including 432 plates.[31] In volume 4 (*Asie*) and in volume 5 (*Amérique*) there are about forty-five illustrations of people of the Pacific area which are based on or inspired by plates after Cook's artists. In this new edition St.-Sauveur goes even further in revising earlier images. In his *Costumes civils* he had shown the figure of a paddler of Hawaii wearing a gourd helmet (Figure 25). In a related plate in this publication, the gourd helmet has been given to the "Danseur des Iles Sandwich" to whom ethnologically speaking it does not belong[32] (figure 23). But St.-Sauveur coupled two images in order to arrive at what he must have regarded as a more spectacular and arresting picture.

There are a number of similarly heterogeneous and nonsensical elements in St.-Sauveur's plates which render his figures picturesque and their costumes impractical to wear. A case in point is his "Homme de l'Isle de Pâques."[33] Eager to show as many different nations as possible, all varied and quite distinct from each other, St.-Sauveur is anxious that all his natives are individually and "ingeniously" clothed. Following the late eighteenth-century popular idea of noble savages of superior physical constitution living in agreement with nature, the bodies of St.-Sauveur's male figures are often athletic and their gestures brave and commanding. Examples of this are the dignified and strenuous warriors of New Zealand or of the Sandwich Islands,[34] whose representations in profile are indebted to neoclassical taste and whose outfits make them akin to Greek heros in battle. St.-Sauveur, and with him his age, admired the moral and physical power of native people who were brave

FIGURE 23. "Insulaire d'Owhyhee," pen and wash drawing by St.-Sauveur for a plate in his *Costumes civils*, National Library of Australia, Canberra.

FIGURE 22. "Pirogue Sandwich," etching from St.-Sauveur, *Costumes civils* (Paris, after 1784).

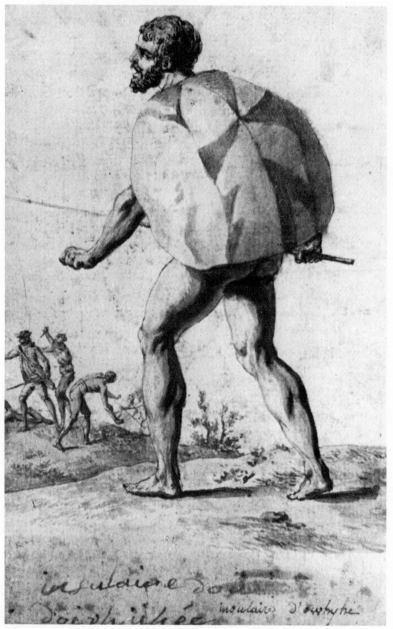

FIGURE 24.  "Danseur des Iles Sandwich," etching from St.-Sauveur, *Encyclopédie des voyages* (1795-96).

and resistant when attacked, and indulgent, reflective, and hospitable when left at peace.

St.-Sauveur repeated these figures in a hand-coloured etching called *Tableau des découvertes de Cap^ne Cook & de la Pérouse*, published in 1797[35] (figure 25). It is an unique historic document in that it represents most of the Pacific nations whom Cook and la Pérouse had visited.[36] A key explains their country of origin.[37] Among the figures represented, there are some such as the paddler of Hawaii or the woman of New Caledonia who are already familiar from plates in St.-Sauveur's volumes, and they may stand for several others which were likewise repeated.

The juxtaposition of the different nations and the publication of this plate may well have been a point of national pride for St.-Sauveur. The atlas of the voyage of la Pérouse had just been published in 1797, and a French audience would have expected to see their naval hero in line with Cook. The plate is a commemorative tribute to two great explorers who had greatly enriched the world with their discoveries and who had both lost their lives during their mission. At the same time the plate, imaginative as its costumes are, may have pursued an instructive intention, comparable to that of the print by Page (after Samuel) about twenty years earlier (figure 17). With many people placed side by side, their costumes become an object of comparative study.

The figures are placed so as to form interlocking groups and "conversation pieces." Most nations are represented by both sexes, some attended by their children. The landscape is stage-like, decorated with trees, houses, and canoes as suggestive props. Though some of the natives wear weapons, the general impression conveyed is idyllic and peaceful. The plate has great folkloristic charm and leaves no doubt about St.-Sauveur's belief in the noble savage.

Among the works mentioned so far, it seems that St.-Sauveur's publications were widely popular. Not only was a second edition of the *Costumes civils* published in 1800 in four volumes by Sylvain Maréchal, apparently an early collaborator of St.-Sauveur's, but also his designs were frequently used in foreign costume books of the period.[38]

They found their most notable distribution when in 1804 the French wallpaper factory of Josef Dufour in Macon published a series of wallpapers entitled *Sauvages de la mer Pacifique*, later to be called *Les voyages du Capitaine Cook* (figure 26), after a design by Jean Gabriel Charvet

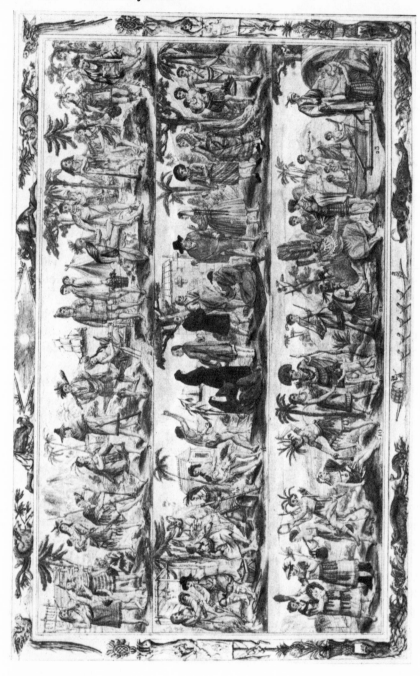

FIGURE 25. *Tableau des découvertes du Cap.^ne Cook & de La Pérouse.*

FIGURE 27. "Nieuw-Zeelanders," aquatint from Martinus Stuart and Jacques Kuyper, *De Mensh...* (Amsterdam, 1803).

FIGURE 26. Wallpaper stripe from Dufour's series *Sauvages de la mer Pacifique* (1804).

(1750–1829).[39] It was the first of the famous "papiers panoramiques" which proved so immensely popular in France and Europe during the first half of the eighteenth century. Like the panoramas from which they took their name, they were organized as a succession of vertical stripes of printed and coloured paper which covered the whole room. They mostly showed landscape and figures that gave the illusion of looking out into an infinite nature. Exotic scenery was particularly favoured as a subject, as it was both diverting and instructive.

The *Sauvages de la mer Pacifique* was sold with an accompanying prospectus in which the purchaser was advised that: "We thought it would be advantageous to have united a great number of nations in a commodious way which otherwise are separated from us through oceans. Not having to leave one's home and simply by contemplation, the reader of histories of travel can imagine himself among those nations and compare text and illustration. Thus he will become familiar with their costumes and the diversity of nature. . . . "[40] On twenty different stripes of wallpaper 2 m high and 50 cm in width, inhabitants of the major islands and areas of the Pacific are represented: natives from Hawaii, New Caledonia, New Zealand, Nootka, the Pelew Islands, Prince William Sound, the Society Islands, Tana, and Tonga. They are loosely arranged in groups of nations. Populating an ideal tropic landscape and surrounded by lush vegetation, they are engaged in characteristic occupations such as hunting, fishing, dancing, or playing sportive games.[41] With a few exceptions[42] all the scenes and natives depicted in Dufour's wallpapers relate to engravings first published in connection with Cook's voyages. However, they are not directly copied from the plates but only indirectly, by way of the illustrations which St.-Sauveur had published in his *Encylopédie des voyages* and *Tableau des découvertes du Cap^ne Cook & de la Pérouse*. A case in point is the representation of St.-Sauveur's "Femme de la Nouvelle Calédonie" with a carrier basket on her back who is introduced into one of the stripes as she is plucking bananas from a palm tree (figures 21 and 26).

A further stage of alienation from Cook's illustrations is reached in the figures of young girls of Tahiti dancing, represented on stripes 4 to 6.[43] Dressed in chiffon-like skirts, wearing long shawls, bracelets, girdles, elements of fancy costumes like feathers, and diadems in their hair, these dancers look vaguely oriental but can no longer be located ethnographically. In fact, Cook's illustrations have been so much altered and modified that the results have lost every degree of possible authenticity. However, it was because Cook's illustrations proved to be such fertile, inspiring material in the hands of the designers and decorative artists that they could be successfully transferred into different media.[44] Dufour's wallpaper is another, and by its particular character a striking example of the appeal that Cook's *Voyages* and their illustrations exerted among a general class of people who were not foremost naturalists or anthropologists. Retreating from the original source but using the name of Cook as a catchword, Dufour, like St.-Sauveur before him, successfully propagated an image of the Pacific which was entirely European in its making but which still claimed to serve the needs of geographical and human education.

At the same time that Dufour issued his wallpaper, another book was published in Europe that had plates devoted to costumes of Pacific nations. This was Martinus Stuart's and Jacques Kuyper's *De Mensch, zoo als hij voorkomt op den bekenden Aardbol...* (Amsterdam 1802-07),[45] a geographical history of man which ranks among the most outstanding and important examples of early nineteenth-century ethnographic literature. Its first three volumes are devoted to the people of the Pacific including the northwest coast of America, one to inland America, and two to Africa. There is no volume on the nations of Europe, since the work remained unfinished when the illustrator, Jacques Kuyper (born 1761), died in 1808.

Stuart's text is eminently erudite and attests to the author's wide reading. For the area of the Pacific he quotes all relevant eighteenth-century sources: Cook, La Pérouse, La Billardière, Billings, Keate, etc., and makes references both to passages of text and to plates. Every nation is anthropologically described and discussed according to customs, laws, education, religion, and other phenomena of culture. By compiling all information available, Stuart's picture is concise and carefully researched. At the same time it is philosophically oriented and thus tends to idealize the natives as noble and happy savages. Kuyper in his illustrations follows Stuart in this view and shows an equally sympathetic and romantic approach to his subject, to which the technique of the plates as hand-coloured aquatints greatly contribute.

*De Mensch* is one of the few costume books considered here in which the illustrations were actually drawn by a fully professional artist. As an illustrator, Kuyper had been tried by Stuart before on a book on Roman history, and in *De Mensch* they continued their collaboration.[46] Seventeen of the original drawings for this work have survived[47] and verify a later judgement that his "style is noble, and in his compositions he proceeded with consideration and with poetical sense. He was always concerned with historical truth in custom and costume, as well as with correct drawing."[48]

For the six volumes of *De Mensch* Kuyper designed forty-one plates of which nineteen refer to Pacific nations. Almost all of the Pacific plates are in one sense or another dependent upon illustrations first published in the editions of Cook's voyages.[49] It is notable that Kuyper has added few major elements of his own invention but has followed the principle of combining different sources. His plate of "Nieuw-Zeelanders," for example, is made up from at least three different engravings[50] (figure 27). The figure of the warrior is easily recognizable from a plate in Parkinson's *Journal* entitled "A New Zealand warrior in his proper dress & completely armed according to their manner,"[51] with the only difference that his head has been turned and replaced by Parkinson's "The head of a Chief of New Zealand."[52] The topknot fashion of the Maoris' binding their hair, ornamented by three feathers and a comb, had been recorded by Parkinson in some detail, and Kuyper was perceptive enough to take note of this. Another kind of hair style is shown on the young woman in the back and is copied from a print illustrating the edition of the voyage of D'Entrecasteaux, the French explorer who had called at New Zealand in 1793.[53] The treatment of hair is only one detail of a more important message which Stuart and Kuyper make in this plate: that of the superb craftsmanship and taste for ornamentation possessed by the Maoris. This is alluded to in several details: in the different kinds of cloak, in ornaments, pendants, and weapons, as well as in objects of basket work and carving. The effect is grand and dignified, apt for a self-assured race, eminently brave and skilled. The visual elements which Kuyper needed for this representation he copied conscientiously from earlier engravings, but it was not before he carefully added and amalgamated these that he arrived at a picture which became a synthesis of the earlier information.

An illustration that is similarly constructed is Kuyper's "Inwooners van Nootka"[54] (figure 28). Anyone who is familiar with the plates published in the account of Cook's last voyage will instantly recognize the

FIGURE 28. "Inwooners van Nootka," aquatint from Stuart and Kuyper, *De Mensch* . . . (1804).

sources that have been used and blended. Thus the portraits of the man and the woman are a rather exact copy of corresponding plates after Webber,[55] and so is the wooden idol in the background of the hut.[56] Where an immediate source is not available among the original illustrations, Kuyper supplements the necessary details from other plates or from descriptive evidence. His method of designing is reconstructive and his approach archaeological. By this means Kuyper sought to come to a representation that was both truthful and exact. And yet his pictures are independent in composition and imbued with a moral spirit about the happiness of the native way of life.

As in this illustration, many of Kuyper's natives are represented as couples. They are frequently depicted as amorous and tender people who, like the inhabitants of Nootka, rear their children lovingly. Kuyper's predilection for happy family scenes, and especially for sweet and chubby children, is also borne out in the plates of the "Marquisen—Eilanders"[57] or of the "Nieuwe Hebrides."[58] In the work of Cook's artists, conjugal or parental relations had played a very subordinate role. But since then family portraits had advanced to a distinctly popular subject of European art, expressing contemporary beliefs in human innocence, domestic happiness, and the benefit of education. It is obvious that the authors' scale of measure is entirely romantic and European in outlook. However favourable and sentimentally tinted their view may have been, it was the most accurate and best informed to date.

The fourth and last work in this sequence to be discussed is Giulio Ferrario's *Il costume antico e moderno o storia del Governo, della Milizia, della Religione, delle Arti, Scienze ed Usanze di tutti i popoli antichi e moderni,* published in twenty-one folio volumes in Milan between 1816 and 1834.[59] Giulio Ferrario (1767–1847) was a native of Milan, head librarian of the Braidense, and the owner of a printing house.[60] As a man who possessed great erudition and comfortable financial means he was well equipped to direct an undertaking which became noteworthy not only for its colossal scope but also for the quality of its text and illustrations. It is the most extensive and erudite work of its kind of the first half of the nineteenth century, a gigantic gathering of knowledge about all nations, European and non-European, from antiquity to modern times. It was lavishly illustrated with some 1,350 hand-coloured folio plates which up to twenty draughtsmen and etchers had produced.

The plates represent physiognomical portraits, scenic events in the profane and sacred life of the nations, their rituals and feasts, their habitations, landscape views and products of nature, as well as objects of their arts and crafts. As far as these concern the Pacific, the majority of them, about thirty, are based upon engravings from all three of Cook's voyages. Engravings after John Webber are the most often copied.[61]

In the use of source material, Ferrario is the most puristic of the publishers considered here. He makes no attempt to reconstruct images from diverse sources or to add to them from his own invention. Instead, his illustrations are generally direct copies and, even though he has had them redrawn by his artists, the composition of the original source and its general character is largely maintained.

For the plate of the natives of the northwest coast of America[62] (figure 29), Ferrario employs two engravings after Webber from the third voyage (the upper two),[63] as well as from a Spanish expedition to the Strait of Juan de Fuca in 1792 (the lower three).[64] Ferrario invites comparison of the heads by placing them side by side. The original drawings of the sitters had been done thirteen years apart and by different artists. Ferrario treats them as equal by pointing to the design and material of their costumes, their hair style, or to the ornamentation of their heads.[65] Very consciously he makes his readers aware of the relativeness of field observation, and offers a wide range of evidence in pursuit of objective information.

Besides Ferrario's head-and-shoulder portraits, there are whole-length and multi-figure representations, landscape views, and interior scenes among his plates. One of these represents the inside of a house at Nootka[66] (figure 30), after Webber's engraving of the same subject.[67] The Lipperheidesche Kostumbibliothek in West Berlin owns Ferrario's own proof copy of *Il costume antico e moderno*; and it contains—bound into the book—a great many pen, pencil, and wash sketches, as well as different states in the preparation of the plates. One of them is a pen and wash drawing for the print mentioned[68] (figure 31). A comparison between Ferrario's aquatint and Webber's engraving shows some small adjustment and restyling of the interior scene but without substantially changing the source. The material possessions of the room have been maintained, but the room has been tidied up and the figures wear spotless clothes. Consistent with the spirit of embellishment, the number of openings in the roofs have been reduced and functionalized as windows or smoke traps. Webber's dilapidated-looking house appears somewhat

FIGURE 29. "Natives of the North-West Coast of America," from Giulio Ferrario, *Il costume antico e moderno* (Milan, 1820).

FIGURE 30. "The Inside of a House at Nootka," from Ferrario, *Il costume antico e moderno* (1820). *Cf.* Figure 4, p. 94.

FIGURE 31. "The Inside of a House at Nootka," pen and wash drawing, Lipperheidesche Kostumbibliothek, Berlin.

more respectable in the aquatint. It is apparent that, in spite of all the demands of objectivity, Ferrario wishes to present his natives in quite a favourable light. But we must concede that his monumental undertaking could not have been carried out without the profound conviction that the representation of the nations of the world was a deserving subject.

A more detailed and extensive survey of costume books and other geographical and ethnographical publications of the period would show that the dominance of illustrations from Cook continues throughout the 1820s and 1830s.[69] In this connection it is odd that publications in this field were almost exclusively Continental and that many of a very popular appeal were published in Germany. The publications that I have singled out are only the tip of an iceberg. They were chosen because of their ambitious illustrative material, because of their artistic merit, and because they showed continuous as well as changing concerns in the representation of exotic nations from overseas. They also indicate that until the time of Ferrario's *Il costume antico*, prints from Cook's voyages clearly dominated the field of illustrations from the Pacific. It was the plates of the third voyage that were predominantly copied, whereas those of the first and second had a noticeably smaller impact.

But even so, for a whole generation, if not more, illustrations from Cook's voyages were foremost in educating people in Europe about Pacific nations. The reason for this unchallenged position must be sought in Cook's success as an explorer, whereas the undertakings of some of his successors were struck by misfortune and disaster. Also, because Cook's orbit as a voyager was so much greater than that of his followers, the illustrations in his accounts were more varied in people and places. During all his three voyages, artists were on board his ships, but subsequent explorers like Bligh or Vancouver sailed without them. But if for many decades illustrations from Cook's narratives proved particularly influential, this was also due to Cook's personal interest in drawing and recording. Last but not least was the influence of Sir Joseph Banks, who not only instigated the practice of taking artists on voyages but also helped considerably in the publication of the accounts and assured a high standard in engraving. Executed in representative size by the foremost engravers in the country, the illustrations in themselves could be considered valuable works of the graphic arts, and thus helped to prolong the reputation of the official accounts of Cook's voyages.

# Two Centuries' Perceptions
# of James Cook:
# George Forster to
# Beaglehole

*Michael E. Hoare*

DURING the long winter of 1786–87, the third spent in his "savage and dreary retreat" in the spiritual and intellectual isolation of Vilna, capital of Polish Lithuania in an ever troubled land, George Forster, the poignant, pleasant sire of Cook scholars, wrestled with his translation into German of the official account of the third voyage of Captain James Cook. More than that, he was constrained to better the "intolerable Introduction" to the first English edition of that long delayed work, wherein everything on Cook had "already long been heard; and everything is so loathsomely expressed."[1] Forster laboured hard at this Introduction to *Des Capitain Jacob Cook's dritte Entdeckungs-Reise*... (two volumes, Berlin 1787–88), and what emerged was his 106-page essay, "Cook the Discoverer: Attempt at a Memorial," which first appeared in 1787.[2] The proper critical study of Cook, his life, times, and work had begun.

That, indeed, was how Forster intended it, for he had himself learned his literary, scientific, and geographical criticism in the hard and rigorously intellectual school of his father, J.R. Forster.[3] He had also learned his exploring at the feet, on the quarterdeck, of James Cook on that epic second voyage in the *Resolution* (1772–75), and had produced in English and German an account of the voyage which is still regarded as the literary-scientific masterpiece among all of Cook's narratives.[4] More ably than any Englishman living, George Forster and his father became the "Pacific experts": the critics, interpreters, and purveyors to the learned and popular-reading public in Europe, especially Germany, of James Cook's, his companions', and his successors' contributions to knowledge and of their place in the contemporary world of progress and Enlightenment. "I have done justice to Cook," wrote George Forster in April 1787, one month after completing his Cook essay, "or rather procured it for the first time, for his merits have been until now incompletely recognized."[5]

We might say the same of Forster's essay on Cook: its merits, outside of German scholarship, have "until now been incompletely recognized." Leslie Bodi gave us an English resumé of it and George's other Pacific writings in 1959,[6] and ten years later I published short excerpts in English from it.[7] Professor Beaglehole, in his writings at least, chose, it seems, to ignore it, except for a single reference in his posthumous opus, *The Life of Captain James Cook* (London, 1974). Yet it is one perception of Cook, the most profound and rounded by any contemporary, that we must notice. It is, in the words of that meticulous Pacific and Cook bibliographer Rolf Du Rietz, "one of the earliest and most important biographies of Cook."[8] There is nothing in perception to compare with it until John Cawte Beaglehole became Cook's Boswell.

The New Zealander is, indeed, anticipated by Forster in "Cook the Discoverer!" "Once, when time will have scattered what we are now collecting so zealously, a learned scholar will recognize Cook's real greatness from the fragments he'll pull from the rubble."[9] For who, on Cook, pulled more fragments from the rubble of two centuries than Beaglehole?

Forster possesses, too, other perceptions that make his Cook essay prescient and precocious: he foresees the rise of European civilizations and settlements in Australia, New Zealand, and western North America; he foresees and lives through the early beginnings of the new trade, Pacific contacts with Asia and Europe, and further explorations—philosophical, commercial, penological, evangelical, and scientific,—which would draw our European ancestors, and now draw us, to the shores and islands of the Pacific, north and south, in the wake of James Cook. "What Cook has added to the mass of our knowledge is such that it will strike deep roots and long have the most decisive influence on the activities of men.... Only our present century could satisfy Cook's burning ambition by putting resources at his disposal, thus enabling him to become a discoverer, and Cook alone could come up to the expectations of his times."[10]

Forster sees Cook, therefore, against a canvas bigger than even the extensive Pacific, Europe's last unknown to master by sea; he sees him as the quintessence of his times in all that scientific discovering implied; sees him as a European and not simply an English mariner serving

British ends. Cook's work delineated an era, presaged the rise of new world civilizations and, suggests Forster, certainly spells change or decay in those with whom they, the Europeans, fatally or fatefully "impacted." Where, tell me, is the Englishman or anyone else who so early perceived and put into such perspective this and much more on Cook and his times?

Our great loss and our bitter regret must be that these first profound perceptions came only from a memory—vivid albeit—of events enacted twelve years before or, vicariously, through correspondence, reading, translation, and all-too-rare conversations with participants; memories and insights penned in the intellectual desolation of a Vilna far removed from London.[11]

For in London, as in other parts of Europe, they were penning mostly encomiums on Cook; from England came pious plaudits for a national hero, corporate yet grateful grief for the man of his times. Forster knew this; Beaglehole came to know it. As Cook biographers they had much in common: their liberalism; their humanity; their modesty; their love of their native languages and the writing of them; their Pacific, and their striving for critical truth. Perhaps, in that long winter of poorer perceptions on Cook from 1787 to the 1950s, a long fallowness when so few cultivators strove critically in the field of Cook scholarship, fate was leaving it to our century's historians, biographers, and scientists to do what Cook's contemporaries and nineteenth-century historians, for all their new theories, advances, and methodologies—in Germany particularly—could not achieve: the proper critical perceptions of Cook and his times.

Beaglehole's perceptions of Cook we find sifted, expanded, distilled, refined in his monumental *Life of Cook*, "one of the great biographies," suspects Geoffrey Moorhouse, "in the English language."[12] But there are, too, his reflective essays on Cook, a mine, I suspect, rarely visited, but yielding much concerning the growth of the editor's and biographer's perceptions of Cook.

Yet J.C. Beaglehole also had his prejudices and, although his Cook perspectives are the least likely ever to be rivalled, there are some dimensions that even he missed or ignored, some angles he blunted or measured falsely. And what is the taking of true perspective if not the art of delineating solid objects on a plane surface "so as to give some impression of relative positions, magnitudes" and so on? If our Cook sun is too large, how sadly out of orbit, how much out of perspective, will be our other planets. If our angles are English, how blunted may seem our Germans, how diminished our Welsh, Scottish, Russians, Polynesians, Melanesians, and so on.

"Down under" we claimed Cook early—forgetting, alas, for long years the brave Dutchmen.[13] In cheaper days of plundering, our forefathers sought out Cook's and his intimate contemporaries' manuscripts, correspondence, drawings, and the return of some of our artifacts and relics of material culture. What could not be bought, begged, borrowed, or stolen was copied for our great libraries. We still buy, but with more stealth, more discrimination, since Europeans are more tenacious and North Americans richer.

From Australian deserts came or dwelt at the fringes critical prophets of Cook and his times like Bernard Smith and, now, Howard T. Fry. From New Zealand, for reasons ethnically obvious, there arose an anthropological Pacific tradition of scholarship producing writings as diverse as those of Peter Buck, Jim Davidson, Andrew Sharp, and John Beaglehole. Other "Australasian" scholars, like Averil Lysaght and Harold Carter, left their own shores to pursue their Cook perceptions elsewhere. If today I can briefly use the now tabu word "Australasia"— once so acceptable geographically and historically—then from that former group of Cook-inspired, Cook-explored colonies, Australia and New Zealand, from those obstinately contracted remnants of *Terra australis incognita*, has come, for clear cultural reasons, much that is great in Cook scholarship. Cook helped, rightly or wrongly, in those countries' search for identity in the past.

But now, since the pendulum of Cook scholarship is moving back to Europe, to the north Pacific, its islands and coasts, some attempt at *critical assessment*, in the truest sense, of Cook scholarship is timely.[14]

Old J.R. Forster, who took on many odds, great or small, long and short, was wont, in his own quaint words, to "lift his cloth" regularly in the *Resolution*, wash it, and hang it out to dry. Standing away from Staten Island, off Tierra del Fuego, on 4 January 1775, "to pass our third summer season to the southward" after but recently doubling the Horn east to west, Cook lost a starboard maintop studding-sail boom. The same squall, wrote Forster ruefully, "carried 3 of my Shirts off."[15]

Squalls can presage winds of change, gales of fury or fortune. Here, for the sake of permissible possible new perceptions, we risk a shirt or two.

Boswell, Beaglehole tells us, could have been a useful member of Cook's voyages, certainly as an observer: "There were characters just as odd, and less amiable, on the voyages, men just as improbable as sailors."[16] Who were those strange men, these incubi, these disturbing sunspots? Well, Banks and the elder Forster, of course, were two: they were awkward, demanding, contrary, self-opinionated, and much more. They were also rivals to Cook, and Cook, I have more than just a suspicion, did not like rivals. And Beaglehole does not like the un-amiable men, the contentious men; he does not like the non-sailors and the non-excellent Englishmen, although genial Swedes, like Solander and Sparrman, may pass. However much the former offended Linnaeus, in affairs of the heart and science, he did become comfortable, respec-table, and English.[17]

But even Britons, too, err! What about that geographical "sciolist," that Scot, Alexander Dalrymple, whose "leading characteristics" (Beaglehole told us in 1955) "were intellectual indiscipline and self-conceit, a perfect inability to discriminate."[18] But, by 1969, after "pro-longed meditation," this unflattering "name of sciolist" is, somewhat grudgingly, retracted in a footnote. "Unfortunately his scholarship," we are informed, "valuable as it was, could never be disinterested—he could not help being propagandist as well as historian, on his favourite subject he had no reserve of scepticism. He is a figure ripe for more extended study."[19] Such ripening, some new Cook perspectives, came through Fry's scholarship in 1970 and, by 1974, our hydrographer and geogra-pher is become a gentleman whose "weaknesses . . . succeeding genera-tions . . . have tended to accentuate . . . rather than his virtues, his failures rather that his strength." He is, too, a "passionate man."[20]

Grudging or not, this twenty-year shift in Beaglehole's perception of one of Cook's leading contemporaries was important. It encouraged me, who (striving, I suppose, after "disinterested" scholarship) was labour-ing with Forster, "one of the Admiralty's vast mistakes," "the patently conspicuous phenomenon" of Cook's *Resolution* voyage.[21]

For the moment, however, let us leave our unamiable men to fester and, with Beaglehole, briefly survey the long winter of poorer percep-tions of Cook and his times from George Forster to Beaglehole.

Lacking Boswell and ignoring George Forster, we come in 1788 to Andrew Kippis's two-volume *Life of Captain James Cook* (and it is over five hundred pages) which, in different editions, impressions, and translations, remains with us, remarkably, until 1889 and in the U.S.A., it seems, until 1924.[22] Kippis, "a professional literary man, a professional biographer" is not, however, "a devoted amateur" like Boswell. He did not go to Whitby or Marton and so, in Cook's case, too, "the annals of the poor" remained "obscure."[23] "If we possessed the story of his youth," Forster had written in 1787, "how much information would it not furnish to the student of human nature," as Cook, boy, apprentice, and almost master in the mercantile service, "struggled with fate," against "indigent circumstances" and "in spite of everything was victorious."[24] Kippis, therefore, concludes Beaglehole, "let us down": he failed to apply any "critical intelligence" to the documents, the correspondence, and even the rare interviewing he did do. "When one thinks of his chances as a contemporary, and what he did with them; when one considers how full of positive error is the little he did gather, one almost weeps as one throws him away."[25]

To which, if George Forster had also not pounced upon the negligent Kippis for review in the influential *Göttingischen Anzeigen von gelehrten Sachen* on 4 October 1788,[26] we could have said amen! And, perhaps lachrymose too, stomped on in our seven-league-boots-of-time with Beaglehole fifty years later to visit Reverend George Young of Whitby with his *Life and Voyages of Captain James Cook* (London, 1836). This clerical gentlemen "had a real feeling for the hero, for family history, for the illuminating anecdote, and professed to supply much original information,"[27] but he is withal still not our man.

Away with Walter Besant and his *Captain Cook* of 1890; pass over those grabbing, grubbing, copying centennial-conscious colonial Australians striving—precariously albeit—in Cook to collect or create the first vestiges of a history, a national heritage untainted by convicts, and we come to Arthur Kitson's *Captain James Cook...* (London, 1907), the next perception "that could lay claim to originality." But he, unlike Kippis, is "not a professional biographer or a professional historian" but a businessman who wrote "at some length about currency reform and thought that Pacifism was a Great Conspiracy." But forget his prejudices, his unscholarly occupation; for Beaglehole he will do *pro tempore* since "in relation to Cook he was an amateur who became devoted." And what we want—demand, indeed—is devotion, total and absolute. Cook captivates.

First and foremost Kitson has heard of original documentation: has heard of and visited the Public Record Office, the British Museum, Cook's manuscript journals; has even got "some good letters," sorted out some confusion and "disentangled two Cooks, and ended by writing a biography which has since been leant on as heavily as his predecessors leant on Kippis."[28] But Kitson's "sense of proportion is not impeccable, his style, like his imagination, is rather pedestrian; he had rather a fondness for revising the spelling and punctuation of his extracts; he knew nothing about the Pacific. He is still useful."[29] He has, in short, a few redeeming features: he advances, scientifically, historically speaking, our Cook perceptions.

But now, horror upon horrors, we are in modern times with many short lives: "Some have virtues, some are dreadful," and about them Beaglehole will be silent. His task, that of "any serious writer," is "to supersede Kitson."

But should we, too, be silent about those Mooreheads, MacLeans and Villierses? Have they not, as George Forster claimed was necessary for his day, popularized the twentieth-century image of that "popular" eighteenth-century man, the folk hero, Cook? Have they not given us catchwords to remember Cook's work, the language and explanations to interpret the sailor's jargon? Their sins are perhaps that they, too, inherited the time-worn perceptions.

To supersede Kitson, Beaglehole must reflect deeply upon how to represent, to weigh up, a taciturn "man of action," one who may have been more than what he did, certainly than what he said. "I have sometimes considered," muses the biographer, "paradoxically enough, that the acts of a man of action are the least important thing about him."[30]

George Forster mused on all that, too, 180 years before. "Nature," he wrote,

> bestowed gifts in full measure on our discoverer, born in the modest cottage of a crofter. The fundamental strength of his personality was his successful striving for action and for performing deeds. This urge was never at rest, it needed no stimulation by the senses, and enjoyment of sensuality meant nothing to him. Cook's abstemiousness was in a way an innate virtue, not the result of a persistent struggle. His curiosity could only be satisfied by knowledge.... Thus this need or pleasure produced

that untiring diligence, that perseverance and pertinacity we admire so much, and by which he achieved such great things; he remained unsurpassed in his work, in his way of overcoming difficulties, dangers and troubles. He had an imagination which quickly grasped a situation, the ability to judge correctly and make unerring decisions. He possessed sensitivity of feeling, whose excess sometimes brought about passionate fits of temper, but, still more frequently, it was ruled by reason, turned towards justice, kindness and humaneness....[31]

Let me repeat: this is George Forster in 1787, not Beaglehole in 1974, and there were over one hundred pages of biography, history, geography, science and—more tedious to read today, philosophy—intertwined. George Forster, a contemporary writing in the white-heat tension of his publisher's deadlines, less ordered sometimes but still, in Friedrich Schlegel's words, "a master of German style," is the prominent essayist of Enlightenment Germany: he wrote here the blueprint, the prelude, the *Ur-Cook* of which Beaglehole wrote the *Meisterwerk*; the Cook I and II. Forster knew, too, his Pacific, his Quiros, his Magellan, his times, and his history of exploration and of science.

For an eighteenth-century person, says Beaglehole, Cook is better known to us than most.[32] That, I contend, is absurd. We know more, indeed, about the Forsters and about Banks, let alone about other figures political, literary, and scientific. "Experimental gentlemen" and natural philosophers wrote volumes of correspondence, and their relics were often dauntingly immense and varied. Sailors, unless say a James Burney, rarely were so obligingly literary or epistolary.

Beaglehole's great merit as Cook's Boswell is that he gave us in print all the known extant journals and drafts, the official and the rather meagre private correspondence, to put alongside the scientific reports and second and third voyage accounts, which are mostly Cook himself. For the unlettered Cook, all agree, learned to write:

Cook's writings, as well as his actions, are distinguished by true diligence, observant acumen, manly reasoning, ingenuousness and simplicity. The man who had every means at his disposal to reach his final goal, was also able to find words when he wanted to describe expressively what he felt deeply about the natives in their natural state, which he studied so carefully. He wrote with inimitable art when he related deeds, boldly achieved, without arrogance but full of seriousness and with great emphasis. His unadorned but pure, clear style was formed without outside help, and without any acquaintance with great models, but by that inner urge which also made him a discoverer.[33]

So wrote Forster in 1787.

In 1970 Beaglehole gave us that thoughtful little essay *Cook, the Writer* as the sixth G.A. Wood Memorial Lecture.[34] It had been Beaglehole's privilege to correct some of Wood's Cook "slips." Cook learned, we are told, "to shape his experience in words"; learned possibly from "that easy, vivid, within limits eloquent writer Banks."[35] I believe, indeed, Cook learned from all his literary and literate scientific companions: from Wales, from his officers and, even, from the Forsters. And why not? Cook was perceptive, intelligent and teachable.

He served a long "apprenticeship for discovery"—much of it in eastern Canada—and underwent, too, a preparation for writing which lasted until after the *Endeavour* voyage. Then something happened. Cook read that "compilation" by Hawkesworth of Byron, Carteret, Cook and Wallis, read it on the way home in the Atlantic in *Resolution* and smarted about its embarrassing exaggerations concerning St. Helena, the Cape, and much more beside. He decided to become his own author, edited politely by Douglas. And so we got *A Voyage towards the South Pole and round the World* (two volumes, London, 1777), which "apart from small things [is] Cook's own book," consciously prepared for publication, Beaglehole believed, throughout the second voyage. To Cook the author and publisher we will return anon.

Beaglehole strove to get inside the sometimes impenetrable Cook for forty years: his life's work as an historian, so his son, T.H. Beaglehole, tells us, was directed towards this end.[36] He stuck reflectively, ruminatingly, perceptively, and devotedly to his task, but not without some prejudices, some of them prodigious, developing. As yet the complete Beaglehole correspondence is not available to us publicly. One day it will be. Then we shall see, I suspect, the deeper reasons why Beaglehole chose Cook as his life's subject, as his never-to-be forgotten Faust upon whom he lavished his life, labour and love, pride and prejudice, style and self. We shall see, too, incidentally, the catholicity of a New Zealand intellect devoted to New Zealand; for, although Cook grew on Beaglehole, the New Zealander showed historical insights, literary taste, and liberal concern for men, things, ideas, and principles in many other spheres. The outside world applauds him in Cook: New Zealanders did that nearly last and least of all. How much he was like George Forster! Prophets at home indeed!

Circa 1934-35 Beaglehole wrote in Wellington a "Memorandum on proposed work on the life of Captain Cook"[37] for submission to the Carnegie Corporation of New York. "While working," wrote the New Zealander, "on the history of discovery in the Pacific Ocean for my book *The exploration of the Pacific* (London, A. & C. Black, 1934) I became interested in the career of Captain Cook, the chief figure in that discovery, and convinced that no adequate study of his life exists. Such a study I should like to make."[38] And, as we know, he made it.

Already by the mid-1930s, therefore, Beaglehole had read his secondary sources; had reached, indeed, some of the perceptions and strictures on Cook's former biographers examined briefly above. During these Pacific researches, Beaglehole had found and utilized Cook's instructions for the first two voyages and so reaped the first fruits of the harvest we now enjoy in Cook documentation. He found early, too, some of the "critical work" done by experts in disparate disciplines on Cook, and foreshadowed the necessary interdependence we as life scientists, geographers, historians, anthropologists, and so on today maintain. How well I recall his eager exhortations to me in 1971 to exploit the every willing "specialists" for Forster's "Journal."[39]

In the 1930s the Beaglehole Cook recipe was this: write it well; study the times and the Pacific; write, in short, a "standard work." The subject Cook demanded literary and historical excellence, no less: "A thoroughly satisfying life of Cook must first, I think, remedy [earlier] failings, and furthermore should take account of the great advance in knowledge of the Pacific ethnology made in recent years—for while it does not seem satisfactory to regard discovery purely from the standpoint of the discoverer, Cook himself was also a principal founder of Pacific ethnology."[40]

As a writer on Cook, Beaglehole knew he must move, however, far beyond his acquaintance with Pacific geography, "beyond my limited New Zealand and Australian experience." He will, he proposes, go to New South Wales—how successful had been those copying, scribbling, grubbing builders of a national heritage on documents!—to examine the "great body of Cook papers and records," both public and private, in that state. He will have in his hand the "exhaustive" Public Library of

New South Wales *Bibliography of Captain Cook*... (Sydney, 1928), for he was hunting pre-Holmes, pre-Cox, pre-Spence, pre-Du Rietz in the bibliographical frontier terrain of Cook researches.[41]

Australia for Beaglehole in the 1930s will be his main Cook port of call. He may, he thinks, need to visit England briefly "to clear up possible points or fill up small gaps." But "certainly the great bulk of the work involved could be done in Sydney."[42] Alas, poor Sydney, the Carnegie did no cooking!

How limited in the 1930s were our perceptions of Cook; how small then our awareness of the documentary spread and provenance of those great voyages, their journals, correspondence, artifacts, specimens, writings, and implications! On all continents there is the mark, in most there are the relics of Cook.

Beaglehole, rooted once more in his country's affairs and history in Wellington, let Cook simmer on during the 1930s and 1940s. After the initial Cook research visit to London in 1949–50, the first of a number, he published his first Cook piece in the *New Zealand Listener*.[43] Five years later came the *"Endeavour" Journal* (1955) and then, over the next twenty years, the Banks journal and diversions (1962); the further Cook journals and documents (1961 and 1967); and, between 1950 and 1971, some thirty-five essays, reviews, corrective pieces and other writings on Cook and his times. Like the *Voyage* of tragic Mathew Flinders, Beaglehole's life's odyssey, Cook's *Life*, was posthumous and he did not even see the great work fresh from the press.

Throughout this Cook odyssey, Beaglehole strove to find Cook the man: whether he rated as "a character or a chronological list of deeds." It was, it seems, an honest search: "One would rather like him to have done something wrong: is there a problem there? Did he ever do anything wrong in the sphere of navigation or seamanship? One would, in a rather mean-spirited way, like to see something wrong, to tie him up with our poorer humanity, and prove that the biographer has a fair mind, and is not overwhelmed and besotted with the majesty of his subject."[44]

George Forster knew this problem, too: the danger of deification, the worry of few seemingly negative, deprecating Cook sources. He, like Beaglehole, chose to ignore or play down *in his essay*, but not earlier, the more obvious. Which brings us back to those two men we left to fester: J.R. Forster, the "odd" and Joseph Banks, the "preposterous."

Most biographers, Beaglehole explains, were landsmen and "therefore incapable of a just, critical analysis, and seamen have been quick to put down hostile commentary."[45] But William Wales was not a seaman: he was the "humane," altogether excellent English astronomer of the *Resolution*, a man "quite austerely devoted to a fine sense of duty."[46] He was a sea lawyer, a defender of tars, a witness who is valid for Beaglehole. One duty was to deprecate, despise, diminish, and defrock that ersatz, parvenu philosopher, that eminently lampoonable charlatan, that taker-in of "so many excellent persons," that man of "a rather romantic imagination ... fed on Druids and certain ingredients of the forested Teutonic past," the "odd," inimitable, mimicable Johann Reinhold Forster.[47]

Beaglehole looks at the phenomenon Forster through the distorted telescope of Wales. What a penumbra to behold! Like Venus beheld on Tahiti in 1769, we have an "Atmosphere or dusky shade," disturbing the observations and results! And so we get Forster observed and "Dalrymple exploded": two men, Beaglehole assures us, "of large hopes."

One wonders what Forster's prominent friends of rationalist Enlightenment Berlin, Göttingen and Halle would have made of their Druid-captivated friend; what even that pleasant little intellectual circle in Warrington would have made of their erstwhile German tutor, of all this satirical baiting of Sir "Hudibras," which Beaglehole perpetuates, of the demeaning—and here the grossest error—of intellect and scholarly competence.

Listen to Wales, the outraged, the righteous: "[Cook] has not told a single untruth, or scarce slipped into a mistake from the beginning of his book to the end of it, whilst some others contain more misrepresentations than pages, but the opinion of the public may be judged from the sale of the two books."[48] Forget that, under legal threat, the Admiralty took away the Forsters' rights to plates and engravings, including to those they had drawn and supervised themselves; forget that Cook's two-volume *Voyage towards the South Pole* had over sixty plates and was deliberately underpriced to sell at two guineas, while George's *Voyage*, meagrely illustrated, sold for the same price.[49] Forget, too, says Wales, that the critical reviewers read Forster "with rapture, while Captain Cook's simple matter-of-fact passes unregarded!"

Beaglehole advises a little more caution than Wales: Forster exasperates us but he cannot be ignored. Let him, therefore, like Dalrymple, be relegated to footnotes and ironical asides; let him be diminished by intellectual one-upmanship, by ridicule and stealth. Let us, like Sir Toby Belch and cronies, hidden behind our Teutonic bushes, mimic his preening and pride; his pretensions and weaknesses; for, like Malvolio, he is a vain steward of his science, his gifts, his philosophy. Let us ignore Forster's *Observations made during a Voyage round the World* (London, 1778), "solid not only with observations, but with the characteristics of its author,"[50] says Beaglehole; full, says Wales, who took six years to read the book, of "hypotheses" only.[51] Let us, if we so continue, diminish, distort, destroy our perceptions of Cook, his contemporaries and his times! We will be the poorer.

Back now to Cook's biography of which all this is part. Despite, argues Beaglehole, all attempts to find "something wrong," something to link ourselves and Cook together in "our poorer humanity," "One is, as it were, condemned to admire, much as one craves to see the man steadily and see him whole, even if it means seeing him in pieces."[52] More than that, Beaglehole, the biographer, "cannot help sighing wistfully after omniscience."

But, although Cook did not, in Beaglehole's eyes, apparently sin, he had at least a temper: that "sensitivity of feeling," George Forster calls it, "whose excess sometimes brought about passionate fits of temper"[53] when iron reason and will broke temporarily. Now it worried Beaglehole that Cook "was himself a very stubborn, persistent man." But these traits were the key to his "whole professional career." Add technical competence and abilities to Cook's "stubbornness, persistence and patience" and he emerges "among the great."[54] But, says Beaglehole, the impatience, the passion still worry him.

But why worry about Cook's *heivas*, his stampings, rantings and railings? Must he always shrive himself or be shriven before letting us have a rare key to his heart, a rare clue to any weaknesses? Consider— Beaglehole admittedly could not because the "Journal" was then unknown—J.R. Forster's illuminating, brooding, pent-up anger over Cook's stubborn persistence in the summer of 1773–74, when he risked ship, life, and expedition, and made a gamble which nearly did not succeed, to go his "furthest south":

> But we must submit, there are people, who are hardened to all feelings, & will give no ear to the dictates of humanity & reason, false ideas of *virtue* & *good conduct* are to them, to leave nothing to *chance*, & future discoverers,

by their *perseverance*: which costs the lives of poor sailors or at least their healths. These people should be constantly employed by Government upon such Schemes: as for instance the N.W. or N.E. Passage; there they will find a career to give their Genius full Scope; but wo! the Crew under them.[55]

What a mournful prophetic glimpse of Cook's career and its mainsprings in 1774! Forster's emphases, his italics, usually bespoke what men said; and "virtue," "good conduct," "nothing to chance," "perseverance," were, perhaps, echoes of Cook at table in the great cabin. From Robert Falcon Scott of the Antarctic, the same region that nearly claimed Cook 140 years earlier, we learned how fine was the line between persistence for fame and persistence for future—to return at least.

But, says Beaglehole, forgetting his own plea for a weakness and echoing Cook's spartan spirit, " . . . these voyages are not made for the sake of exultations, or for the improvement of a literary style. They are made for the improvement of Geography and Navigation. The fewer despairs we have the better; and exultations will only take our minds off the business we have in hand."[56] But why? Are all men spartan, all men automatons, all men Cooks? And, if George Forster is again our witness, the psychology of men: their interactions, exultations, despairs, hopes, feelings; their social divisions, the "strict subordination," the all-too-quickly forfeited sociability and loss of convivial conversation, the descent to brusque or hostile bickering were all part of those small vessels' way of life. "In a few weeks the small supply of real adventures, anecdotes, the jovial or witty ideas, which everyone can conjure up, are exhausted, and received at the second and third repetition with only a yawn."[57] Our excellent mariners *were* human.

More humanity, more failings, more humour, more of life, it has been whispered, and Cook would be less of a god, more a man. Here in men—in all their meanness or greatness, their deeds and failings—lay all the potential for a *Bounty* story in fact or a *Caine* story in fiction. Why not, therefore, the odd discordant note; a real baring of self; the stating of despairs and exultations; in short, the revelation of that ambivalence that is in most men? Mercifully, Forster senior gives us the despairs and exultations, the human ambivalence, flowing over.

Forster père gives us, too, a slightly modified Cook, one displaying some of the weaknesses for which Beaglehole asks. Cook and Forster were men ripe to clash: both ambitious, both intelligent, both stubborn, and both with tempers. Forster also did not dissimulate in his writing, privately or publicly. He is not one of those uncritical "admiring shipmates of the third voyage."[58]

He tells us of the captain's passions and weaknesses; the unexpected susceptibility to promptings of underlings and of the shipboard intrigues around, but not aimed at, the great man. Cook's taciturnity exasperates Forster, as does his willingness to defer to the not always unbiassed testimony of his officers. Once Cook is himself "exasperated by some false Insinuations from his first Servant," "& so some hot & unguarded Expressions came out on both sides & he sent me [Forster] by Force out of his Cabin, the use of which he agreed upon I should have, in consideration of bearing so great a share in the Mess, & because he could not procure me the Enlargement of my Cabin which he had promised me."[59]

Cook's disdain for and neglect of scientific opportunity outraged Forster constantly. The captain, sometimes petulantly, chose the times and places to suit himself. Once, off Vatoa in June 1774, records Forster, "to avoid a flat refusal & ... an altercation I kept silence." But still he got not ashore. It is, we are told, the self-centred, self-important officers and subordinates who "Lord & Bashaw it over others," and who influence Cook: "I mean not to say Capt *Cook* acted thus ... but he seemed to be prompted to act thus in respect to me by people who had such principles ... "[60]

Is Cook, the incorruptible, susceptible then—subtly or otherwise—to "influence" and "insinuation"?

Yes, says George Forster, ghosting albeit for an embittered parent: "Dr. Hawkesworth's publication which had been sent to meet Capt Cook at the Cape, with the news of the prodigious profits of the compiler, inspired [Cook] with the desire of becoming an author."[61] And so, after the return to England, in the autumn of 1775, Cook became one party to a wider "conspiracy" to do the Forsters out of a large share and profit in the official publication. Cook tried unsuccessfully to suppress *Characteres generum plantarum* (London, 1775), the first botanical work, "being desirous to profit even by this" scientific work.[62] Science again became the whipping-boy.

"This study of nature," George boldly affirms, "was only the secondary object of the voyage." They came to regard "those moments as peculiarly fortunate, when the urgent wants of the crew, and the interest of the sciences, happened to coincide."[63] Banks the "proposterous" recalled something similar in 1803: "Had Cook paid the same attention to Naturalists, we should have done more at the time" in the *Endeavour*.[64]

By 1974 Beaglehole has moved more to accommodate the naturalists' claims vis-à-vis Cook, who "laid the foundations of Pacific geography as a science, of Pacific anthropology, of antarctic hydrography", but

> If one does not make even greater claims, and bring in the sciences of natural history, it is because one is speaking of Cook, and not of his voyages. As a commander of ships he very efficiently brought the scientists to their material, when that chimed with his own larger purposes; he had an observant eye, he could ask relevant questions, he could learn; but without Banks and Solander, Anderson, the Forsters, the artists, the voyages would not, in natural science, have been great.[65]

So we have Cook the avaricious, Cook sometimes the baulker of scientific endeavour, Cook the bad-tempered, Cook the jealous and impatient. Avaricious? Yes, says George again, "with the utmost reluctance," but seeing "the failing of a man whom I respect as a navigator of distinguished ability"; Cook fleeced the Forsters mightily in overcharging for their commons and contribution to his table in the *Resolution*.[66]

Where has this Cook sprung from? Are we too "mean-spirited," despite Beaglehole's suggestion so to be? No, says old Forster again in 1781, translating and introducing in German John Rickman's surreptitious *Journal of Captain Cook's last Voyage to the Pacific Ocean* (London, 1781): "the Captain's character is not the same now as formerly." "His head seems to have been turned." Behind it is Lord Sandwich—he had done it to others like Sir Hugh Palliser—and, relates that high-minded officer James King, "a scholar by profession," Cook is also jaundiced against all philosophers and philosophy. Curse them and it![67] Our Captain is become "...a grumpy fellow, sometimes ruled by avarice and bad temper, to which was added arrogance, the result of having his head turned by Lord Sandwich."[68] On the third voyage Cook became tired, lost his self-control, got more cruel and wanton, and perished.

This, Beaglehole accepts in part. Cook became "a very tired man" on that "wearing, worrying voyage": he "lost his sense of proportion."[69]

Death was not a result of hubris, which is, roughly speaking, Forster's suggestion. Nonsense to both of these explanations, says Gordon Parsonson of Otago, New Zealand, in 1976! According to his controversial thesis the fatal happenings of Kealakekua Bay in February 1779, "perhaps one of the most famous events of Pacific history," is a question of understanding the complexities, divisions and religion of Hawaiian society. Cook is dedicated to the ancient secondary inferior god, Lono, whose followers are tributary to an upper class, "a true military aristocracy," who worship the war god Kukulaimoku. Cook, before "a somewhat unrehearsed death or sacrifice," laid "sacrilegious hands on Kalani'up'u," chief of the higher order. Cook, in Hawaiian terms, was no god but "a lesser being, the representative of a lesser god, a popular god."[70]

Thus, even in death, new perceptions of Cook are possible after two centuries; even, indeed, post-Beaglehole. In terms of anthropology and culture-contact research, such perceptions are now more profound and better researched. Beaglehole's perceptions changed noticeably in forty years of Cook scholarship: he was, indeed, influenced by the very bicentenary studies he helped generate. Cook is no god: he is mortal and sacrificial.

He was, too, in the widest sense a *European*. The fatal news came from Petropavlovsk, Kamchatka, in 1779 overland to St. Petersburg, whence, through P.S. Pallas, the naturalist, it got into A.F. Büsching's influential *Wöchentlichen Nachrichten* of 10 January 1780, one day before London heard of it.[71] In Cassel, George Forster read of this "most unfortunate & must-to-be-lamented End" and craved more detail for biography.[72] In 1780 and 1781 he and that Anglophile extraordinaire, Georg Christoph Lichtenberg of Göttingen, gave the Germans two smaller, more fragmentary accounts of Cook,[73] accounts that prelude the greatest eighteenth-century piece: "Cook the Discoverer."

"Those who know Cook," wrote Lichtenberg, "only from his circumnavigations know him too little ... he deserved a wider reputation long ere that." He "has become known throughout the civilized world and the greater portion of that which we cannot include within this designation."[74]

Fame, then, is not to be denied. Are failings? We have examined Cook's greatest biographer Beaglehole, Plumb in mouth, as it were. "I know," Beaglehole wrote in 1966, "about George's *Cook der Entdecker*, & I have seen it highly praised."[75] But it was not yet read, although it seems to have been perused in a Wellington translation before 1971.[76] Was Beaglehole influenced by Forster? There are many parallels. I think he was, although perhaps unconsciously.

Let us conclude with that truth of all polemic, quoted by George Forster and William Wales in 1777–78 from César de Missy (1703–75), a truly international if minor man of letters:

> *On ne repousse pas la vérité sans bruit;*
> *Et de quelque façon qu'on l'arrête au passage,*
> *On verra tôt-ou-tard que c'étoit un outrage,*
> *Dont il falloit qu'au moins la* honte *fut le fruit.*[77]

# Notes

## Introduction:

1. Quoted in *The Auckland Star*, 23 March 1970.

2. *Ibid.*

3. For a full listing of his varied writings see *John Cawte Beaglehole: a Bibliography* (Wellington: Alexander Turnbull Library and Victoria Univ. of Wellington, 1972) 1; for an account of other work relating to Cook's voyages see M.K. Beddie, ed., *Bibliography of Captain James Cook R.N., F.R.S., Circumnavigator*, 2nd ed. (Sydney: Library of New South Wales, 1970).

4. J.C. Beaglehole, *The Life of Captain James Cook* (London, 1974). As far as we know the only gainsayer was J.H. Plumb in the *New York Review of Books*, XXI, No. 9, 30 May 1974, a review which says more about the reviewer than the book reviewed.

5. Michael E. Hoare has more fully reassessed the career of Forster senior in *The Tactless Philosopher: Johann Reinhold Forster (1729-98)* (Melbourne, 1976). The son, George Forster, awaits similar attention.

6. Quoted in Beaglehole, *The Life*, p. 714. Appropriately, the phrase was also used to describe Beaglehole by his colleague, F.W.L. Wood, in a tribute that appeared in the *New Zealand Listener*, LXVIII, no. 1670, 1 November 1971, 11.

7. The point was previously made by Christopher Lloyd and Jack L.S. Coulter, *Medicine and the Navy 1200-1900: Volume III—1745-1815* (Edinburgh and London, 1961), pp. 307-18.

8. Bernard Smith, *European Vision and the South Pacific, 1768-1850: A Study in the History of Art and Ideas* (London, 1960).

9. Beaglehole, *The Life*, p. xi.

10. J.C. Beaglehole, ed., *The Journals of Captain James Cook on His Voyages of Discovery, Vol. I: The Voyage of the Endeavour, 1768-1771* (Cambridge, 1968), pp. clxxii-cxcii.

11. The strength and persistence of this notion is examined by K.R. Howe, "The Fate of the 'Savage' in Pacific Historiography," *The New Zealand Journal of History*, XI (October 1977), 137-54.

## New Geographical Perspectives and the Emergence of the Romantic Imagination:

1. Edward Heawood, *A History of Geographical Discovery in the Seventeenth and Eighteenth Centuries* (New York, 1965); J.N.L. Baker, *A History of Geographical Discovery and Exploration*, rev. ed. (London, 1937); and J.C. Beaglehole, *The Exploration of the Pacific*, 3rd ed. (Stanford, 1966).

2. Alan Frost, "The Pacific Ocean: the eighteenth century's 'new world,'" *Studies on Voltaire and the Eighteenth Century*, CLII (1976), 779-822.

3. John Ellis to Linnaeus, 16 July 1771, J.E. Smith, ed., *A Selection of the Correspondence of Linnaeus, and other naturalists* (London, 1821), I, 263.

4. The first phrasing is from *Gentleman's Magazine*, L (1780), 44; Sir John Pringle used the second, when he presented the Copley Metal, which the society awarded to Cook, to Mrs. Cook. Pringle's address was included as an appendix to Cook's *A Voyage towards the South Pole* (London, 1777), II, 369-96.

5. J.R. Forster, "The Translator's Preface," to Lewis de Bougainville, *A Voyage round the World* (London, 1772), p. v.

6. William Coxe, *Sketches of the Natural, Civil, and Political State of Swisserland* (London, 1779), which Wordsworth knew in the French version by Ramond de Carbonnière, *Lettres de M. William Cox à M. W. Melmoth sur l'état politique, civil, et naturel de la Suisse*, 2 vols. (Paris, 1782); William Gilpin, *Observations on the River Wye* (London, 1782), *Observations... on several Parts of England; particularly the Mountains, and Lakes of Cumberland, and Westmorland*, 2 vols. (London, 1786), *Remarks of Forest Scenery*, 2 vols. (London, 1791), *Three Essays* (London, 1792); H.B. de Saussure, *Voyages dans les Alpes*, 4 vols. (Neuchâtel, 1779-96); [Thomas West], *A Guide to the Lakes, in Cumberland, Westmorland, and Lancashire* (London, 1778).

The quoted phrases are, respectively, Gilpin's and John R. Nabholtz's, and appear in Nabholtz "Dorothy Wordsworth and the Picturesque," *Studies in Romanticism*, III (1964), 118-28. See also Christopher Hussey, *The Picturesque* (London, 1927); Samuel H. Monk, *The Sublime* (New York, 1935); John R. Nabholtz, "Wordsworth's *Guide to the Lakes* and the Picturesque Tradition," *Modern Philology*, LXI (1964), 288-97; Martin Price, "The Picturesque Moment," in *From Sensibility to Romanticism*, ed. F.W. Hilles and Harold Bloom (New York, 1965), pp. 259-92; Christopher Salvesen, *The Landscape of Memory* (London, 1965); and J.R. Watson, *Picturesque Landscape and English Romantic Poetry* (London, 1970).

7. *Cf.* Andrew Kippis, *The Life of Captain James Cook* (London, 1788), pp. 497-98, "It is not to the enlargement of natural knowledge only, that the effects arising from Captain Cook's voyages are to be confined. Another important object of study has been opened by them; and that is, the study of human nature, in situations various, interesting, and uncommon. The islands visited in the centre of the South Pacific Ocean, and the principal scenes of the operations of our discoverers, were untrodden ground. As the inhabitants, so far as could be observed, had continued, from their original settlement, unmixed with any different tribe; as they had been left entirely to their own powers for every art of life, and to their own remote traditions for every political or religious custom or institution; as they were uninformed by science, and unimproved by education, they could not but afford many subjects of speculation to an inquisitive and philosophical mind. Hence may be collected a variety of important facts with respect to the state of man; with respect to his attainments and deficiencies, his virtues and vices, his employments and diversions, his feelings, manners, and customs, in a certain period of society."

8. For example Cook's description of the perils of navigating the east Australian coast given in J.Hawkesworth, *An Account of the Voyage taken by the Order of His Present Majesty for making Discoveries in the Southern Hemisphere* (London, 1773), III, 606-7: "Rocks and shoals are always dangerous to the mariner, even where their situation has been ascertained; they are more dangerous in seas which have never before been

navigated, and in this part of the globe they are more dangerous than in any other; for here they are reefs of coral rock, rising like a wall almost perpendicularly out of the unfathomable deep, always overflowed at high-water, and at low-water dry in many places; and here the enormous waves of the vast Southern Ocean, meeting with so abrupt a resistance, break, with inconceivable violence, in a surf which no rocks or storms in the northern hemisphere can produce."

There are numerous parallels to this passage and sentiments in other explorers' narratives. See for example George Forster's descriptions of Tahiti, *A Voyage Round the World* (London, 1777), I, 253-54, 268-69, 288-89, 312-13; J.R. Forster's description of Easter Island, *Observations made during a Voyage Round the World* (London, 1778), p. 155; William Bartram's descriptions of the alligators, *Travels through North and South Carolina, Georgia, East and West Florida* (New York, 1928 [1791]) pp. 114-24; Hearne's description of the shamen, *A Journey...to the Northern Ocean* (London, 1795), pp. 218-19; Bruce's of Egypt, *Travels to discover the Source of the Nile* (London, 1790), I, 7-113; and Park's descriptions of the Moors of Benown, *Travels in the Interior Districts of Africa* (London, 1799), pp. 121-60.

See also Smith, *European Vision*.

9.  Aged twelve, Southey wrote "a satirical description of English manners, as delivered by Omai, the Taheitean, to his countrymen on his return": Southey to John May, 29 June 1824, C.C. Southey, ed., *The Life and Correspondence of...Robert Southey* (London, 1849), I, 119. Wordsworth's teacher at Hawkeshead, Thomas Bowman, lent him "Tours and Travels": T.W. Thompson, *Wordsworth's Hawkeshead*, ed. Robert Woof (London, 1970), p. 344. Coleridge studied geography as a deputy-Grecian at Christ's Hospital in 1787 (perhaps with Guthrie's *Geographical Grammar* as text); and he learned his mathematics from William Wales, "the companion of Cook in his circumnavigation," who liked to entertain the boys with stories of the voyage: S.T. Coleridge, *The Notebooks*, ed. Kathleen Coburn (London, 1957, 1962), II, no. 2894.

10.  The poets saw details of Cook's voyages, for example, in Cowper's *The Task*; of Cook's voyages and Bruce's travels, among others, in Erasmus Darwin's works; and they of course saw reviews of voyages and travels in the magazines.

11.  Southey to G.C. Bedford, 1 June 1793, Robert Southey, *New Letters*, ed. Kenneth Curry (New York, 1965), I, 26.

12.  Coleridge to Poole, 13 December 1796, S.T. Coleridge, *Collected Letters*, ed. E.L. Griggs (Oxford, 1956), I, 273.

13.  "If the *Bounty* mutineers had not behaved so cruelly to their officers I should have been the last to condemn them. Otaheitia independent of its women had many inducements not only for the sailor but the philosopher. He might cultivate his own ground and trust himself and friends for his defence—he might be truly happy in himself and his happiness would be increased by communicating it to others. He might introduce the advantages and yet avoid the vices of cultivated society. I am again getting into my dreams...": Southey to G.C. Bedford, 8 February 1793, *New Letters*, I, 19.

14.  *The Notebooks*, I, no. 296.

15.  Coleridge to Poole [28 November 1796], *Collected Letters*, I, 263.

16.  Coleridge to Cottle, [April 1797], *Collected Letters*, I, 320-21.

17.  Wordsworth to Tobin, 6 March 1798, *The Letters of William and Dorothy Wordsworth*, eds. E. de Selincourt and Chester L. Shaver (Oxford, 1967), I, 212.

18.  *Sir Thomas More* (London, 1829), II, 365.

19. William Bligh, *A Narrative of the Mutiny, on Board His Majesty's Ship "Bounty"* (London, 1790) p. 8; Mary Jacobus, *Tradition and Experiment in Wordsworth's "Lyrical Ballads" (1798)* (Oxford, 1976) p. 28.

20. *The Notebooks*, I, 174/22; Dorothy Wordsworth to Mary Hutchinson, [June 1797], *The Letters*, I, 189. Wordsworth described their beginning "The Ancient Mariner" in his note to "We Are Seven" (William Wordsworth, *The Poetical Works*, ed. E. de Selincourt, rev. H. Darbishire, 5 vols. [Oxford, 1952] I, 360-61).

21. C.S. Wilkinson discussed this possibility in *The Wake of the Bounty* (London, 1953), pp. 85-162.

22. For discussions of this motif in other terms, see: N. Frye, *Anatomy of Criticism* (New York, 1966), *passim*; and Harold Bloom, "First and Last Romantics," and "The Internalization of Quest Romance," in *The Ringers in the Tower* (Chicago, 1971), pp. 3-11, 13-35. Also relevant are: Maynard Mack, "The Jacobean Shakespeare," in *Jacobean Theatre*, eds. J.R. Brown and B. Harris (New York, 1960), pp. 11-41 (especially pp. 33-41); and Donald Davie, "John Ledyard: The American Traveler and his Sentimental Journeys," *Eighteenth-Century Studies*, IV (1970), 57-70.

23. J.L. Lowes, *The Road to Xanadu*, 2nd ed. (London, 1930), *passim*.

24. See Watson, pp. [65]-78; Price, p. 289; and Salvesen, p. 69 (where the phrase quoted occurs), and elsewhere.

25. Lowes, pp. 325-30.

26. Wordsworth, of course, uses these phrases in his Preface to the 1800 edition of *Lyrical Ballads*: see for example R.L. Brett and A.R. Jones, ed. *Lyrical Ballads*, rev. ed. (London, 1965), p. 245.

27. See for example R.W. Frantz, *The English Traveller and the Movement of Ideas 1660-1732* (New York, 1968 [1934]).

28. Preface, *Lyrical Ballads*, p. 247. *Cf.* Jacobus's remarks on the abstract landscape of "The Pedlar" in *Tradition and Experiment*, p. 96; and Kroeber's on particularized landscapes and states, in *Romantic Landscape Vision* (Madison, 1975), pp. 29 ff.

29. For discussions of this aspect, see for example Jacobus, p. 116, and Salvesen, *passim*.

30. *The Prelude*, ed. E. de Selincourt, rev. H. Darbishire (Oxford, 1959), pp. 623-28.

31. For a comprehensive discussion of what constitutes a "spot of time," see Jonathan Bishop, "Wordsworth and the 'Spots of Time,'" *English Literary History*, XXVI (1959), 45-65.

32. William Gilbert, *The Hurricane* (London, 1796), pp. 68-69. For Wordsworth's, Coleridge's, and Southey's knowledge of Gilbert and his poem, see Joseph Cottle, *Reminiscences* (Highgate, 1970 [1847]), pp. 42-47; Southey, *New Letters*, I, 120; Coleridge, *Collected Works*, ed. Kathleen Coburn, et al. (London, 1970- ) II, 350-51. In a note to *The Excursion*, Wordsworth called this passage "one of the finest... of modern English prose" (*Poetical Works*, V, 422-23); and Keats afterwards turned to it for "On First Looking into Chapman's Homer."

33. *Gentleman's Magazine*, LV (1785), 40; Watkin Tench, *A Narrative of the Expedition to Botany Bay* (London, 1789), p. 97; cited in J.C. Beaglehole, ed., *The Journals of Captain James Cook On his Voyages of Discovery, Vol. III: The Voyage of the Resolution and Discovery, 1776-1780* (Cambridge, 1967), p. lxxi; Poole to Warwick, 6 February 1796, in M.E. Sandford, *Thomas Poole and his Friends* (London and New York, 1888),

I, 132; George Vancouver, *A Voyage of Discovery to the North Pacific Ocean* (London, 1798), I, vi-vii.

34.   I have adopted some of Cook's self-descriptions here.

## A Presiding Genius of Exploration: Banks, Cook, and Empire, 1767-1805:

1.   Details of the *Porpoise* voyage are in the Mitchell Library, Banks Papers, M.L. Banks X, A79/3, including the report of the commander, 6 February 1799, fols. 199-200.

2.   A general account of the incident is in J.C. Beaglehole, ed., *The Journals of Captain James Cook on His Voyages of Discovery, Vol. II; The Voyage of the Resolution and Adventure, 1772-1775* (Cambridge, 1961) pp. xxviii-xxxii. The calendar of documents has the letters of Cook and Clerke on the instability of the vessel, pp. 930-31.

3.   J.C. Beaglehole, ed., *The Endeavour Journal of Joseph Banks* (Sydney, 1962), I, 24.

4.   A.M. Lysaght, *Joseph Banks in Newfoundland and Labrador* (London, 1971), p. 251.

5.   Beaglehole, *The Life,* p. 291.

6.   *Historical Records of New South Wales (H.R.N.S.W.)*, I, ii, p. 113. Phillip to Banks, 3 December 1791, M.L. Banks XVIII, A81, fols. 33-43.

7.   Banks to Nepean, 7 June 1789, Public Record Office (P.R.O.) Adm. 1/4154. Banks to Grenville, 7 June 1789, Home Office (H.O.) 28/6, fols. 234-35.

8.   A list of the plants on board is in H.O. 28/7, fols. 110-11, 7 December 1789. Riou's account of the wreck is in Adm. 1/2395, 25 December 1789, and 22 February 1790.

9.   In 1792 crewmen of a whaler threw salt water on some cochineal insects destined for Banks, see Enderby to Banks, 16 February 1793, Kew Herbarium Library, Banks Correspondence (Kew B.C.) II, 91. Archibald Menzies complained to Vancouver about fowls destroying plants in the *Discovery*'s plant cabin, Menzies to Vancouver, 18 November 1793, in M.L. Banks IX, A79/2, fol. 30.

10.   J. Banks to S. Banks, 26 April 1773, M.L. Banks XVI, A80/4, fol. 21.

11.   On the breadfruit, see D.L. Mackay, "Banks, Bligh and Breadfruit," *New Zealand Journal of History,* VIII (April 1974), 61-77. On the Indian experiments, D.L. Mackay, "Exploration and the Economic Development of Empire, 1782-1798; with Special Reference to the Activities of Sir Joseph Banks" (London: Ph.D. thesis, 1970).

12.   R. Schofield, *The Lunar Society of Birmingham* (Oxford, 1963); A.E. Musson and E. Robinson, *Science and Technology in the Industrial Revolution* (Manchester, 1969), pp. 138-42, 190-99.

13.   D. Hudson and K. Luckhurst, *The Royal Society of Arts, 1754-1954* (London, 1954); *Premiums Offered by the Society Instituted at London for the Encouragement of Arts, Manufactures and Commerce* (London, 1765-90).

14.   H. Lyon, *The Royal Society* (Cambridge, 1944), p. 217.

15.   The record of the growth of the family can be traced in J.W.F. Hill, *Letters and Papers of the Banks Family of Revesby Abbey, 1704-1760* (Lincoln, 1952). Young's opinion is in his *General View of Lincolnshire* quoted in G. Mingay, *English Landed Society in the Eighteenth Century* (London, 1963), pp. 173-74.

16.  J. Banks, *A Short Account of the course of a Disease in Corn, called by farmers the blight, the mildew and the rust* (London, 1805). It went through four editions up to 1834. Banks's only other publications also related to agricultural topics: *The Propriety of Allowing a Qualified Exportation of Wool, discussed historically* (1782); and *Some circumstances Relating to Merino Sheep* (1809).

17.  Young Edward Parry made this point in 1817: "Having obtained a *Carte blanche* from Sir J., I shall of course go to his library without any ceremony, whenever I have occasions: for his invitations are not those of fashionable life, but are given from a real desire to do everything which can in the smallest degree tend to the advancement of every branch of science...," quoted in Lysaght, p. 285.

18.  On these aspects, see Mackay, "Exploration and Economic Development," also R.P. Stearns, *Science in the British Colonies of America* (Illinois, 1970), ch. 9; L.J. Ragatz, *The Fall of the Planter Class in the British Caribbean, 1763-1833,* (New York, 1928); W.H.G. Armytage, *The Rise of the Technocrats* (London, 1965), ch. 4.

19.  King to Banks, October 1780, British Museum (Natural History) Dawson Turner Copies of Banks's Correspondence (D.T.C.) I, fol. 304.

20.  J. Ibbetson to E. Nepean, 25 August 1785, H.O. 28/5; Dryander to Banks, 12 August 1785, Fitzwilliam Museum, Banks Papers; Banks's instructions to Hove are in Adm. 2/1342, 15 September 1785.

21.  See Mackay, "Banks, Bligh and Breadfruit."

22.  Menzies to Banks, 21 August, 7 September 1786, Kew B.C., I, 239, 243.

23.  Grenville to Lords of Adm., 3 October 1789, Adm. 1/4154; also H.O. 28/6, fols. 304-5.

24.  Banks to Maskelyne, 16 February 1791, Kew B.C., II, 30.

25.  As in his outburst to Lieutenant King: Beaglehole, *Journals*, II, xlvi.

26.  Quoted in R. Hallet, *The Penetration of Africa* (London, 1965), pp. 244-45.

27.  Banks to Hawkesbury, 8 June 1799, British Museum, Banks Papers, Add. MSS 38233, fols. 94-95. See also his views on the Sandwich Islands: Banks to T. Haweis, 6 May 1799, B.M. Add. MSS 33980, fol. 185.

28.  Adm. 1/9800, undated. There is a draft in M.L. Banks XI, A79/4, fols. 195-212, May 1801.

29.  Instructions to Menzies, 22 February 1791, B.M. Add. MSS 33979, fols. 75-78. These also appear in Grenville to Lords of Adm., 23 February 1791, Adm. 1/4156, 17, and D.T.C., VII, fols. 197-201.

30.  A. Menzies, "Journal of Vancouver's Voyage," B.M. Add. MSS 32641, fols. 30-31. There is a similar description of Admiralty Inlet on the North American coast: "...a pleasant & desirable tract of both pasture & arable land where the Plough might enter at once without the least obstruction...," fol. 119.

31.  Banks to Hawkesbury, 30 March 1787, D.T.C., V, fols. 143-46: H.O. 42/11, 42, 30 March 1787; D.T.C., V, fol. 247, 9 September 1787.

32.  On these expeditions see Mackay, "Banks, Bligh and Breadfruit."

33.  Banks to Nepean, 15 February 1790, H.O. 42/16.

34.  "Memorandum for Mr. Nepean," December 1790, H.O. 42/17.

35.  H.O. 42/18, enclosure 2, 20 February 1791. See also M. L. Banks IX, A79/2, fols. 7-8 on Rennell and Bligh. In the end Bligh's notes were not used.

36. Banks to King, 15 May 1798, *H.R.N.S.W.*, III, 382-83. Manuscript note on voyage, 12 December 1800, M.L. Banks XI, A79/4, fols. 3, 12; Flinders to Banks, 6 September 1800, *ibid.*, XX, A83, fols. 59-62.

37. Banks to Sir Hugh Inglis, 24 April 1801, *ibid.*, XI, A79/4, fols. 169-70. This volume contains documentation of the other aspects of the voyage, including the appointment of the astronomer, fols. 9-11; instructions for the scientists, fols. 13-24; appointment of a miner, fol. 253; salaries, fol. 73.

38. Flinders to Banks, 18 February 1801, *ibid.*, fol. 259.

39. Banks to Nepean, and reply, 28 April 1801, *ibid.*, fol. 177.

40. *Ibid.*, fol. 33.

41. Beaglehole, *The Life*, p. 443.

42. 30, 9 May 1787, Adm. 3/103/30.

43. Bligh to Banks, 15 August 1787, M.L. Banks V, A78/4, fol. 40.

44. 18 September 1787, Adm. 2/117, 507-8.

45. 11, 12 February 1791, Adm. 3/106, 96; Adm. 3/108.

46. Flinders to Banks, 18 February 1801, *H.R.N.S.W.*, IV, 303.

47. Banks to Nepean, 9 January 1801, M.L. Banks XI, A79/4, fol. 73.

48. Etches to Banks, 14 March 1785, Kew B.C., I, 195.

49. Strange to Banks, 3 December 1785, *ibid.*, 216.

50. Hallett, pp. 156-59.

51. Dryander to Banks, 19 September 1785, Fitzwilliam Museum, Banks Papers; Flinders to Blanks, 1 July 1807, M.L. Banks XI, A79/4 fols. 371-73.

52. "Substantially intact": the main exception being the men who contracted malaria at Batavia on the *Endeavour* voyage.

53. Beaglehole, *The Life*, p. 451.

54. Burney to Banks, 6 July 1791, D.T.C., VII, fol. 230.

55. For example Banks to Reverend Weedon Butler, 13 May 1792, Kew B.C., II, 68.

56. W. Parsons to Banks, 27 August 1789, B.M. Add. MSS 33978, fols. 258-59. The flatterer was Lieutenant Colonel Antonio De Pineda y Ramirez of the Spanish Guards.

57. W. Bligh, *A Voyage to the South Sea* (London, 1792), p. 5. The editing and publication of Bligh's journal was arranged by Banks and Burney, see Banks to Bligh, 27 July 1791, M.L. Banks V, A78/4, fols. 145-46. There are suggestions that Banks himself wrote the introduction.

58. Banks to Jussieu, 15 October 1791, Kew B.C., III, 2.

59. Banks to Hawkesbury, 18 November 1788, B.M. Add. MSS 38223, fol. 273.

60. Board of Trade (B.T.) 1/14, fol. 362, 29 March 1797. In the terms of the age Banks was a conscientious attender of meetings. From his appointment to December 1801 he attended 98 out of 233 meetings. In 1802 he attended 49 of the 69 meetings; B.T. 5/10, B.T. 5/11, B.T. 5/12. He was always absent in September, October and the first two weeks of November, during the annual visitation to Revesby.

61. *H.R.N.S.W.*, I, ii, 229, February 1789.

62. Banks to Dupont, 18 July 1798, M.L. Banks XVI, A80/4, fols. 223-24.

63. On these aspects of imperial administration, see D.L. Mackay, "Direction and Purpose in British Imperial Policy, 1783-1801," *The Historical Journal*, XVII (1974), 487-501.

64. Banks to Hunter, 30 March 1797, D.T.C., X, fol. 94.

65. F. Grenville to Brown, 14 January 1802, *H.R.N.S.W.*, IV, 677.

66. Navy Board to Banks, 9 February 1799, and reply, 11 February, M.L. Banks X, A79/3, fols. 232-33.

67. P.G. King to Sir Andrew Hamond, September 1799, *H.R.N.S.W.*, III, 719-21.

## *Alexander Dalrymple and Captain Cook: The Creative Interplay of Two Careers:*

1. Beaglehole, *The Life*, p. 125. Since my own book on Dalrymple is included in the bibliography of that posthumous work, it is fair to point out that Beaglehole never saw my book, but only the thesis on which it was based, and from which it differed in important respects.

2. Raffles often referred to Dalrymple's scheme, and it is noteworthy that he was a clerk in India House at the same time that Dalrymple was hydrographer there.

3. On 17 April 1762 the authorities at Fort St. Geroge recommended Dalrymple to the directors in London as "a man of capacity, integrity and unwearied application."

4. "Nautical astronomy [was] a science then little understood in the royal navy"—entry on Captain John Campbell, R.N., in Rev. H.J. Rose, *A New Biographical Dictionary* (London, 1848). See also E.G.R. Taylor, "Navigation in the days of Captain Cook," *Journal of Navigation* XXI (1968), 257. Dalrymple's awareness of the impossibility of his being employed on any purely naval enterprise was shown in his letter to the Earl of Shelburne on 24 November 1766: "I am not insensible, notwithstanding the instances of Dampier, Halley, etc., how foreign to rules of office it is, to form the most distant expectations, that a person may be employed in the publick service by sea, who has no rank in the Navy" (P.R.O. Chatham Papers, 30/48, XXI, fol. 11).

5. A. Dalrymple, *An Historical Collection of the several voyages and discoveries in the South Pacific Ocean* (London, 1770-71), I, xxvi-xxvii.

6. Council Minutes of the Royal Society, Royal Society Library, London, vol. V. (1763-68).

7. A. Dalrymple, *Plan for promoting the Fur-Trade, and securing it to this Country, by uniting the Operations of the East India and Hudson's Bay Companys* (London, 1789), p. 20.

8. His host was Rev. William Hirst, a keen astronomer who had observed the 1761 transit at Madras, with Dalrymple's friend Governor Pigot. Nevil Maskelyne had just been appointed astronomer royal and had notably advanced the means for accurately determining longitude.

9. Beaglehole's assertion that Dalrymple "was not particularly interested in observing the transit of Venus or the far reaches of astronomy" was unfounded (Beaglehole, *The Life*, p. 106). Dalrymple's large and valuable library was particularly strong in works on astronomy.

10. On 3 December one member had proposed for the command "Captain Campbell or some such lover of astronomy (a captain of a man of war)."

11. *Encyclopaedia Britannica* (1974), Micropaedia V, "Halley," p. 861.

12. For Tudor times see Richard Hakluyt, *Voyages*, 8 vols. (London, 1962), Introduction by John Masefield, p. xxiii.

13. A. Dalrymple, *An Account of what has passed between the India Directors and Alexander Dalrymple* (London, 1769), pp. 16 ff. Dalrymple's interpretation of the duties and responsibilities of a captain was not at variance with the definition of the duties of captain, master, and mate in William Falconer's *An Universal Dictionary of the Marine* (London, 1780).

14. See entry for 3 April 1768 Council Minutes of the Royal Society for confirmation of Dalrymple's appointment.

15. Journals of the Royal Society, Royal Society Library, London.

16. Rose, V.

17. "Memoirs of Alexander Dalrymple Esq," *The European Magazine and London Review* (November 1802), p. 325. The records show that on 23 March the Admiralty ordered the Navy Board to make a survey of the *Valentine* and of the *Earl of Pembroke* (P.R.O. Adm. 3/75 and National Maritime Museum ADM./A/2605). This was done, and on 27 March Deptford Yard reported that: "Pursuant to your warrant of the 23rd instt. we have survey'd and measur'd the undermentioned ships, recommended to your Honrs to proceed on Foreign Service and send you an Acct of their Qualities, Condition, Age and Dimensions with our opinion of the value of their Hull, Masts and Yards as may be proper to purchase with *either* [my italics] of them." (P.R.O. Adm. 106/3315). To this report on these two ships (which was written in black ink), there has been added, roughly and in red ink, another set of figures in either margin, under the heading: "The Red Figures are the Dimensions of the Ann and Elizabeth." When these red figures were added, and for what purpose, is not clear, but there was no report and opinion on the latter vessel's "Qualitites, Condition, Age" etc., as Beaglehole stated (*Journals* I, 606), and the latter's summary and derisive dismissal of Dalrymple's claim seems to have been based not upon evidence but upon personal antipathy.

18. *Mr. Dalrymple's Observations on Dr. Hawkesworth's Preface to the Second Edition* (Printed 18 September 1773, not published), p. 19. Dalrymple's account of the bureaucratic reaction rings true: "A navy oracle told me, 'I was much mistaken if I thought I should have just what stores I pleased, that there was an *Establishment*, altho' *I might* be allowed an anchor and cable extraordinary on such a voyage,' my reply was that on such an expedition, I thought there was no Establishment but what the ship could carry." Dalrymple's claim was made in his first letter to Hawkesworth, and repeated in the 1802 *Memoirs*. The records show that on 22 March the Navy Board advised the Admiralty that a cat-built vessel would be most suitable "on account of the advantage of stowing a large quantity of provisions" (P.R.O. Adm. 3/75). The report on both vessels was highly favourable, with the *Valentine* appearing to show slightly better sailing qualities. But the *Earl of Pembroke* weighed 368 (71/94) tons against the *Valentine's* 316 (35/94) tons, "and comes nearest to the tonnage mentioned in your warrant." She thus had the greater carrying capacity.

19. Cook, *A Voyage towards the South Pole*, I, xx, xxiv.

20. For Dalrymple's account, see *European Magazine* (November 1802) and his two letters to Hawkesworth. Kippis, perhaps relying upon Palliser, was clearly wrong in the

melodramatic response that he attributed to Hawkesworth. Regarding the latter's role, Dalrymple told Hawkesworth: "I am very far from intending the most distant insinuation of resentment to, or dissatisfaction with, the worthy and brave old officer...; his ideas on the subject of discovery were clear and just in the only conference I ever had with him, and I have been told that afterwards 'He lamented I did not go'; but his open, honest, unsuspecting nature, I think, exposed him to the insinuations of cunning men." He mentioned the threat of impeachment in *The European Magazine*, adding that "as the persons by whose insinuations (I) was set aside, on that occasion, are now dead, it would be improper to enter into further detail of the subject." The most likely persons were Palliser (1723-96) and Palliser's close friend and former commander at the capture of Quebec, Sir Charles Saunders (d. 1775); they might have been supported by Saunders's friend and paliamentary mentor, Keppel (1725-86). It is significant that as early as 12 April Palliser knew that "Mr Cook who is...employed in surveying the coasts of Newfoundland, is to be employed elsewhere." (P.R.O. Adm. 3/75).

There is no reason to suppose that any of the five civilian Lords Commissioners, who were in numerical control of the Board, were opposed to Dalrymple's appointment, which lends weight to his remark about "the Admiralty approving of his being employed for this service." Palliser, Saunders and Keppel were not on the Board in March 1768.

21. *European Magazine* (November 1802).

22. A. Dalrymple, *An account of the discoveries made in the South Pacifick Ocean previous to 1764* (Printed 1767, but not published until 1769, after Bougainville's return).

23. The first volume concentrated on the Spanish voyages, the second (London, 1771) the Dutch. The first volume contained the dedication "to the man who, emulous of...the heroes of former times...shall...succeed in establishing an intercourse with a Southern Continent." That was written in January 1770, when the only man who still might have that opportunity before him was Cook. It was a curious aberration of memory that led Beaglehole to see this dedication as self-serving, "wherein the hero, the companion in history of heroes, is Alexander Dalrymple." Beaglehole, *The Life*, pp. 121-22.

24. Banks confessed that he still believed in a southern continent, though he thought that the counter-weight theory was "a most childish argument."

25. That was why it had been intended, had the *Endeavour* not run aground, to follow up the survey of the east coast of New Holland with a search for the lands discovered by Quiros in 1606, so as "to make discoveries more interesting to trade...than any we had yet made." Beaglehole, *Journal of Banks*, II, 38.

26. J. Hawkesworth, *An account of the voyages undertaken...for making discoveries in the Southern Hemisphere, and successively performed by Commodore Byron, Capt. Carteret, and Capt. Cook* (London, 1773), III, 438-46.

27. *Plan by Messieurs Franklin and Dalrymple for benefiting distant unprovided countries* (London, 29 August 1771).

28. V.T. Harlow, *The founding of the Second British Empire* (London, 1964), II, 392 ff.

29. A. Dalrymple, *A Collection of Voyages chiefly in the Southern Atlantick Ocean* (London, 1775), p. 2.

30. A. Dalrymple, *Memoir of a Chart of the Southern Ocean* (London, 1769). A close examination of the relevant maps by Ortelius and Mercator makes it appear probable that this detailed gulf, as opposed to the vague outline of other parts of the supposed

Southern Continent in regions far removed from the Strait of Magellan, was derived from some genuine discovery.

31. Beaglehole, *Journals*, II, ci.

32. *Ibid.* 609. Characteristically, this very page is headed "Dalrymple exploded."

33. Various writers have quoted with approval Bougainville's well known comment: "Geography is a science of facts; in studying it authors must by no means give way to any system, formed in their studies, unless they would run the risk of being subject to very great errors, which can be rectified only at the expense of navigators." It was fortunate that there were geographers willing to take these risks in the cause of promoting exploration. All exploration was inevitably performed "at the expense of navigators," and it was Dalrymple's greatest ambition to be the navigator who investigated his own theories.

34. Alexander-Gui Pingré, *Mémoire sur les lieux óu le Passage de Vénus, le 3 Juin 1769, pourra être observé avec le plus d'avantage* (1767), which contained this map.

35. See H.T. Fry, *Alexander Dalrymple and the expansion of British Trade* (London and Toronto, 1970), p. 122*n*.

36. *A Letter from Mr. Dalrymple to Dr. Hawkesworth* (London, 1773), pp. 1-2.

37. The second letter was never published, first because some of his friends told him that it contained "too much asperity," and then because of Hawkesworth's death.

38. See H.T. Fry, "The commercial ambitions behind Captain Cook's last voyage," *The New Zealand Journal of History*, VII (October 1973), 186-91.

39. Beaglehole, *Journals*, III, cliv.

40. Dalrymple argued against the "premature attack upon the exclusive rights and privileges of the East India Company," both in the Eastern Islands and in the proposal "to open the trade to the South Seas and the North West Coast of America to all British ships that may chuse to proceed thither" in his *A Fragment on the India trade* (London: written in 1791, published 1797), pp. 3-15. For the impact of the "country trade," see Holden Furber, *Rival empires of trade in the Orient, 1600-1800* (Minneapolis, 1976).

41. For a fuller treatment of this danger, see H.T. Fry, "'Cathay and the way thither': the background to Botany Bay," *Historical Studies*, XIV (April 1971), 497-510. See also A. Dalrymple, *A Serious Admonition to the Publick on the Intended Thief-Colony at Botany Bay* (London, 1786 [ed. G. Mackaness, Australian Historical Monographs no. 7, Sydney, 1943], pp. 30, 32.

42. See H.T. Fry, "Alexander Dalrymple and New Guinea," *The Journal of Pacific History*, IV (1969), 83-104.

43. See Fry, *Dalrymple*, pp. 217-18.

44. See A. Dalrymple, *A Fragment on the India trade*, pp. 26 ff., and James Colnett, *Voyage to the South Atlantic and round Cape Horn into the Pacific Ocean . . . 1793-4* (Newton Abbot, 1968 [London, 1798]), p. 12. Colnett, a veteran of Cook's second voyage, agreed that Isla Grande, if found, "would prove a much greater acquisition than the Island Georgia, to which many profitable voyages had been made...."

45. Frédéric Metz wrote a letter, headed "Géographie. Aux Rédacteurs de la Revue," which was published in *La Revue ou Décade philosophique, littéraire et politique*, xlvii, (11 novembre 1805), 261-66. The Bibliothèque Nationale, Paris, who kindly provided me with a copy of this letter, inform me that they have been unable to unearth any information about its author.

46. Dalrymple expressed this belief in a footnote in his *Memoir Concerning the Chagos Archipelago* and in his *A Serious Admonition to the Publick on the Intended Thief-Colony at Botany Bay*. See also J. Burney, *A Chronological History of the Discoveries in the South Pacific Ocean* (London, 1803), I, 381.

47. R.H. Major, ed., *Early Voyages to Terra Australis, now called Australia* (London, 1859). Major commended Metz for the "sound sense" of his reasoning. It is significant that Metz did not quote the footnote at all, while Major quoted it only in part, omitting the key sentence which made Dalrymple's meaning clear. This interpretation of Metz and Major was repeated by Beaglehole (*Journals*, I, clxiv and note), who stated that Major had "settled" the question of Dalrymple's "foolish innuendo."

48. Major, p. xxxv. Barbié du Bocage was referring to the charts of the Dieppe school of cartography, including the Dauphin and Rotz maps. It is noticeable that Metz could not name Dalrymple's *Memoir* but merely described it as "one of his works."

49. Burney, I, p. 381.

50. In the introduction he expressed his "Warmest acknowledgement" to "my friend Sir Joseph Banks," the latter having been knighted in 1781.

51. A. Dalrymple, *Historical Collection Concerning Papua* (no date or place of publication known: the British Museum possesses an incomplete copy), p. 3.

52. Similarly, he was silent about the Dauphin map when he wrote his *Memoir on the Passages to and from China* in 1782, despite the fact that he there discussed at some length the very same problem of place-names which was the subject of the footnote in which he first referred to the Dauphin map.

53. Dalrymple had made the same point in *An Historical Collection of the Several Voyages and Discoveries in The South Pacific Ocean*, (London, 1770), I, 39. See also Beaglehole, *The Life*, p. 590.

54. Dalrymple's critics have failed to spot the significance of that part of his footnote which reads: "So that we may say with Solomon 'There is nothing new under the sun.'" For that biblical quotation continues: "It hath been already of old time. There is no remembrance of former things." (Ecclesiastes 1:10-11.) That last sentence, in itself, would have been incompatible with any suggestion that Cook knew of the Dauphin map. Dalrymple cannot be held responsible for his twentieth-century critics' ignorance of the Bible!

## Myth and Reality: James Cook and the Theoretical Geography of Northwest America:

1. Beaglehole, *Journals*, I, 288-89.

2. See F.A. Golder, ed., *Bering's Voyages* (New York, 1922-23); Raymond H. Fisher, *Bering's Voyages: Whither and Why* (Seattle and London, 1977).

3. See Glyndwr Williams, *The British Search for the Northwest Passage in the Eighteenth Century* (London, 1962), ch. 7.

4. See James R. Masterton and Helen Brower, *Bering's Successors 1745-1780: contributions of Peter Simon Pallas to the history of Russian exploration towards Alaska* (Seattle, 1948).

5. For this see O.M. Medushevskaya, "Cartographic Sources for the history of Russian geographical discoveries in the Pacific Ocean in the second half of the 18th Cen-

tury," *Cartographica*, Monograph no. 13, trans. J.R. Gibson (Toronto, 1975), pp. 67-89. On the secrecy surrounding the Russian discoveries at this time, and the consequent problems which afflicted Müller and the geographers working at the Academy of Sciences, see A.I. Andreyev, "Trudy G.F. Millera, o vtoroy kamchatskoy ekspeditsii," *Izvestiya Vsesoynznogo Geograficheskogo Obshchestva*, XCI, no. 1 (Jan.-Feb. 1959), 1-16. I am indebted to Professor Raymond H. Fisher for sending me his notes on this article.

6. See Warren L. Cook, *Flood Tide of Empire: Spain and the Pacific Northwest, 1543-1819* (New Haven and London, 1973), ch. 3.

7. See Council Minutes and correspondence of the Royal Society, 10, 17 February, 7 March 1774: Council Minutes, VI, 214, 216, 220, Archives of the Royal Society, London.

8. D. 1778, v. 286, Dartmouth MSS, William Salt Library, Stafford.

9. See the Introduction by Dr. John Douglas to James Cook and James King, *A Voyage to the Pacific Ocean* (London, 1784), I, xlvi.

10. Beaglehole, *Journals*, III, ccxxi.

11. *London Evening Post*, 29 May 1776.

12. See journals of Midshipman Henry Martin, 14 August 1777, Adm. 51/4531, Pt.I, fol. 44d.

13. G.B. Hill, ed., L.F. Powell, rev., *Boswell's Life of Johnson* (Oxford, 1934-50), III, 7.

14. Beaglehole, *Journals*, III, 293-94.

15. *Ibid.*, 335.

16. Journal of Lieutenant James King, Adm. 55/122, fol. 31.

17. *Ibid.*, fol. 31d.

18. Beaglehole, *Journals*, III, 343.

19. Burney, p. 221.

20. [John Rickman], *Journal of Captain Cook's Last Voyage to the Pacific Ocean on Discovery* (London, 1781), p. 247.

21. Journal of David Samwell, British Library Eg. MSS 2591, fol. 114.

22. Journal of Lieutenant John Gore, Adm. 55/120, fol. 154.

23. Beaglehole, *Journals*, III, 353.

24. *Ibid.*, 356-57, 358-59.

25. *Ibid.*, 360-61.

26. Adm. 55/120, fol. 160d.

27. Log of Midshipman Edward Riou, Adm. 51/4529, P. III, fol. 90d.

28. [Rickman], *Journal*, p. 252.

29. Journal of Lieutenant James Burney. Add. MSS 8955, p. 30.

30. Beaglehole, *Journals*, III, 368n.

31. Adm. 55/122, fol. 42.

32. *Ibid.*, fol. 72.

33. Beaglehole, *Journals*, III, 424.

34. *Ibid.*, p. 449.

35. Adm. 55/122, fol. 98.

36.　Beaglehole, *Journals*, III, 456.

37.　*Ibid.*, I, cxxi.

38.　G. Müller, *Voyages from Asia to America, for Completing the Discoveries of the North West Coast of America*, 2nd ed. (London, 1764), pp. 108, 114, 115.

39.　William Coxe, *An Account of the Russian Discoveries between Asia and America* (London, 1780), p. 283n.

40.　J. von Stählin, *An Account of the New Northern Archipelago, Lately Discovered by the Russians in the Sea of Kamtschatka and Anadir* (London, 1774), p. 14.

41.　Daines Barrington, *The Probability of Reaching the North Pole Discussed* (London, 1774), p. 14.

42.　Beaglehole, *The Life*, p. 633.

## Cook and the Nootka:

Research for this paper was made possible by financial assistance from the Canada Council and Simon Fraser University.

1.　Alan Moorehead, *The Fatal Impact: An Account of the Invasion of the South Pacific 1767-1840* (New York, 1966).

2.　See for example W.H. Pearson, "European Intimidation and the Myth of Tahiti," *Journal of Pacific History*, IV (1969), 199-217.

3.　Beaglehole, *The Life*, p. 133.

4.　Philip Drucker, *The Northern and Central Nootkan Tribes*, Smithsonian Institute Bureau of American Ethnology, Bulletin 144 (Washington, 1951), p. 11; Martin Robin, *The Rush for Spoils: The Company Province 1871-1933* (Toronto, 1927), p. 30.

5.　Dates are given in civil time following Cook's journal.

6.　Beaglehole, *Journals*, III, 300.

7.　"The Instructions," 6 July 1776, Beaglehole, *Journals*, III, ccxxii.

8.　Pearson, "European Intimidation," 215 *passim*.

9.　The point is made by J.M.R. Owens, *Prophets in the Wilderness: The Wesleyan Mission to New Zealand 1819-1827* (Auckland and Oxford, 1974), pp. 126-27.

10.　Drucker, p. 2.

11.　Anonymous, log, Adm. 51/4530/66, fols. 221-32; and William Harvey, log, Adm. 55/121, fols. 45-46.

12.　John Ledyard, *A Journal of Captain Cook's Last Voyage to the Pacific Ocean... Performed in the Years 1776, 1777, 1778, and 1779* (Chicago, 1963), pp. 71-72.

13.　Beaglehole, *Journals*, III, 323-30.

14.　Gilbert Malcolm Sproat, *Scenes and Studies of Savage Life* (London, 1868), pp. 134-37.

15.　Beaglehole, *Journals*, III, 1412.

16.　Beaglehole, *Journals*, III, 1092, 1329, 1414; Williamson, journal, 25 April 1778, Adm. 55/117, fol. 100; William Bayly (journal, p. 122, Alexander Turnbull Library, Wellington, [A.T.L.]) claimed that he conducted an experiment similar to Williamson's with the same result. The dubious nature of the evidence on cannibalism has not deterred some historians from making confident assertions on the subject, see Warren L. Cook, p. 87.

17. James Burney, journal, 22 April 1778, Adm. 51/4528, fol. 229. Apparently estimates ranged from 500 to 2,000.

18. Beaglehole, *Journals*, III, 1406-7.

19. Beaglehole, *Journals*, III, 314; Bayly, log, Adm. 50/20, fol. 117.

20. See Captain J. Laskey, *A General Account of the Huntarian Museum, Glasgow* (Glasgow, 1813), p. 72. I am indebted to Mr. J.C.H. King, Assistant Keeper, the Ethnology Department of the British Museum, for pointing out the existence of this piece.

21. J.H. Parry, *The Spanish Seaborne Empire* (London, 1960), p. 65.

22. Beaglehole, *Journals*, III, 1395, 1398, 299; Thomas Edgar, journal, 29 March 1778, B.M. Add. MSS 37528, fol. 90.

23. William J. Folan and John T. Dewhirst, "Yuquot: Where the Wind Blows from all Directions," *Archaeology*, XXIII (1970), 284.

24. Beaglehole, *Journals*, III, 295.

25. Bayly, journal, p. 116, A.T.L.

26. See for example George Gilbert, journal, 1, 2, 18 April 1778, Adm. 51/4559/214, fol. 183.

27. Beaglehole, *Journals*, III, 1400.

28. See for example Warren L. Cook, p. 87.

29. Beaglehole, *Journals*, III, 297, 302, 314.

30. Burney, journal, 24 April 1778, Adm. 51/4528/45, fol. 230.

31. See Edgar, journal, 25 April 1778, B.M. Add. MSS 37528, fol. 94. Edgar cites Gerhard Friedrich Müller, presumably having read his *Voyages from Asia to America for Completing the Discoveries of the North-West Coast of America* (London, 1761), p. 66; see also Coxe, pp. 234-35.

32. Beaglehole, *Journals*, III, 312, 1407-8.

33. *Ibid.*, III, 1413.

34. *Ibid.*

35. There is more than one reference in the journals to the sale of masks. See Beaglehole, *Journals*, III, 1091, 1414; Burney, journal, 5 April 1778, Adm. 51/4528/45, fol. 228; Edward Riou, log, 30 March 1778, Adm. 51/4529/42, fol. 76. See also Cook's remark about the Indians' willingness to part with carved images (Beaglehole, *Journals*, III, 320). It is therefore curious that Erna Gunther should claim that masks "were never offered for sale or trade" while Cook was at Nootka and that those remaining in collections "have no references in the texts of the journals giving clues as to where they were acquired": see *Indian Life on the Northwest Coast of North America as Seen by the Early Explorers and Fur Traders during the Last Decades of the Eighteenth Century* (Chicago and London, 1972), pp. 21-22.

36. Beaglehole, *Journals*, III, 1091-92, 1394; Riou, journal, 30 March 1778, Adm. 51/4529/42, fol. 76; Bayly, journal, fol. 120, A.T.L.

37. Beaglehole, *Journals*, III, 307.

38. *Ibid.*, III, 1091.

39. *Ibid.*, III, 307-8.

40. *Ibid.*, III, 299, 1398.

41. *Ibid.*, III, 1400-1, 1329.

42. *Ibid.*, III, 302.

43. Beaglehole, *Journals*, III, 299, 315, 1398; Clerke, journal, 4 April 1778, Adm. 55/33, fol. 152.

44. Drucker, p. 229.

45. Burney, journal, 5 April 1778, Adm. 51/4528/45, fol. 228. Cook also writes that "our first friends, or those who lived in the Sound" were controlling the trade, perhaps implying that the visitors were from outside the sound. Beaglehole, *Journals*, III, 299.

46. Beaglehole, *Journals*, III, 301, 1327, 1400; Drucker, pp. 126-27.

47. Gunther provides some ethnographic evidence in support of her assertion, but offers no artistic evidence and her use of the written record is very confused. King's journal is cited, but on the page referred to the only outside group he mentions is clearly the one that came on 12 April, not the quite different group described by Gunther which actually came on 22 April. There is no evidence, in any journal, that the group arriving on 22 April brought masks. See Gunther, p. 26; Beaglehole, *Journals*, III, 1414. Two pages earlier (p. 24) Gunther warns against the uncritical use of the journals.

48. It would seem that Warren Cook's mistake arises largely from the fact that he has not read Cook's journals. Instead he cites the *Voyage* compiled under the editorship of Dr. John Douglas and first published in 1784. Presumably it is Clerke whom Douglas uses as his source in this instance, since in his own journal Cook appears to discount any evidence of a prior Spanish presence at Nootka Sound. Even in the *Voyage*, however, the spoons are simply presumed to be of Spanish manufacture and nothing is said about their being proof of a Spanish presence in the area. See Warren L. Cook p. 65, n. 43; Cook and King, II, 282; Beaglehole, *Journals*, III, 321-22, 1329.

49. Beaglehole, *Journals*, III, 1398, 1406; Drucker, p. 254.

50. Beaglehole, *Journals*, III, 306, 1407.

51. Riou, journal, 20 April 1778, Adm. 51/4529/42, fol. 79.

52. Webber to Douglas, 31 December 1783, Letters to Dr. Douglas Relating to Cook's Voyages, 1776-1784, B.M. Eg. MSS 2180.

53. Beaglehole, *Journals*, III, 305.

54. Beaglehole, *Journals*, III, 1326, 1095; Burney, journal, 4 April 1778, Adm. 51/4528; Williamson, journal, Adm. 55/117; Bayly, journal, pp. 115-16, A.T.L.; W. Ellis, *An Authentic Narrative of a Voyage Performed by Captain Cook and Captain Clerke, in His Majesty's Ships Resolution and Discovery during the Years 1776, 1777, 1778, 1779 and 1780* (London, 1782), I, 203, 216. I would like to thank Sir James Watt, who pointed out this possibility.

55. Bayly, journal, pp. 97, 115, A.T.L.; Ellis, I, 216-17; Drucker, pp. 304-9.

56. Beaglehole, *Journals*, III, 1329, 1407.

57. *Cf.* Pearson, "European Intimidation," 215.

58. Beaglehole, *Journals*, III, clvi, 1350-51.

59. *Ibid.*, 1100.

60. Portlock, journal, 4 April 1778, Adm. 51/4531, fol. 293.

61. *Ibid.*

62. The points made here are based on Drucker, pp. 332-44, 453-54; and Morris

Swadish, "Motivations in Nootka Warfare," *Southwestern Journal of Anthropology*, IV (1948), 76–93.

63. Beaglehole, *Journals*, III, 1350; Robin Fisher, "Arms and Men on the Northwest Coast, 1774–1825," *B.C. Studies*, 29 (Spring 1976), 10.

64. Bayly, journal, 21, 22, April 1778, A.T.L.; Adm. 55/20, fol. 117.

65. [Rickman], *Journal*, p. 237. Similar words were used by Bayly (journal, fol. 104, A.T.L.) to describe the Nootka.

66. Beaglehole, *Journals*, III, 307–8.

67. I have developed this argument in detail in Robin Fisher, *Contact and Conflict: Indian-European Relations in British Columbia, 1774–1890* (Vancouver, 1977), ch. 1.

68. Beaglehole, *Journals*, III, xxxiii.

69. Allen Curnow, "The Unhistoric Story," *A Small Room with Large Windows: Selected Poems* (London, 1962), p. 7.

## The Spanish Reaction to Cook's Third Voyage:

1. *Enciclopedia Universal Ilustrada* (Madrid, 1964), XXXVIII, 1062.

2. Francisco Javier de Viana, *Diario de viaje* (Montevideo, 1958), II, 62.

3. Alexander von Humboldt, *Political Essay on the Kingdom of New Spain* (London, 1811), II, 385.

4. Javier de Ybarra y Berge, *De California a Alaska: Historia de un descubrimiento* (Madrid, 1945), pp. 25–27; Warren L. Cook, pp. 54–55; and Michael E. Thurman, *The Naval Department of San Blas: New Spain's Bastion for Alta California and Nootka* (Glendale, Cal., 1967), p. 118.

5. Antonio María Bucareli y Ursúa to General de Flota Luis de Córdoba, 25 August 1773; and Córdoba to Bucareli, 1 September 1773, Archivo General de la Nación, México (A.G.N.), Sección de Historia, LXI.

6. Bucareli to Juan Pérez, 18 July 1773, A.G.N., Hist., LXI.

7. Bucareli to Pérez, 29 September 1773, A.G.N., Hist., LXI.

8. Pérez to Bucareli, 15 December 1773, A.G.N., Hist., LXI.

9. Pérez to Bucareli, 28 December 1773, A.G.N., Hist., LXI.

10. Instrucción que debe observar el Alférez de Fragata graduado D. Juan Pérez..., 24 December 1773, A.G.N., Hist., LXI.

11. *Ibid.*, Articles 15, 16.

12. *Ibid.*, Articles 20, 22, 30.

13. Diario de la exploración practicada por el Alférez graduado D. Juan Pérez en la fragata *Santiago*, A.G.N., Hist., LXI.

14. Diario de la navegación y exploración del Piloto Segundo D. Esteban José Martínez; and Martínez to Bucareli, Monterey, 31 August 1774, A.G.N., Hist., LXI.

15. *Ibid.*

16. Martínez to Manuel Antonio Flórez, Archivo General de Indies, Seville, Sección de Méjico (A.G.I., Mexico), legajo 1529.

17. *Ibid.*

18. Bucareli to Pérez, 14 November 1774, A.G.N., Hist., LXI; and Bucareli to Julián de Arriaga, 26 November 1774, in "La administración de D. Frey Antonio María de Bucareli y Ursúa, cuadragésimo sexto virrey de México," *Publicaciones del Archivo General de la Nación* (Mexico, 1936), XXX, 226.

19. Juan Francisco de la Bodega y Quadra, "Ano de 1775: Navegación hecha por Juan Francisco de la Bodega y Quadra, Teniente de Fragata de la Real Armada y Comandante de la Goleta *Sonora;* a los descubrimientos de los Mares y Costa Septentrional de California," ed. Roberto Barreiro Meiro, *Coleccion de Diarios y Relaciones para la Historia de los Viajes y Descubrimientos* (Madrid, 1944), II, 107.

20. *Ibid.*, p. 118.

21. Diario de la navegación hecha por el Teniente de Navío de la Real Armada, D. Bruno de Hezeta, 1775, A.G.N., Hist., CCCXXIV.

22. Juan Francisco de la Bodega y Quadra, "Ano de 1775: Navegación," p. 123.

23. *Ibid.*, p. 124.

24. Bucareli to José de Gálvez, 26 June 1776, in "La administración de Bucareli," (Mexico, 1936), XXIX, 307.

25. *Ibid.*, pp. 308–309.

26. Warren L. Cook, p. 91.

27. Beaglehole, *The Life*, p. 508; and Charles E. Chapman, *A History of California: The Spanish Period* (New York, 1923), p. 264.

28. Beaglehole, *Journals*, III, 296, 322.

29. Beaglehole, *The Life*, p. 585.

30. Beaglehole, *Journals*, III, 1329.

31. The journals of Teniente de Navio Fernando Bernardo Quirós, Piloto José Camacho, Piloto Juan Pantoja y Arriaga, Piloto José Cañizares, and Piloto Juan Bauptista de Aguirre are in A.G.N., Hist., LXIV; and of Alférez Francisco Antonio Mourelle, in Museo Naval, Madrid, DCXXII.

32. Diario de la navegación de Teniente de Navío D. Ignacio de Arteaga mandando la fragata *Princesa*, A.G.N., Hist., LXIII.

33. Tercera exploración hecha en el año de 1779 con las fragatas del Rey la *Princesa* y *Favorita*; Observaciones sobre el genio, carácter, armas, y alimientos de aquellos naturales..., Museo Naval, Madrid, DLXXV-bis.

34. Diario de Arteaga, A.G.N., Hist., LXIII, entry for 11 June 1779.

35. *Ibid.*, entries for 9, 10 June 1779.

36. *Ibid.*, and Tercera exploración hecha en el año de 1779, Museo Naval, DLXXV-bis.

37. Diario del Segundo Piloto de la fragata *Princesa*, D. Juan Pantoja y Arriaga, 1779, A.G.N., Hist., LXIV.

38. Diario de la navegación de Teniente de Navío D. Bernardo de Quirós, A.G.N., Hist., LXIV.

39. Thurman, pp. 257–59; and Henry R. Wagner, *The Cartography of the Northwest Coast to the Year 1800* (Amsterdam, 1968), p. 202.

40. Warren L. Cook, pp. 112–13.

41. Martínez to Flórez, 7 August 1789, A.G.N., Hist., LXV.

42. Conde de Revillagigedo to Valdés, 8 December 1789, A.G.N., Hist., LXVIII; Martínez to Flórez, 5 December 1788, A.G.I., leg. 1529; reports on the 1788 expedition, A.G.I., Guadalajara, leg. 43; and Martínez to Valdés, 5 December 1788, Archivo Histórico Nacional, Madrid, leg. 4289.

43. Flórez to Valdés, 23 December 1788, Mexico, leg. 1529.

44. Instructions for Martínez, 23 December 1788, A.G.I., Mexico, leg. 1529; and Esteban José Martínez, "Diario," Meiro, VI, 25.

45. See W.R. Manning, "The Nootka Sound Controversy," *Annual Report of the American Historical Association for 1904* (New York, 1905), pp. 279–478; Warren L. Cook, pp. 146–99; Christon I. Archer, "The Transient Presence: A Re-Appraisal of Spanish Attitudes toward the Northwest Coast in the Eighteenth Century," *B.C. Studies*, 18 (Summer, 1973), 11–19.

46. See for example, Joseph Ingraham to Martínez, Description of Nootka Inhabitants, 1789, A.G.N., Hist., LXV.

47. Esteban José Martínez, "Diario," p. 63.

48. *Ibid.*, p. 83.

49. Martínez to Flórez, 13 July 1789, A.G.N., Hist., LXV.

50. Reflexiones a la noticia que da Martínez en carta de 13 de Julio de 1789 sobre haber hallado entrado o estrecho de Juan de Fuca, A.G.N., Hist., LXV.

51. Martínez to Flórez, 24 July 1789, A.G.I., Mexico, leg. 1530.

52. *Ibid.*, and Archivo Histórico Nacional, Madrid, leg. 4289.

53. Revillagigedo to Valdés, 12 January 1790, A.G.I., Mexico, leg. 1530.

54. Revillagigedo to Valdés, 27 December 1789, A.G.I., Mexico, leg. 1530.

55. Noticias que se han recibido de Monterey, 1792, Museo Naval, Madrid, DLXXV-bis.

56. Instrucciones secretas para el Teniente de Navío D. Francisco Eliza, 28 January 1790, A.G.N., Hist., LXVIII.

57. Revillagigedo to Pedro de Lerena, 31 March 1791, A.G.I., Mexico, leg. 1540; and Revillagigedo to Diego de Gardoqui, 30 June 1792, A.G.I., Mexico, leg. 1548.

58. Viaje a la costa N.O. de la América Septentrional por D. Juan Francisco de la Bodega y Quadra, 1792, Provincial Archives of British Columbia.

59. Pedro de Novo y Colson, ed., *La Vuelta al Mundo por los Corbetas Descubrimiento y Atrevida al mando del Capitán de Navío Don Alejandro Malaspina desde 1789-1794* (Madrid, 1885), p. 372.

60. Revillagigedo to Floridablanca, 1 April 1792, Archivo Histórico Nacional, leg. 4288; Revillagigedo to Conde de Aranda, 24 October 1792, Archivo Histórico Nacional, leg. 4290; and Revillagigedo to Malaspina, 20 November 1791, Museo Naval, Madrid, CCLXXX.

61. Instrucciones secretas para el Teniente de Navío D. Francisco Bodega y Quadra, 28 January 1790, A.G.I., Mexico, leg. 1537.

62. The murder of the Nootka Chief Callicum, several reprisals against the Indians for thievery, and the firing on a canoe at Nuñez Gaona (Neah Bay) were the worst examples. See Salvador Fidalgo to Bodega y Quadra, 4 July 1792, and 30 September 1792, A.G.N., Hist., LXVII; and Martínez to Bodega y Quadra, 2 December 1790, A.G.N., Hist., LXVII.

63. Instrucción que deben observar los capitanes de fragata, D. Dionisio Alcala Galiano y D. Cayetano Valdés en la exploración... del Estrecho de Juan de Fuca, 31 January 1795, Museo Naval, Madrid, DCXIX.

64. *Ibid.*

65. Manuel Godoy to Revillagigedo, 23 February 1793, A.G.N., Hist., LXVII; and Memorandum of the Conde de Aranda, 1793, Archivo Histórico Nacional, Madrid, leg. 4288.

66. Revillagigedo to Francisco de Eliza, 17 November 1790, A.G.N., Hist., LXVIII.

67. Salvador Fidalgo to Revillagigedo, 13 November 1790, A.G.N., Hist., LXVIII.

68. Iris H. Wilson, ed., *Noticias de Nutka; An Account of Nootka Sound in 1792 by José Mariano Moziño* (Seattle, 1970).

69. Beaglehole, *The Life*, pp. 358-59.

70. Beaglehole, *Journals*, II, 1329, 1414, 1092.

71. Ingraham to Martínez, Description of Nootka Inhabitants, 1789, A.G.N., Hist., LXV.

72. Esteban José Martínez, "Diario," p. 124.

73. Informe de D. José Tobar y Tamiriz, 29 August 1789, A.G.N., Hist., LXV.

74. Martínez to Flórez, 13 July 1789, A.G.N., Hist., LXV.

75. John Meares, *Voyages Made in the Years 1788 and 1789 from China to the Northwest Coast of America* (New York, 1972), pp. 255-57; Marqués del Campo to the Conde de Floridablanca, London, 26 November 1790, Archivo Histórico Nacional, Madrid, leg. 4291.

76. Carácter, vida y costumbres de los Indios de Noka, y sus inmediaciones, Jacinto Caamaño, 1789, A.G.N., Hist., LXIX.

77. Nuevo Método o Gobierno de las Misiones, Colegio Apostólico de San Fernando, October 1772, in A.G.N., Documentos para la História de México, Segunda Serie, XV.

78. Fray Severo Patero to Flórez, 13 July 1789, A.G.N., Hist., LXV; and Noticias de Nutka, Fray Lorenzo Socies, 1789, A.G.N., Hist., XXXI.

79. Marqués de Branciforte to the Duque de Alcudía (Manuel Godoy), n.d., Archivo Histórico Nacional, Madrid, leg. 4290.

80. Beaglehole, *Journals*, II, 1054.

81. Beaglehole, *The Life*, p. 500.

82. José Porrúa Turanzas, ed., *Relación del viage hecho por las Goletas Sútil y Mexicana en el Año de 1792 para reconocer el Estrecho de Fuca* (Madrid, 1958).

## Cook's Reputation in Russia:

The author wishes to thank G.R.V. Barratt, A.G. Cross, S.G. Fedorova, and Ya.M. Svet for their help and advice.

1. The facts about the voyage are taken from Beaglehole, *Journals*,III.

2. Recorded, no doubt with many frills, in Maurice Benyowsky, *Memoirs and Travels* (London, 1790). One romantic interpolation was that he abducted the Russian's daughter; but as she was not living in Kamchatka, he could never have met her.

3. S.G. Fedorova, "Issledovatel' Chukotki i Alyaski kazachiy sotnik Ivan Kobelev," *Letopis' Severa*, V (1971), 159.

4. *Ibid.*, 160.

5. M.I. Belov, *Arkticheskoye moreplavaniye s drevneyshikh vremen do serediny XIX veka* (Moscow, 1956), p. 423.

6. James Gibson, *Imperial Russia in frontier America: the changing geography of supply of Russian America, 1784-1867* (New York, 1976).

7. A.J. von Krusenstern, *Voyage round the world in the years 1803, 1804, 1805 and 1806*, trans. R.B. Hoppner (London, 1813), I, 190, 216; II, 203, 222.

8. U. Lisyansky, *A voyage round the world in the years 1803, 4, 5 and 6* (London, 1814), p. 109.

9. *Ibid.*, p. 59.

10. *Ibid.*, p. 228.

11. O. von Kotzebue, *A voyage of discovery into the South Sea and Beering's Straits . . . in the years 1815-1818* (London, 1821), I, 155.

12. F. Debenham, ed., *The voyage of Captain Bellingshausen to the Antarctic seas*, Hakluyt Society Second Series nos. 91-92 (London, 1945).

13. A.A. Samarov, ed., *M.P. Lazarev Dokumenty* (Moscow, 1952), p. 231.

14. V.M. Golovnin, *Puteshestviye na shlyupe "Diana" iz Kronshtadta v Kamchatku . . . v 1807-1811 godakh* (Moscow, 1961), p. 231.

15. V.M. Golovnin, *Sochineniya* (Moscow and Leningrad, 1949), p. 338. Later Russian commentators have made similar charges, the latest being a report by Moscow Radio on 6 August 1977 that the recently rediscovered logs of Bering and Chirikov for their voyages of 1741 show that they discovered places later named by, and credited to, Cook. Golovnin's comment is again apt: how could Cook have known if the discoveries were never publicized? Some of the place-names indignantly attributed to Cook are in fact imaginary, such as "Cookshaven" for the north-east tip of Asia. Cook may reasonably be thought to have erred in propriety, however, by naming the western tip of Alaska Cape Prince of Wales, for on Müller's map, which he knew, that piece of coast was plainly marked "coast discovered by surveyor Gwosdew in 1732"—whose name might more appropriately have been attached to the cape. But he was probably misled through using Stählin's highly imaginative map of 1774. See Beaglehole, *Journals*, III, lx-lxiv. S.G. Fedorova has examined many of these points in *Soviet Studies in History*, XIX, nos. 1-2, (1975), 198-201.

16, In *Mesyatsoslov na 1779 god* (St. Petersburg, 1778), p. 21-83, an annual publication of the Academy of Sciences.

17. M.I. Belov, "Shestaya chast' sveta otkryta russkimi moryakami," *Izvestiya Vsesoyuznogo Geograficheskogo Obshchestva*, XC (1962), 107-108.

18. "Vyderzhki iz dnevnika krugosvetnogo puteshestviya na korable 'Nadezhda,'" *Yakhta* XVI (1876), quoted by Ye.Ye. Shvede in the introduction to his edition of F.F. Bellinsgauzen, *Dvukratnyye izyskaniya v yuzhnom ledovitom okeane* (Moscow, 1949), p. 30.

19. O. von Kotzebue, *A new voyage round the world in the years 1823, 1824, 1825, and 1826* (London, 1830), II, 173.

20. Who first put about the baseless story of the East India Company connection is not clear, but it is reapeated by Belov, p. 356. The idea might have been given some

currency by the fact that the company was asked to advise on the third voyage; in any case it had a monopoly on British trade to the Pacific at that time.

21. See T.E. Armstrong, "Bellingshausen and the discovery of Antarctica," *Polar Record*, XV (1971), 887-89. The Soviet case is put by Belov on pp. 890-91.

22. The statement is in Beaglehole, *Journals*, II, 643. For Soviet comment see D. Golubev, *Russkiye v Antarktike* (Moscow, 1949), p. 22; and M.Ya. Kotukhov, *Velikiy podvig* (Moscow, 1951), pp. 8-9. It should be added that more scholarly commentators like D.M. Lebedev, M.I. Belov, and V.L. Lebedev did not follow this line. Indeed V.L. Lebedev points out its shortcomings in his article in *Antarktika. Doklady Komissii 1960 g.* (Moscow, 1961), pp. 7-24.

23. V.N. Vladimirov, *Dzhems Kuk* (Moscow, 1933).

24. I.P. Magidovich, *Ocherki po istorii geograficheskikh otkrytiy* (Moscow, 1967), pp. 405-21.

25. For Russian versions see p. 128.

26. James Cook, *Vtoroye krugosvetnoye plavaniye kapitana Dzhemsa Kuka*, trans. Ya.M. Svet (Moscow, 1971), pp. 5-6.

27. *Ibid.*, p. 26.

## Medical Aspects and Consequences of Captain Cook's Voyages:

1. S. Henderson, "An Account of the Means of Preserving the Health of Seamen on Board His Majesty's Ship Astrea," *The Medical and Physical Journal* (1799), I, 91-96.

2. Sir John Pringle, *A Discourse upon some Late Improvements of the means for Preserving the Health of Seamen* (London, 1776), pp. 1-37; James Cook, "The Method Taken for Preserving the Health of the Crew of His Majesty's Ship the 'Resolution' during her Late Voyage round the World," *Philosophical Transactions* (1776), LXVI, 402-406.

3. C. Fletcher, *A Maritime State Considered as to the Health of Seamen* (Dublin, 1786), p. 18.

4. Beaglehole, *Journals*, II, 33.

5. *Ibid.*, 64.

6. Anders Sparrman, *A Voyage Round the World with Captain James Cook in HMS Resolution*, ed. Owen Rutter (London, 1944), p. 40.

7. E. Philipp, quoted in Beaglehole, *Journals*, II, 75.

8. Alexander Armstrong, *A Personal Narrative of the Discovery of the North-West Passage* (London, 1857), pp. 326-29.

9. Beaglehole, *Journals*, II, 111.

10. Sparrman, p. 44.

11. A.P. Meiklejohn, R. Passmore and C.P. Stewart, "The Importance of Ascorbic Acid to Man"; and James Lind, *Treatise on Scurvy*, ed. C.P. Stewart and D. Guthrie (Edinburgh, 1953), p. 425.

12. Sparrman, p. 61.

13. Tobias Furneaux, log, 23, 28 July 1773, Adm. 55/1.

14. Beaglehole, *Journals*, II, 186.

15. Sparrman, P. 62; Père Labat, *Nouveaux voyages aux Iles de l'Amérique (La Haye*, 1724), I, 201; Armstrong, p. 616.

16. Beaglehole, *Journals*, II, 1188.

17. *Ibid.*, 232.

18. *Ibid.*, 317.

19. *Ibid.*, 349, 369.

20. J. François Galaup de La Pérouse, *A Voyage Round the World, Performed in the Years 1785, 1786, 1787 and 1788* (London, 1799), II, 53.

21. Beaglehole, *Journals*, II, 443.

22. W. Anderson, "Letters to Sir John Pringle, 5 March and 23 April, 1776," *Philosophical Transactions* LXVI (1776), 544-74.

23. Clerke, journal, 16 March 1775, B.M. Add. MSS 8951.

24. Anders Sparrman, *A Voyage to the Cape of Good Hope* (Dublin, 1785), p. 121.

25. G.J. Milton-Thompson, "The Changing Character of the Sailor's Diet and its Influence on Disease," *Problems of Medicine at Sea, Maritime Monographs and Reports*, No. 12 (1974), pp. 20-27.

26. J. Cook to Sir John Pringle, 7 July 1776, *Philosophical Transactions*, LXVI (1776), 406.

27. Beaglehole, *Journals*, II, 33; T. Trotter, *Medical and Chemical Essays* (London, 1795), pp. 71-78.

28. J. Huxham, *De Scorbuto* (Venice, 1766), D.N.B., 1908, X, 364; "A Method for Preserving the Health of Seamen in Long Cruises and Voyages, 1747," *The Works of John Huxham MD FRS* (London, 1788), II, 259-65; and *Observations on the Air and Epidemic Diseases* (London, 1759), Appendix, p. 32.

29. T. Trotter, *Medicina Nautica* (London, 1797), I, 174, 189.

30. F.A. Klipstein and J.J. Corcino, "Seasonal Occurrence of Overt and Subclinical Tropical Malabsorption in Puerto Rico," *American Journal of Tropical Medicine and Hygiene*, XXIII (1974), 1189-96.

31. W.B. Monkhouse, journal, B.M. Add. MSS 27889, fols. 83-96.

32. 30 May 1768, N.M.M. ADM/C/590; 10 June 1768, N.M.M. ADM/E/40; 10 June 1768, P.R.O., Adm. 2/94.

33. Sick and Hurt Commissioniers to Cook, Canberra Letter Book, 19 July 1768.

34. 30 September 1768, Adm. 2/94.

35. 15 June 1768, Adm. 111/64.

36. Beaglehole, *Journals*, I, 13.

37. *Ibid.*, 51.

38. Beaglehole, *Journal of Banks*, II, 301.

39. *Ibid.*, I, 243, 249.

40. 12 July 1771, Adm. 1/1609.

41. Beaglehole, *Journals*, I, 138.

42. Beaglehole, *Journal of Banks*, I, 475.

43. Beaglehole, *Journals*, I, 418.

44. Beaglehole, *Journal of Banks*, II, 152.

45. *Ibid.*, 193.

46. *Ibid.*, 242.

47. *Ibid.*, 233.

48. Beaglehole, *Journals*, I, 466.

49. J. Bontius, "An Account of the Diseases, Natural-History and Medicines of the East Indies, 1769," *Opuscula Selecta Needlandicorum de Arte Medica*, X (1931), 121, 123.

50. Beaglehole, *Journal of Banks*, II, 242-43.

51. D. Schoute, *Occidental Therapeutics in the Netherlands East Indies during Three Centuries of Netherlands Settlement (1600-1900)* ([Batavia], 1937), p. 9; H.B. Morse, *The Chronicles of the East India Company Trading with China (1635-1834)* (Oxford, 1926), V, 154.

52. Pringle, *Observations on the diseases of the Army*, 6th ed. (London, 1768), p. 200.

53. J. Lind, *An Essay on the Most Effectual Means of Preserving the Health of Seamen* (London, 1774), pp. 65-87.

54. J. Millar, *Observations on the Management of the Prevailing Diseases in Great Britain Particularly in the Army and Navy* (London, 1779), p. 107.

55. Millar to Melville, 5 February 1792, Melville Papers, Scottish Record Office, GD 51/1/593.

56. Beaglehole, *Journals*, I, 438.

57. Hawkesworth, I, 291.

58. 13 March 1772, Adm. 98/10 and Adm. 99/47.

59. 12 July 1771, Adm. 1/1609.

60. James Lind, *Treatise of the Scurvy* (London, 1757), pp. 149-53.

61. John Reid Muir, *The Life and Achievements of Captain James Cook...* (London, 1939), p. 25.

62. D. MacBride, *Experimental Essays on Medical and Philosophical Subjects* (London, 1767), p. 57.

63. D. MacBride, *An Historical Account of a New Method of Treating the Scurvy at Sea* (London, 1768), p. 3; 29 June 1762, ADM/C/576; 1 July 1762, ADM/F/23.

64. MacBride, *Experimental Essays*, p. 171; J.D.H. Widdess, "Robert Adair," *Irish Journal of Medical Science* (March 1948), pp. 1-5.

65. A. Young, "Surgeon's Journal of HMS 'Jason'"; MacBride, *New Method of Treating the Scurvy at Sea*, pp. 8-62; Lloyd and Coulter, III, 308.

66. H. Wallis, *Cartaret's Voyage Round the World 1766-1769* (Cambridge, 1965), II, 444-54.

67. 20 January 1772, ADM/E/41; 3 October 1775, ADM/FP/18; 30 October 1771, ADM/C/604; A. Harden and S.S. Zilva, "An Investigation of Beer for Antineuritic and Antiscorbutic Potency," *Journal of the Institute of Brewing* XV (1918), 197-208.

68. 1 July 1767, ADM/FP/10.

69. Gilbert Blane, *A Brief Statement on the Progressive Improvement of the Health of the Royal Navy* (London, 1830), p. 23; 4 February 1796, ADM/F/26.

70. A. Armstrong, *Observations on Naval Hygiene and Scurvy* (London, 1858), pp. 17-19; A. Armstrong, *Discovery of the North-West Passage*, pp. 614-16.

71.  R.E. Hughes, "James Lind and the Cure of Scurvy: an Experimental Approach," *Medical History*, XIX (1975), 342-51.

72.  H.V. Wyatt, "James Lind and the Prevention of Scurvy," *Medical History*, XX (1976), 433-38.

73.  W. Bartley, H.A. Krebs and J.R.P. O'Brien, *Vitamin C Requirements of Human Adults*, Medical Research Council, Special Report Series No. 280, (London, 1953), p. 179; R.E. Hodges, J.Hood, J.E. Cannam, H.F. Sauerbuch and E.M. Baker, "Clinical Manifestations of Ascorbic Acid Deficiency in Man," *American Journal of Clinical Nutrition*, XXIV (1971), 439-44.

74.  Blane, p. 13; A. Carré, "La Santé et l'histoire maritime Anglaise du XVIe siècle à 1815," *La Revue maritime*, 310 (1976) 27-47.

75.  E.M. Baker, "Vitamin C Requirements in Stress," *American Journal of Clinical Nutrition*, XX (1967), 583-90.

76.  C.R. Markham, ed., *The Hawkins Voyages* (Cambridge, 1878), p. 164; Schoute, pp. 18-23; James Lind, *An Essay on Diseases Incidental to Europeans in Hot Climates* (London, 1771), p. 352; Lind, *Preserving the Health of Seamen*, pp. 87-90.

77.  H. Brunschwig, *Das Buch zu Distillieren* (Strasburg, 1519).

78.  Hawkesworth, I, 515.

79.  Louis Antoine de Bougainville, *Voyage autour du monde par la frégate du roi La Boudeuse et La Flute L'Étoile en 1766, 1767, 1768, et 1769*, 2nd ed. (Paris, 1772), II, 19, 20; C.J. Phipps, *A Voyage towards the North Pole* (London, 1773), pp. 205-21.

80.  J.A. Shepherd, *Spencer Wells, The Life and Work of a Victorian Surgeon* (Edinburgh, 1965), p. 132.

81.  Lloyd and Coulter, III, 316.

82.  John Law, journal, B.M. Add. MSS 37327.

83.  D. Samwell, *A Narrative of the Death of Captain James Cook to which are Added Some Particulars Concerning his Life and Character and Observations Respecting the Introduction of the Venereal Disease into the Sandwich Islands* (London, 1786).

84.  W.L. Davies, "David Samwell (1751-1798)," *Transactions of the Honourable Society of Cymmrodion*, Session 1926-7 (1928), pp. 70-133; Ellis, *passim*.

85.  Beaglehole, *Journals*, III, 473.

86.  Cook to James Snagg, 4 August 1778, Canberra Letter Book.

87.  Beaglehole, *Journals*, III, 59.

88.  Ellis, I, 60.

89.  Beaglehole, *Journals*, III, 214, 215; Bayly, journal, 13 October 1777, Adm. 55/20.

90.  Beaglehole, *Journals*, III, 274.

91.  Samwell, journal, June 1777, LXII, B.M. Eg. MSS 2591.

92.  Beaglehole, *Journals*, III, 927; Bontius, p. 181.

93.  Beaglehole, *Journals*, III, 210.

94.  *Ibid.*, 1370; Samwell, journal, 13 August 1777, LXX.

95.  Beaglehole, *Journal of Banks*, I, 374.

96.  F.Wilkinson, journal, 14 April 1769, Adm. 51/4547.

97.  Bougainville, journal 1766-1769, 4JJ 144K.

98.  Beaglehole, *Journal of Banks*, I, 374-75.

99. G. Robertson, log, 28 December 1766, Adm. 51/4540; Bougainville, journal, 1766-1769, 4JJ 142, Archives Nationales-Marine.

100. C.C. Dennie, *A History of Syphilis* (Springfield, 1962), pp. 7-12.

101. I. Van de Sluis, *The Treponematosis of Tahiti: Its Origin and Evolution—A Study of Sources* (Amsterdam, 1969); H.M. Smith, "The Introduction of Venereal Disease into Tahiti: A Re-examination," *Journal of Pacific History*, X (1975), 38-45.

102. C.J. Hackett, "On the Origin of the Human Treponematoses," *Bulletin of the World Health Organisation*, XXIX (1963), 7-41.

103. C.J. Hackett, *Diagnostic Criteria of Syphilis, Yaws and Treponarid* (Berlin, 1976), pp. 112-15.

104. W.F. Bowers, "Pathological and Functional Changes Found in 864 Pre-Captain Cook Contact Polynesian Burials from Sand Dunes at Mokapu, Oahu, Hawaii," *International Surgery*, XLV (1966), 206-17; C.E. Snow, *Early Hawaiians: An Initial Study of Skeletal Remains from Mokapu, Hawaii* (Lexington, 1974), p. 60.

105. T.B. Turner, D.H. Hollander and K. Schaeffer, *Biological Investigations on Treponemes*, First International Symposium on Yaws Control, World Health Organisation (Geneva, 1953), pp. 7-16.

106. K.R. Hill, *Non-Specific Factors in the Epidemiology of Yaws*, First International Symposium on Yaws Control, World Health Organisation (Geneva, 1953), pp. 17-47.

107. A. Duncan, *Medical Cases Selected from the Records of the Public Dispensary at Edinburgh*, 3rd ed. (Edinburgh, 1778), pp. 219-20.

108. J. Wilson, "Observations on the Natural or Spontaneous Cure of Syphilis," *Transactions of the Medico-chirurgical Society of Edinburgh*, III (1829), 58.

109. Beaglehole, *Journals*, II, 232.

110. *Ibid.*, III, 97, 480 and II, 647; John White, *The Ancient History of the Maori, his Mythology and Traditions* (Wellington, 1887-91), V, 121-30.

111. [Rickman], *Journal*, p. 175.

112. Beaglehole, *Journals*, III, 1083.

113. H. Roberts, log, 25 January 1778, Dixon Library, Sydney.

114. Ellis, I, 216.

115. Beaglehole, *Journals*, III, 303.

116. King, journal, 28 November, 1 December 1778, 1 March 1779, Adm. 55/116; M.L.A. Milet-Mureau, *Voyage de La Pérouse autour du monde* (Paris, 1797), II, 337.

117. J. Sparks, *Travels and Adventures of John Ledyard*, 2nd ed. (London, 1834), pp. 124, 135.

118. Beaglehole, *Journals*, III, 506.

119. Sparks, p. 135.

120. G. Forster, *A Voyage Round the World in His Britannic Majesty's Sloop Resolution Commanded by Capt. James Cook, during the Years 1772, 3, 4, and 5* (London, 1777), I, 538, 547; Beaglehole, *Journals*, III, 315.

121. Beaglehole, *Journals*, III, 506.

122. G. Forster, *A Voyage*, I, 543, 547-48.

123. W. R. Thrower, "Contributions to medicine of Captain James Cook, FRS, RN," *Lancet* (1951), pp. 215-19.

124. J. Pringle, *Observations on the Diseases of the Army* (London, 1768), pp. 210-11.

125. R. Hoeppli, *Parasites and Parasitic Infections in Early Medicine and Science* (Singapore, 1959), p. 388.

126. G. Forster, *A Voyage*, II, 36; Beaglehole, *Journals*, II, 535.

127. R. Buzina, "Early Signs of Niacin Deficiency," *Bibliotheca Nutricio et Dieta*, XXIII (1976), 89-94; F. Bicknell and F. Prescot, *The Vitamins in Medicine* (London, 1953), pp. 216, 354.

128. Beaglehole, *Journals*, III, 214-15.

129. E. Kodicek, "Some Problems Connected with the Availability of Niacin in Cereals," *Bibliotheca Nutricio et Dieta*, XXIII (1976), 86-7; "Forms of Bound Niacin in Wheat," *Nutrition Reviews*, (April 1974), p. 32.

## Cook's Posthumous Reputation:

1. Colville to Cleveland, 30 December 1762, Adm. 1/482, quoted in Beaglehole, *The Life*, p. 59.

2. Quoted in Muir, p. 22.

3. See Beaglehole, *The Life*, p. 471.

4. "Ce n'est ni dans les forêts du Canada ni sur le sein des mers, que l'on se forme à l'art d'écrire," from *Voyage autour du monde*, quoted in Peter France, *Rhetoric and Truth in France* (Oxford, 1972), p. 79.

5. Thomas Sprat, *History of the Royal Society*, eds. J. Cape and H.W. Jones (Seattle, 1958), pp. 111 ff.

6. *Oeuvres complètes*, II, 208, quoted by France, p. 79.

7. "To choose incidents and situations from common life, and to relate or describe them, throughout, as far as was possible in a selection of language really used by men," *Anglistica*, IX (1957), 115.

8. Peter Gay, *The Enlightenment: an Interpretation* (London, 1973), p. 3.

9. See France, p. 73.

10. *Les Jardins, ou l'Art d'embellir les Paysages* (Paris, 1782), trans. in *Gentleman's Magazine*, LIII (December, 1783), 1044-45.

11. *Elogio del Capitano Giacomo Cook letto da M. Gianetti nella pubblica adunanza della Reale Accademia Fiorentina* (with parallel texts in Italian and English), (Firenze, 1785).

12. Gianetti, *Elogio*, p. 25.

13. Pierre Lémontey, *Éloge de Jacques Cook avec des notes: discours qui a remporté le prix d'éloquence au jugement de l'Académie de Marseille*, le 25 Août 1789, (Paris, 1792).

14. Pierre Louis Paris, *Eloge de Cook* (Riom, 1790).

15. "La vie d'un homme seroit à ses yeux, plus précieuse que la connoissance d'un continent," Paris, p. 62.

16. *Frederick the Great* (London, 1858-65), bk., iv, ch. 3.

17. Beaglehole, *Journals*, III, 556.

18. Gordon Browne, "Death of Captain Cook," in C.R. Low, ed., *Captain Cook's three voyages round the World* (London, 1895), p. 470.

19. Will Robinson, "A few of the natives brandished spears," in John Lang, *Story of Captain Cook* (London, 1906), p. 58.

20. Charles Mitchell, "Zoffany's Death of Captain Cook," *Burlington Magazine*, LXXXIV (1944), 56-61.

21. Benjamin West, *The Death of Wolfe*, oil, National Gallery of Canada, Ottawa.

22. Louis Le Vieux, Captain James Cook, marble, 1790, National Portrait Gallery, London.

23. For the *theory* of repressive tolerance (in relation to Auguste Comte) see Herbert Marcuse, *Reason and Revolution* (Boston, 1960), pp. 355 ff.

24. See W.S. Howell, "Adam Smith's Lectures on Rhetoric: an Historical Assessment," *Essays on Adam Smith*, eds. A.S. Skinner and T. Wilson (Oxford, 1975), pp. 11-43.

25. Joseph Burke, *English Art 1714-1800* (Oxford, 1976), p. 249.

26. Sir Henry T. Wood, *A History of the Royal Society of Arts* (London, 1913), p. 76.

27. Quoted by Burke, p. 249.

28. On the posthumous veneration of Cook on Hawaii as Lono, see J.F.G. Stokes, "Origin of the Condemnation of Captain Cook in Hawaii," Hawaiian Historical Society, Annual Report XXXIX (1930), 69-104; E.S.C. and E.G. Handy, "Native Planters in Hawaii. Their Life, Lore and Environment," Bishop Museum Bulletin, CCXXXIII (1972), 372.

29. J. Williamson, "I Now Took Possession in Right of His Majesty King George III," frontispiece to J. Barrow, ed., *Cook's Voyages of Discovery* (London, 1904).

30. Beaglehole, *Journals*, III, 556-57.

31. *Ibid.*, 1492.

32. G. Forster, *A Voyage*, I, 29.

33. Gerald Fitzgerald, *The Injured Islanders: or, the Influence of Art upon the Happiness of Nature* (Dublin, 1779).

34. Lémontey, p. 51 (author's trans.).

35. Stokes, pp. 68-104.

36. I am indebted to Professor Manning Clark for drawing my attention to this point. I should also like to acknowledge the valuable assistance of Miss Jane De Teliga in collecting material related to this paper.

## The Artistic Bequest of Captain Cook's Voyages—Popular Imagery in European Costume Books of the Late Eighteenth and Early Nineteenth Centuries:

Initial research on this subject was carried out in autumn 1975, when, as a Visiting Fellow of the Humanities Research Centre at The Australian National University, Canberra, I was given the opportunity to work in the Pictorial Section of the National Library of Australia. To both institutions I am very grateful. The National Library of Australia and the Lipperheidesche Kostumbibliothek have both kindly given permission to reproduce originals which are in their custody; this is herewith gratefully acknowledged.—*R.J.*

1. In the extended version of my paper submitted to the Cook Conference and duplicated and issued by the organizers during the conference in April 1978, I have drawn attention to a number of these works and pointed to the immediate impact which Cook's voyages had upon the arts.

2. Beaglehole's *Journals* published and reproduced for the first time many of the drawings and paintings produced during Cook's voyages. A complete survey of the visual material has been prepared by Professor Bernard Smith of Melbourne and myself, and will be published under the title *Catalogue Raisonné of Coastal Views, Landscapes, Portraits, Depictions of Events and Ethnographical Artifacts drawn or painted by artists and others who travelled with Captain James Cook on his three voyages around the world, 1768-71, 1772-5, 1776-80.*

3. Bernard Smith, *European Vision*, p. 79.

4. J.G. Herder, *Ideen zur Philosophie der Geschichte der Menschheit* (1784), trans. by T. Churchill as *Outlines of a Philosophy of the History of Man* (London, 1803), I, 289.

5. Opp. p. 37. The print bears the publisher's line "London Published Jan$^y$. 26$^{th}$ 1778, by J. Johnson S$^t$. Pauls Church Yard."

6. "AAA. A Man, Woman & Child of Easter Island—B. Woman of New Zeeland—C. A New Zeeland Warrior—D. Native of New Caledonia—E. Woman of New Holland—F. Woman of O-Taheitee—G. Another Woman of O-Taheitee, with a Bonnet of Leaves to shade the Sun—H. Man of O-Taheitee—I. Man of Mallicollo—KK. Man and Woman of S$^t$. Christina, in the Marquesas—L. A Priest of the Society Islands—M. Dancing Girl at Ulietea—M. A Musician playing on a Lute from his Nose—M. The Drum of Ulietea—N. The very singular habit of mourning worn at O-Taheitee—O. A Tupapow or Bier, with a Corpse; being the manner of disposing the dead at the Society Islands—P. A Canoe of the Friendly Islands—Q. A Hippah, or fortified Village of New Zeeland—R. A Canoe of O-Taheitee—S. A Branch of the Bread fruit Tree, with the Fruit—T. The Kanguroo, an animal peculiar to New Holland—U. The manner of constructing the Houses at O-Taheitee—X. A Species of the Fig Tree found at New Caledonia—Y. A Floating Ice Island, numbers of which were seen towards the southern Frigid Zone."

7. The sources used are engravings from Hawkesworth (see for instance his chief mourner in pl. 5, the dancers and musicians in pl. 7 and the kangaroo in pl. 20); from S. Parkinson, *Journal of a Voyage to the South Seas in his Majesty's Ship, The Endeavour* (London, 1773), (see for instance his priest of Ulietea opp. p. 71, or his New Zealand warrior in his proper dress opp. p. 88); and from James Cook, *A Voyage towards the South Pole*, (see for instance the portraits of the man and the woman of Easter Island, pls. 46, 25, or of the chief of S$^{ta}$. Christina, pl. 36).

8. These and the following works discussed below, all of which seem to be comparatively rare, are kept in the Lipperheidesche Kostumbibliothek in West Berlin. On Viero and St.-Sauveur see Eva Nienholdt and Gretel Wagner-Neumann, *Katalog der Lipperheideschen Kostumbibliothek* (Berlin, 1975), I, 13-14. A copy of Viero's publication—in three separate parts—is also in the British Library, London.

9. Engraved by J. Basire, pl. 27 in Cook, *A Voyage towards the South Pole*.

10. Teodoro Viero, *Raccolta di... Stampe*, pt. 3, pl. 106 (for plate numbers I have followed the edition in the British Library).

11. Beaglehole, *Journals*, II, 597; Cook, *A Voyage towards the South Pole*, II, 183.

12. Viero, pt. 3, pl. 99.

13. Cook, *A Voyage towards the South Pole*, pl. 56.

14. Pencil and red crayon, 18 x 25 cm. (Nan Kivell Collection 236).

15. The only plate not borrowed from Hodges is pl. 108 representing "Omai, nativo di Ulaietea," based upon Bartolozzi's engraving (1774) after the famous drawing by Nathaniel Dance now in the Public Archives of Canada, Ottawa.

16. Viero, pt. 3, pl. 93.

17. Engraved by J. Hall in Cook, *A Voyage towards the South Pole*, pl. 48.

18. *Ibid.*, pl. 50.

19. "Femme de la Nouvelle Calédonie," coloured etching in J. Grasset de Saint-Sauveur's *Encyclopédie des voyages* (1796), V (America), no plate number.

20. No special study on St.-Sauveur seems to have been undertaken. For biographical details see the *Biographie universelle (Michaud) ancienne et moderne, nouvelle edition* (Paris, 1857), XVII, 375.

21. J. Grasset de Saint-Sauveur, *Costumes civils* (Paris, 1784), I, i-viii.

22. *Ibid.*, vi.

23. *Ibid.*, III, no plate number.

24. Cook and King, pl. 66.

25. *Ibid.*, pl. 62.

26. In the edition of St.-Sauveur's *Costumes civils* which I consulted at the Lipper-heidesche Kostumbibliothek in West Berlin, this plate is not among the group of plates illustrating the natives of the Sandwich Islands in vol. III. Instead, it is listed separately in a supplement at the back of the volume together with plates which are based on illustrations of the voyage of La Pérouse. These plates were most likely issued in 1797 or some time later, after the atlas of the voyage of La Pérouse had been published that year. (While vol. I is dated 1784, vols. II-IV are without a date.)

27. Now in the Dixson Library, Sydney. To compare with St.-Sauveur's plate see Smith, fig. 7 in this volume.

28. Bartolozzi's and Byrne's engraving seems to have been first published in complete state on 1 January 1784 (see Beddie, *Bibliography*, no. 2603); Mitchell, 59, mentions an edition of 1 July 1785; other editions have been recorded for 1 January 1785 and 4 January 1787.

29. Pen and wash, 16.8 x 10.8 cm. (Nan Kivell Collection 146).

30. Nienholdt and Wagner-Neumann, I, 14.

31. Alterations between the first and the second of St.-Sauveur's costume books primarily concern the format, the order, and the presentation of the plates. To distinguish the plates from one work to another, the later ones show thin frames around the figures as well as around the titles below. There are also variations in the colouring of the plates and in composition. Many illustrations not in the first work have been added to the second, but some have also been cropped. From the author's line "J.G.S^t. Sauveur inv & direx" frequently found underneath the plates, it appears that again St.-Saveur was responsible for the plates.

32. J. Grasset de Saint-Sauveur, *Encyclopédie des voyages* (Paris, 1796), V, no plate number.

33. *Ibid.*

34.  *Ibid.*, see plates such as "Sauvage de la Nouvelle Zéelande," "Guerrier de la Nouvelle Zéelande," "Guerrier de Sandwich," or "Insulaire des Isles Sandwich."

35.  In the author's line this plate which measures 43.6 x 51.1 cm. is inscribed: "J.G. St. Sauveur Fecit-Phelipeau Sculp." A copy of it is owned by the National Maritime Museum, Greenwich. For a reproduction in colour see Rex and Thea Rienits, *The Voyages of Captain Cook* (London, 1968), p. 144.

36.  One other nation, discovered by the English captain Henry Wilson, are the inhabitants of the Pelew Islands, in St.-Sauveur's plate in the second row, far right; the figures are based upon illustrations in G. Keate, *An Account of the Pelew Islands* (London, 1788).

37.  "1. Hab$^{ts}$ de Nootka—2. Hab$^{ts}$ de la Zeeland—3. Hab$^{ts}$ de l'Entrée du Prince Guillaume—4. Hab$^{ts}$ de l'Isle de Pâques—5. Hab$^{ts}$ de la Baye de Norton—6. Hab$^{ts}$ des Iles Sandwich—7. Hab$^{ts}$ de Tanna—8. Hab$^{ts}$ de S$^{te}$ Christine—9. Hab$^{ts}$ de la Baye de Castries—10. Hab$^{ts}$ de la Baye ou Port des Français—11. Hab$^{ts}$ de Maouna—12. Hab$^{ts}$ de Macao—13. Hab$^{ts}$ de la Baye de Langle—14. Hab$^{ts}$ de la Conception—15. Hab$^{ts}$ de la Baye des Manilles—16. Hab$^{ts}$ des Iles Pelew—17. Hab$^{ts}$ d'Oonalaska—18. Hab$^{ts}$ d'Ulietea—19. Hab$^{ts}$ des Iles Marquises—20. Hab$^{ts}$ de l'Ile des Amis—21. Hab$^{ts}$ de la Nouvelle Calédonie—22. Hab$^{ts}$ d'Otaiti—23. Hab$^{ts}$ d'Anaamoka—24. Hab$^{ts}$ de Hapaée."

38.  See Friedrich Gottlob Leonhardi, *Bildliche Darstellung aller bekannten Völker nach ihren Kleidertrachten, Sitten, Gewohnheiten* (Leipzig, 1798-1801); *Gallerie der Menschen. Ein Bilderbuch zur Erweiterung der Kenntnisse über Länder und Völker* (Pest, 1813); J.A.C. Löhr, *Die Länder und Völker der Erde oder vollstandige Beschreibung aller fünf Erdtheile mit deren Bewohner* (Leipzig, 1818-19); or *Abbildungen verschiedener Völker der Erde in ihren eighetenthümlichen Trachten* (Breslau, 1826); all works are in the Lipperheideschen Kostumbibliothek in West Berlin.

39.  See Josef Leiss, *Bildtapeten aus alter und neuer Zeit* (Hamburg, 1961), pp. 41-46.

40.  My translation from an extract quoted in Leiss, p. 43.

41.  The whole panorama of the wallpaper is reproduced in Henri Clouzot, *Les Chefs-d'oeuvres du papier peint, tableaux—teintures de Dufour & Leroy* (Paris, 1903), pls. 2 and 3, and in N. McClelland, *History of Wall-papers* (Philadelphia-London, 1924), pp. 367-70. A complete series of the wallpaper still on the walls is in the home of Dr. H. Seul, Burg Kommern Mechernich, W. Germany and in the Musées d'Histoire et de Folklore, Champlitte, France. Individual pieces, others than those listed in McClelland (p. 366), are kept in a number of private and public collections, such as the Deutsches Tapetenmuseum, Kassel, W. Germany (kind communication by Dr. E.W. Mick).

42.  Sources other than Cook's are Keate, *An Account*, and La Billardière, *Relation du voyage à la recherche de La Pérouse* (Paris, 1800) which inspired representations of the inhabitants of the Pelew Islands and of Van Diemen's Land.

43.  See Clouzot, in colour, pl. 1.

44.  An interesting example of the transfer of images first published in the editions of Captain Cook's voyages is also a piece of furnishing fabric (cream-coloured cotton with copperplate-printed designs of South Sea motifs) in the Honolulu Academy of Arts: *A Festival of Fibers. Masterworks of Textile Art from the Collection of the Honolulu Academy of Arts* (Honolulu, 1977), p. 72.

45.  Nienholdt and Wagner-Neumann, I, 376.

46. On Kuyper see Thieme-Becker, *Allgemeines Lexikon der bildenden Künstler*, XXII, 147-48.

47. These are kept in the Historical Museum, Amsterdam (Collection Fodor); in addition there are a drawing for the title page and three drawings for vignettes (kind communication by Mijnheer Jonker, Librarian of the Historical Museum).

48. G.K. Nagler, *Neues allgemeines Künstler-Lexikon* (Leipzig, 1835-52), VIII, 128.

49. Occasionally the plates also employ pictorial elements from La Billardière, *Relation*, after drawings by the French artist Piron. This could be demonstrated by Kuyper's illustration of "Nieuw Caledoniers" (*De Mensch*, II, p. 74), where the native throwing a lance and the woman pleading for mercy are almost exactly copied from engravings after Piron (*Relation*, Atlas, pl. 35). Accessory elements in this plate, however, such as the detail of the hut, or the cap worn by the native, are taken from plates in the edition of Cook's second voyage (pls. 20, 39, 50).

50. M. Stuart and J. Kuyper, *De Mensch* (1803), II, opp. 158.

51. Parkinson, opp. p. 88.

52. *Ibid.*, opp. p. 90.

53. La Billardière, pl. 25.

54. Stuart and Kuyper, III (1804), opp. 202.

55. Cook and King, pls. 38, 39.

56. *Ibid.*, pl. 42.

57. Stuart and Kuyper, II, opp. 82.

58. *Ibid.* opp. p. 100.

59. Nienholdt and Wagner-Neumann, I, 17-18. The edition in the Lipperheidesche Kostumbibliothek in Berlin is dated 1817-1834, whereas the edition in the British Library begins with 1816 as the date of publication. An apparently abridged edition in a French translation was published in Milan in 1822; a copy of this is kept in the National Library of Australia. This was kindly pointed out to me by Mrs. Sylvia Carr of the N.L.A.

60. On Ferrario see *Enciclopedia Italiana di scienze, lettere ed arti* (Milan, 1932), XV, 56.

61. Not only did Webber cover more ground in the Pacific than any other artist but also his representations were held to be generally authentic. There is, on the other hand, some reservation about Hodges's landscape and historical subjects; for example, Ferrario rejects Hodges's view of the monuments in the Easter Islands in favour of Duché de Vancy's view from the voyage of La Pérouse. Other explorers in the Pacific whose travel editions contributed to Ferrario's illustrations are Baudin, Billings, D'Entrecasteaux, Malaspina, Vancouver, Wallis, Wilson.

62. Giulio Ferrario, *Il costume antico e moderno... America*, (1820), I, pl. 17.

63. Cook and King, pls. 38, 39.

64. José Espinosa y Tello, *Atlas para el viage de las goletas Sutil y Mexicana* (Madrid, 1802). The persons represented are "Macuina," the chief of Nootka; "Tetacu," a chief of the district of Juan de Fuca; a native woman, called Maria. The artists are Tomas de Suria and Jose Cardero, who accompanied Malaspina on his trip along the northwest coast of America. The drawings were later used to illustrate the atlas of the Galiano-Valdés expedition published by Espinosa y Tello.

65. See Ferrario's extensive verbal description of this subject in *Il costume*, I, 116-17.

66. *Ibid.*, pl. 19.

67. Cook and King, pl. 42.

68. Pen and wash, 21.7 x 32.6 cm.

69. Examples include Aspin's *Cosmorama. A view of the Costumes and Peculiarities of all Nations* (London, 1827); and F.W. Goedsche's *Vollständige Völkergalerie in getreuen Abbildungen aller Nationen* (Meissen, 1830-1838).

## Two Centuries' Perceptions of James Cook: George Forster to Beaglehole:

1. George Forster to J.K.P. Spener, 28 October 1786, in A. Leitzmann, "Beiträge zur Kenntnis Georg Forsters aus ungedruckten Quellen," *Archiv für das Studium der neueren Sprachen und Literaturen*, LXXXVII (1891), 182-83. Spener was Forster's publisher in Berlin. The object of Forster's strictures in editing was, of course, Canon John Douglas of Windsor, editor of Cook's second and third voyage journals. On Forster's lot in Vilna see also G. Forster to Pennant, 5 March 1787, ML Doc. 489b, Mitchell Library, Sydney.

2. In vol. I of the Berlin edition of 1787, pp. 1-106. The Cook essay was subsequently published in vol. I of George Forster's *Kleine Schriften*, ed. G. Forster (Leipzig, 1789), pp. 1-232 and in vol. V of Therese Forster, ed., *George Forster's Sämmtliche Schriften* (Leipzig, 1843), pp. 60-172. A more recent expertly annotated edition of the essay and of the earlier German writings on Cook is *Cook der Entdecker: Schriften über James Cook von Georg and Georg Christoph Lichtenberg*, ed. Klaus-Georg Popp (Leipzig: Reclam, 1976). I quote in translation below from the later edition.

3. Hoare, *The Tactless Philosopher*. Much further exploring needs to be done on this fascinating father-son intellectual partnership.

4. *A Voyage round the World in His Britannic Majesty's Sloop, Resolution... during the Years 1772, 3, 4 and 5*, 2 vols. (London, 1777). The German edition first appeared in Berlin in 1778-80, also in 2 vols. The literature on it is now vast. See for example Horst Fiedler, *Georg-Forster-Bibliographie 1767 bis 1970* (Berlin, 1971).

5. G. Forster to C.G. Heyne, Vilna, 2 April 1787, in *Johann Georg Forster's Briefwechsel. Nebst einigen Nachrichten von seinem Leben*, ed. Therese Huber, 2 vols. (Leipzig, 1829), I, 599. Heyne was George's father-in-law.

6. Leslie Bodi, "George Forster, the 'Pacific Expert' of Eighteenth Century Germany," *Historical Studies Australia and New Zealand*, VIII (1959), 345-63.

7. M.E. Hoare, "Cook the Discoverer: An essay by Georg Forster, 1787," *Records Australian Academy Science*, I, no. 4 (1969), 7-16.

8. Rolf Du Rietz, *Bibliotheca Polynesiana* (Oslo, 1969), p. 77.

9. *Cook der Entdecker*, 1976, pp. 66-67. The translation is by Dr. Gerda Bell, Wellington, from our forthcoming edition of Forster's essay to be published by Victoria University Press in Wellington as *Cook The Discoverer and New Holland and the British Colony at Botany Bay*, ed. M.E. Hoare and trans. Gerda Bell.

10. *Cook der Entdecker*, p. 128.

11. As Ludwig Uhlig writes, "the literary output of the Vilna years was relatively meagre," *Georg Forster: Einheit und Mannigfaltigkeit in seiner geistigen Welt* (Tubingen, 1965), p. 8. George was in Vilna 1784-87 and produced, apart from the Cook essay, one on "New Holland and the British Colony in Botany Bay" and several other botanical works directly related to the voyages. We badly need a good biography of George *in any language.*

12. Review in *Guardian,* 12 October 1974.

13. A German working in Holland has recently reminded us of Dutch enterprise. See Günther Schilder, *Australia Unveiled: The Share of Dutch Navigation in the Discovery of Australia* (Amsterdam, 1976).

14. See for example my *In the Steps of Beaglehole: Cook Researches Past and Prospect,* Hocken Lecture (Dunedin, 1977).

15. M.E. Hoare, ed., *The "Resolution" Journal of Johann Reinhold Forster, 1772-1775* (London: Hakluyt Society, at press) and Beaglehole, *Journals,* II, 615. Forster's original six-volume journal is in the Staatsbibliothek Preussischer Kulturbesitz, Berlin, under MS germ quart 222-27.

16. Beaglehole, "Some Problems of Cook's Biographer," in *Employ'd as a Discoverer: Papers presented at the Captain Cook Bi-Centenary Symposium, Sutherland Shire, 1-3 May 1970,* ed. J.V.S. Megaw (Sydney, 1971), pp. 23-54. Also, as a longer version, in *The Mariner's Mirror,* LV (1969), 365-81. These papers were some of the first "perceptions" of the Australian Cook bicentenary: they, too, need some overhaul.

17. See R. Rauschenberg, "Daniel Carl Solander, the Naturalist on the 'Endeavour,'" *Transactions of the American Philosophical Society,* LVIII (1968).

18. Beaglehole, *Journals,* I, ci.

19. *Ibid.,* II, lxxxix, n. 2.

20. Beaglehole, *The Life,* p. 20. For some of the other side see Fry, *Dalrymple* and H.T. Fry, "Captain James Cook: the historical perspective," *The Significance of Cook's "Endeavour" Voyage: Three Bicentennial Lectures* (Townsville, 1970), pp. 1-23. These papers deserve a wider audience.

21. Beaglehole, *Journals,* II, xlii. There is little relief in *The Life,* pp. 302-3. The phenomenon is, of course, J.R. Forster

22. Du Rietz, *Bibliotheca Polynesiana,* 1969, pp. 213-17.

23. Beaglehole, "Problems of Cook's Biographer," pp. 24-25.

24. *Cook der Entdecker,* pp. 134-35.

25. Beaglehole, "Problems of Cook's Biographer," p. 25.

26. George Forster in *Göttingischen Anzeigen von gelehrten Sachen* (1778), St. 158, pp. 1577-79.

27. Beaglehole, "Problems of Cook's Biographer," p. 25.

28. *Ibid.,* pp. 25-26.

29. *Ibid.,* p. 26.

30. *Ibid.*

31. *Cook der Entdecker,* p. 134.

32. Beaglehole, "Problems of Cook's Biographer," p. 26. Beaglehole is talking about Cook's deeds.

33. *Cook der Entdecker,* pp. 131-32.

34. J.C. Beaglehole, *Cook the Writer* (Sydney, 1970).

35. *Ibid.*, p. 9.

36. Beaglehole, *The Life*, p. xi.

37. Typescript 3pp., Beaglehole Room, Library, Victoria University of Wellington.

38. *Ibid.*, p. i.

39. Beaglehole to Hoare, 8 July 1971, in author's possession.

40. Beaglehole, "Memorandum," p. ii.

41. To see how far Australians alone have added to their writings and collecting on Cook, see the second revised edition of Beddie, *Bibliography of Captain James Cook*. Herein are listed many of the Cook MSS copied (for example by James Bonwick) in Australia or elsewhere from 1890 onwards.

42. Beaglehole, "Memorandum," p. iii.

43. "As Captain Cook put it," *N.Z. Listener* (28 July 1950), pp. 12-14.

44. Beaglehole, "Problems of Cook's Biographer," p. 39.

45. *Ibid.*

46. Beaglehole, *Journals*, II, xl-xli; see also Beaglehole, *The Life*, pp. 301-2.

47. For Beaglehole's sketch of Forster see *Journals*, II, xliii-xlix and, for the nonsense on "romantic imagination," 501, n. 2. The Forster portrait in *The Life*, pp. 302-3, is a little toned down. The Wales spleen was vented in the first of an acrimonious trilogy of post-voyage pamphlets, *Remarks on Mr. Forster's Account of Captain Cooks Last Voyage round the World* (London, 1778).

48. *Ibid.*, p. 69.

49. Hoare, *Tactless Philosopher*, pp. 163-70.

50. Beaglehole, *Journals*, II, cliii.

51. Wales to Douglas, 12 April 1784, B.M., Eg. MSS 2180, fol. 196.

52. Beaglehole, "Problems of Cook's Biographer," p. 39.

53. *Cook der Entdecker*, p. 134.

54. Beaglehole, "Problems of Cook's Biographer," p. 40.

55. J.R. Forster, *Journal*, quoted in Hoare, *Tactless Philosopher*, p. 106.

56. Beaglehole, *Cook the Writer*, p. 21.

57. *Cook der Entdecker*, pp. 73-78.

58. Beaglehole, "Problems of Cook's Biographer," p. 40.

59. J.R. Forster, *Journal*, quoted in Hoare, *Tactless Philosopher*, p. 101.

60. *Ibid.*, p. 43.

61. G. Forster, *A Letter to the Right Honourable the Earl of Sandwich* (London, 1778), p. 12.

62. Forster to Banks [n.d.], Botany Dept., B.M. (Natural History), Banks Correspondence, Dawson Turner copies (D.T.C.), I, fol. 173.

63. G. Forster, *Voyage round the World*, II, 373.

64. Quoted in Edward Smith, *The Life of Sir Joseph Banks* (London, 1911), pp. 234-35, and Beaglehole, *Journals*, I, 266, n. 1.

65. Beaglehole, *The Life*, p. 699.

66. *Letter to Sandwich*, p. 6, and Hoare, *Tactless Philosopher*, p. 172.

67.  J.R. Forster, trans., *Tagebuch einer Entdekkungsreise* (Berlin, 1781), pp. [ii-iii].

68.  *Ibid.*, p. [iv].

69.  For Beaglehole on the death of Cook see for example *The Life*, pp. 637-72.

70.  G. Parsonson, "On the death of Captain Cook," unpublished typescript, 1976, 24pp., Hocken Library, Dunedin. I am grateful for the author's permission to study this essay. A more recent book on this theme is Gavin Kennedy, *The Death of Cook* (London, 1978).

71.  See *Cook der Entdecker*, pp. 251-52, n. 191.

72.  G. Forster to Banks, Cassel, 20 January 1780, D.T.C., I, fols. 283-84.

73.  G.C. Lichtenberg, "Einige Lebensumstände von Captain James Cook," *Göttingisches Magazin der Wissenschaft und Litteratur*, I (1780), St. 2, 243-96; and G. Forster, "Fragmente über Capitain Cooks letzte Reise und sein Ende," *ibid.*, I (1780) St. 6, 387-429. The latter was not published until early in 1781. Both are reproduced in *Cook der Entdecker*, pp. 138-99.

74.  *Ibid.*, p. 138.

75.  Beaglehole to Hoare, 23 June 1966, in author's possession.

76.  P.E. Klarwell, trans., "Cook the Discoverer," MS 1485, Alexander Turnbull Library, Wellington. I am informed that Professor Beaglehole consulted this translation which was made in 1969.

77.  G. Forster, *Voyage*, I, title page; and Wales, *Remarks*, title page.

# Index

Académie Française, 162
Académie Royale des Sciences, 64, 79
Acapulco, 106, 113
Adair, Robert, surgeon, 144–45
Adam, Robert, architect, 180
Adelphi, the, 180
Admiralty, Board of; mounts expeditions 6, 34, 46, 55, 183; fixes northern coast of America, 68; and naval medicine, 137, 143, 145, 146; and Banks, 21, 24, 29, 32, 33; and Dalrymple, 49; and the Forsters, 215, 222
Admiralty College, Russia, 124
*Adventure*, H.M.S., 162, 174; health aboard, 129–36, 147, 150, 152
Africa, 5, 29, 30, 35, 203
African Association, 30
Alaskan peninsula, 63, 64, 65, 79, 80
Alaska, 61, 66, 68, 69, 70, 74, 75, 77, 78, 109, 110, 121, 122, 123
Aleutian Islands, 61, 63, 121
Alta California, 101
Amboyna Pox, 150
America, 5, 86, 118, 151, 165; *see also* North America, and northwest coast of America
American War of Independence, 23, 38, 53, 109
Americans, 110–12, 114
Anderson, William, surgeon, 85, 132, 133, 134, 148, 149, 150, 156–57, 226
Andrews, Thomas, surgeon, 135, 152
Anson, George, admiral, 106
Antarctic Ocean, 14, 16
Antarctica, 59, 125–28, 167
Anthropology, 188, 227
*Aquila* (ship), 132
Archer, Christon I., 3, 4
Arctic, 67, 68
Arctic Ocean, 6, 49
Arias, Dr. Juan Luis, memorial to Philip IV, 47

Armstrong, Alexander, surgeon, 131, 135, 145
Armstrong, Terence, 3
Arteaga, Ignacio, navigator, 107–10
Artists, 30, 93, 187, 210, 226
Asia, 60, 68, 114, 212
Association for the Exploration of the Interior Parts of Africa, 6, 29, 30
Atlantic Ocean, 32, 49, 55, 70, 219
Australia, 1, 19, 31, 41, 55, 59, 151, 167, 182, 190, 212, 214, 221
Avacha Bay, Kamchatka, 123

Bacon, Francis, 25–29, 38; *New Organon*, 25
Baffin Bay, 64, 70, 77
Baja California, 101
Baker, George, capt., 42
Baltic Sea, 78
Bankes, Rev. Thomas; *New System of Geography*, 174
Banks, Joseph; on Cook's first voyage, 22–24, 27, 33, 47, 137–40, 142, 145, 150, 219, 221, 226; and health on *Endeavour*, 137–40, 142, 145, 150; and Cook's reputation, 160–61, 167, 215, 218–19, 221, 226; fosters exploration, 6, 21–39, 210; and Vancouver's voyage, 30–32, 34; and the development of colonies, 36–39; and natural history, 5, 21–39; and Dalrymple, 47–48, 52, 56
Barrington, Daines, 68, 77
Barrow, John, 10, 124
Barry, James, artist, 180
Bartolozzi, Francesco, engraver, 174, 195
Bartram, William, traveller, 5, 7, 9, 10, 12, 14, 16
Batavia, 48, 137, 138, 139, 140, 141, 142, 143
Baudin, Nicolas, explorer, 5, 6
Bayly, William, astronomer, 88, 95–96, 148, 149, 150, 155

Beaglehole, John Cawte; contribution to Cook scholarship, 1–4, 160, 211–18; on Cook, 52, 74, 79, 133, 160, 179, 211–28; view of Banks, 22, 33, 215, 221; view of Dalrymple, 42, 43, 46, 50–51, 215, 222; view of the Forsters, 215, 221–23, 227–28; description of Vancouver Is., 76; on indigenous people, 4, 81; Russian translations of, 127; *Cook the Writer*, 219; *Exploration of the Pacific*, 1, 220, *Endeavour Journal of the Pacific*, *Banks*, 1; *Journals of Cook*, 1, 221; *Life of Cook*, 2, 3, 212, 213, 221

Beaglehole, T.H., son of J.C., 3, 219

Bedford, G.C., 9

Behm, Magnus von, governor of Kamchatka, 121, 122

Behm's Canal, 121

Bellingshausen, F.G. von (F.F. Bellinsgauzen), navigator, 123–27

Benyowsky, Maurice, 14, 121

Bering, Vitus, navigator, 58, 60, 61,63, 64, 71, 73, 74, 77, 103

Bering Strait, 6, 64, 69, 75, 77, 78, 79, 80

Berlin, 145, 222

Besant, Walter; *Captain Cook*, 216

Bevis, Dr. John, astronomer, 44, 45

Billings, Joseph, navigator, 122, 203

Biographers of Cook, 1–4, 211–28

Birmingham, 175, 183

Blane, Gilbert, surgeon, 130, 135, 145, 146

Bligh Is., 81, 92

Bligh, William, navigator, 5, 9, 10, 11, 12, 15, 16, 19, 25, 29, 32, 34, 36, 154, 210

Board of Longitude, 49

Board of Trade, 38

Bocage, M. Barbié du, geographer, 56

Bodega y Quadra, Juan Francisco de la, navigator, 66, 67, 104–9, 113

Bodi, Leslie, 212

Boerhaave, Hermann, physician, 142

Bol'sheretsk, 121

Bontius, J., physician, 141, 150

Bossuet, Jacques, 162

Boswell, James, 35, 70

Botanical collecting, 5, 6, 21, 22, 23–25, 28, 29, 30, 32, 33, 114

Botany Bay, 23, 24, 38, 39, 53, 56, 138, 165

Bougainville, Louis Antoine de, navigator, 4, 12, 45, 47, 60, 138, 147, 150, 151, 160

Boulton, Matthew, mechanician, 175, 183

*Bounty*, H.M.S., 10, 11, 15, 25, 29, 34, 36, 224

Bourzes, Father, 14

Bouvet de Lozier, Jean Baptiste Charles, navigator, 49

Bradeley, William, A.B., 153

Branciforte, Marqués de, viceroy, 118

Brazil, 23

Brett, captain, 144

Britain, 48, 54, 55, 125, 162

British Columbia, 67, 76, 79

British Museum, 56, 217

Broughton, William, navigator, 36

Brown, Robert, scientist, 6, 38, 39

Brown, Gordon, illustrator, 172

Bruce, James, traveller, 7, 10, 12, 14, 16

Brunschwig, Hieronymous, 147

Buache, Phillippe, geographer, 49, 63, 64, 76

Bucareli, Antonio María y Ursúa, navigator, 100, 101, 103–08

Bucareli Bay, 66, 105, 107, 108, 110

Bucareli Sound, 67

Buck, Sir Peter, anthropologist, 214

Burke, Joseph, 180

Burney, Dr. Charles, 36, 180

Burney, James, lieut., 19, 52, 56, 73, 152, 218; *Chronological History*, 56

Büsching, A.F.; *Wöchentlichen Nachrichten*, 227

Byrne, William, engraver, 191–95

Byron, George Gordon, 6th lord, 125

Byron, John, navigator, 5, 6, 69, 219

Cabot, Sebastian, navigator, 180

Caley, John, botanist, 6

California, 60, 66, 100, 104, 105, 106, 109

Campbell, John, capt., 44–46

Canada, 160, 219

Cannibalism, 85, 115–16

Canton, 41, 113

Cape Douglas, Alaska, 78
Cape Edgecombe, Alaska, 71
Cape Elizabeth, Alaska, 72
Cape Fairweather, Alaska, 71
Cape Flattery, Wash., 71, 76
Cape of Good Hope, 6, 24, 53, 133, 140, 219, 225
Cape Horn, 48, 51, 53, 106, 133
Cape Hinchinbroke (Hinchinbrook), Alaska, 72
Cape Prince of Wales, Bering Strait, 60, 61
Cape St. Hermogenes, Alaska, 73
Capetown, 130
*Captain Cook* (ship), 35
Carlos III of Spain, 114
Carlos IV of Spain, 115, 118
Carlyle, Thomas, 168
Carré, A., 146
Carter, George, painter, 169
Carter, Harold, 214
Carteret, Philip, navigator, 5, 6, 145, 219
Carver, Jonathan, explorer, 10
Cassel, Germany, 227
Chagos Archipelago, 56
Charvet, Jean Gabriel, designer, 199-202
China, 44, 53, 88, 98, 109, 110, 118, 165
Chirikov, Aleksei, navigator, 61, 103
Christian, Fletcher, lieut., 10, 11, 15, 16
Chukotka, 122
Churchill, Manitoba, 66
Clayoquot Indians, 92
Clayoquot Sound, 92, 112
Cleghorn, George, anotomist, 144
Clerke, Charles, lieut., 21, 39, 80, 92, 94, 96, 106, 115, 121, 123, 133, 148, 149, 156
Cleveley, James, carpenter, 169
Cleveley, John, painter, 169, 172
Coleridge, Samuel Taylor, 8, 9, 11, 12, 14, 15-19; "The Rime of the Ancient Mariner," 12-14
Collingwood, Cuthbert, 1st lord, 124
Colnett, James, captain, 36, 55, 152
*Columbia* (ship), 116
Columbia R., 105
Columbus, Christopher, 12, 17, 86, 151
Colville, Alexander, lord Colville, 159
Company Land, 61

Consumption, 138, 140
Convict settlement, 29, 38, 53-54, 165
Cook, James, 8, 9, 12, 16, 27, 41, 67, 116, 118, 188, 191; and Banks, 21-23, 28, 29, 31, 33, 34, 36, 219, 226; bicentennial celebrations, 2; and Coleridge, 12-15; and critics, 125-26, 183-85; and Dalrymple, 44, 50-52, 55-57, 215; death of, 6, 113, 155, 159, 169-77, 182-83, 226-27; early life, 2; and east coast of Australia, 55-57; and *Endeavour*, 46-47; and extension of knowledge, 5-7, 19, 212-13; and first voyage, 47-48, 50; and the Forsters, 211-13, 214, 217-18, 223-26; health of, 2-3, 154-57; and health of his crews, 3, 129-40, 142-50, 152-54; and illustrative material, 187,210; and indigenous people, 4, 81, 84, 86, 87, 96, 98, 152-54, 183, 184; influence of, 3-4, 35-36, 39, 99-100; journals of, 2, 127, 218; at Nootka Sound, 70-71, 81, 84-87, 90-94, 96-98, 104, 107, 110-111; on northwest coast of North America, 62, 67, 70-79; and Northwest Passage, 59-60, 69-70, 224; reputation of, 2-3, 121-29, 159-85, 213, 227; and Russians, 64, 65, 121-28; and scientists, 30, 215, 219, 225, 226; and Spanish exploration, 66, 105, 106, 109, 112, 114; study of, 1-4, 211-27; and third voyage, 52-53, 70, 80; *A Voyage towards the South Pole and round the World*, 6, 219, 222; *A Voyage to the Pacific Ocean*, 6, 98, 174, 203; and writing, 160-61, 218-19;
Cook's officers, 19, 36, 70, 121, 226
Cook Inlet, Alaska, 74
Cooper, Robert Palliser, lieut., 132
Cooper's Is., 139
Coral Sea, 167
Corcino, J.J., 136
Cornwallis, Sir William, admiral, 124
Costume books, 194-99, 203-210
Cottle, Joseph, 18
Coulter, Jack L.S., 145
Cowper, William, poet, 8
Coxe, William, 7, 65, 76, 77; *Account of the Russian Discoveries*, 65
Critics of Cook, 183-85

Cross Sound, Alaska, 71
Cuddalore (ship), 42
Culture contact, 4, 81–98, 114–19, 183
Cumberland, 12, 16

Dalrymple, Alexander, 2, 34, 35, 41–57,
215, 222; Chart and Memoir, 49; Collection concerning Papua, 54, 56; Historical collection, 47, 51; Memoir concerning the Chagos, 55, 56; Plan for promoting the fur trade, 55
Dalrymple, Hugh, capt., 51
Dampier, William, navigator, 10, 12, 14, 17, 41, 45, 47
Danville, Jean-Baptiste Bourguignon, geographer, 49–50
Dartmouth,William Legge, 2nd earl of, 68
Darwin, Charles, naturalist, 19
Dauphin map, 54, 55, 56, 57
Davidson, J.W., historian, 214
Davies, Robert, surgeon's mate, 148
Davis, John, quartermaster, 149
De Gama Land, 61
Deal, Kent, 23
Dee, John, 55
Delille, Jacques, 162, 163; Les Jardins, 162
De Loutherbourg, Phillip James, painter and designer, 174
Derby Philosophical Society, 26
Diana (ship), 124
Dibble, Rev. Sheldon, 184–85
Diderot, D., 161; Supplement au voyage de Bougainville, 183
Dioscorides, De Materia Medica, 26
Discovery H.M.S., under Cook, 29, 81, 94, 96, 121, 122, 148
Discovery H.M.S., under Vancouver, 25, 30, 32, 34
Dixon, George, navigator, 35
Dodd, D.P., painter, 169
Dolphin (ship), 147
Douglas, John, canon of Windsor, 1, 219
Downs, the, 140
Drake, Sir Francis, 70, 180
Drawater, Benjamin, surgeon's mate, 134
Drucker, Philip, 91, 92
Drury Lane, 172

Dublin, 134, 144
Dufour, Josef, 199, 202, 203
Duncan, A., 152
Dusky Bay, N.Z., 130, 131
Dysentery, 136, 139, 140, 141–42

East India Company, 32, 37, 42–44, 52, 53–55, 56, 125, 142
East Indies, 22
Easter Is., 13, 123, 132, 155, 190
Edgar, Thomas, master, 154–55
Edinburgh, 51, 179
Eliza, Francisco de, lieut., 113
Ellis, William, surgeon's mate, 148, 153, 155
Endeavour, H.M.S., 22, 23, 24, 27, 30, 33, 38, 39, 47, 48, 50, 51, 153, 167, 219, 226; selection of, 42, 46; health aboard, 136–45, 150, 152, 156
Endeavour R., Aus., 138
Engel, Samuel; Mémoires et observations géographiques, 68, 70
England, 3, 13, 19, 28, 30, 42, 48, 52, 68, 76, 79, 130, 139, 140, 144, 148, 165, 187, 213, 221, 225
Engravings, 187–99, 203–10
D'Entrecasteaux, Bruni, navigator, 5, 204
Etches, Richard C., merchant, 29, 34
Ethnography, 84–85, 100, 101, 103, 108–9, 114, 122, 203
Eulogies, 162–67, 203
Europe, 7, 8, 28, 60, 63, 64, 79, 114, 173, 180, 190, 194, 195, 202, 203; Cook's reputation in, 3, 159–85, 210, 211, 213–14; expansion of, 19, 165, 184, 212; venereal disease in, 150–51
Experiment (ship), 35

Falkland Islands, 49, 145
Favorita (ship), 107
Fenton, Henry, 130
Ferrario, Giulio; Il costume antico e moderno, 206–07, 210
Fiji, 153
First Voyage, 6, 22, 29, 43–48, 50, 59, 121, 136–41
Fisher, Robin, 4
Fitzgerald, Gerald, poet, 183
Fletcher, Charles, 129

Flinders, Matthew, navigator, 5, 6, 29–36, 221

Flórez, Manuel Antonio, viceroy, 110, 111, 112

Flower, Peter, surveyor, 137

Fonte, Bartholomew de, admiral of New Spain, 54, 55, 62, 64, 69, 71, 76

Forster, Johann George Adam; contribution to Cook's voyages, 3; account of voyages, 6, 7, 154–55, 160–61, 211–28; concern over outcome of voyages, 183, 212; *Cook der Entdecker*, 228; *Cook's dritte Entdeckungs-Reise*, 211; *Voyage Round the World*, 183, 222

Forster, Johann Reinhold; character of, 215, 221–27; contribution to Cook's voyages, 3, 226; account of voyages, 6, 7, 132–34, 154–55, 160–61, 214, 223–25; influence on George, 211; *Characteres generum plantarum*, 225; *Observations*, 223

Fort St. George, Madras, 41

France, 45, 64, 121, 164, 165, 166, 196, 202

Franciscans, 116

Franklin, Benjamin, 47, 48

Franklin, Sir John, explorer, 29

French East India Company, 49

French exploration, 112

French Revolution, 12, 161, 164, 175

Friendly Cove, 107, 115, 118; *See also* Yuquot

Friendly Islands, 133, 152

Frost, Alan, 3

Fry, Howard T., 2, 214, 215

Fuca, Juan de, 54, 55, 62, 64, 69, 71, 76

Funchal, Madeira Is., 137

Furneaux, Tobias, commander, 131, 135, 136

Fur trade, 29, 34, 54, 64–65, 79, 91, 98, 100, 109, 110, 112–13, 116

Galapagos Islands, 55

Galen, Greek physician, 142

Galiano, Dionisio Alcala, navigator, 114, 119

Gálvez, José de, Minister of the Indies, 106

Gardner, Sir Alan, 145

Gay, Peter, 161

*General Evening Post*, 135

Gentlemen's Society of Spalding, 26

George III, 9, 46

Germany, 210, 211, 213, 218

Gianetti, Michelangiolo, 162

Gibson, James, 123

Gibson, Samuel, marine, 149, 156

Gilbert, Sir Humphrey, 17

Gilbert, William, 18

Gilpin, William, 7

Golenishchev-Kutuzov, L.I., editor, 124

Golovnin, V.M., navigator, 124

Gore, John, lieut., 72, 73

Göttingen, 222, 227

*Göttingischen Anzeigen von gelehrten Sachen*, 216

Great Ayton, Yorkshire, 51

Green, Charles, astronomer, 138, 139, 140, 156

Greenslade, William, marine, 137

Grand Tour, 12, 14

Grenville, William, lord, 31, 32

*Guardian* (ship), 23, 24, 30

Gulf of Alaska, 124

Gunther, Erna, 92

Gwosdev, Mikhail Spiridonovich, explorer, 60, 61, 63, 64, 79

Hackett, C.J., 151

Haida Indians, 103

Hakluyt, Richard, 55

Hakluyt Society, 1

Hall, J., engraver, 191

Halle, Germany, 222

Hallett, Robin, 35

Halley, Dr. Edmund, astronomer, 44, 45, 47, 49

Hamilton, Emma, 175

Hardy, Thomas Masterman, 175

Harleian Library, 56

Harlow, V.T., 49, 57

Harvey, William, midshipman, 155

Haslar hospital, 137

Hastings, Warren, 164

Hawaii, 84, 96, 112, 113, 148, 154–55, 168, 182, 184, 196, 199, 202

Hawke, Sir Edward, lord Hawke, admiral 46, 47

Hawkesbury, Charles Jenkinson Liverpool, 1st earl of, 37, 39
Hawkesworth, Dr. John, editor, 1, 14, 46, 51, 219, 225
Hawkins, Sir Richard, 14, 147
Health, 3, 124, 129-57, 168
Hearne, Samuel, explorer, 7, 10, 16, 66, 68, 69, 70, 78, 80, 112
Henderson, Stewart, 129
Herder, Johann Gottfried, writer, 188
Hergest, Richard, navigator, 36
Herschel, Sir John Frederick William, astronomer, 19
Hezeta, Bruno de, navigator, 104-06
Hicks, Zachary, lieut., 139, 140, 156
Hoare, Michael E., 2, 3
Hodges, William, artist, 6, 191, 194
Holland, 165
Home Office, 23, 24, 32, 38
Hove, A.P., botanist, 6
Howe, Thomas, capt., 41
Huahine Is., Society Islands, 149
Hudson Bay, 64, 66, 106
Hudson Strait, 77
Hudson's Bay Company, 53, 54, 66, 68, 77
Hughes, R.E., 146
Hulme, Dr. Nathaniel, 137, 145
Humboldt, Friedrich Heinrich Alexander von, naturalist, 5, 6, 7, 100
Huntarian Museum, Glasgow, 86
Hunter, John, Governor N.S.W., 39
Hunter, John, surgeon, 144
Hutchinson, John, surgeon, 136, 143, 147
Huxham, John; *Method for Preserving the Health of Seamen, Observations on… Epidemic Diseases*, 135

Inca, the, 165
India, 6, 25, 52, 124, 141, 164
Indians of North America, 16
Indians of northwest coast: artifacts of, 86, 89; ceremonies of, 89-90; claims of cannibalism among, 85, 115-16; dances of, 89; labrets of, 103, 109; and metals, 103, 106-07, 113; and property, 92-93; sexual contact with, 93-96, 118; social organisation, 87; Spanish policy on, 100-01, 109, 114, 115, 118; study of

Indians of northwest coast (*continued*)
their languages, 111, 115; and theft, 88, 96, 107, 108; and trade, 87-93, 104, 105, 108, 112-14; and violence, 96-97, 105, 107-08, 114-15; *See also* Nootka Indians, Haida Indians, Kwakiutl Indians
Indochina, 165
Ingraham, Joseph, trader, 116
*Investigator* (ship), 30, 31, 32, 34
Irkutsk, 122
Irving, Charles, surgeon, 147
Isla Grande, 55
Isle of Georgia, 50
Isle of Pines, 165
Italy, 22, 173

James, Thomas, explorer, 14
James' Powder, 135
Japan, 52
*Jason* H.M.S., 145
Johnson, J., publisher, 188
Johnson, Dr. Samuel, 98
Joppien, Rudiger, 3

Kalani'opu'u (Kalaniopu), of Hawaii, 153, 227
Kamchatka, 60, 61, 64, 76, 100, 121, 122, 227
*Kamchatka* (ship), 124
Kayak Is., 61
Kealakekua Bay, Hawaii, 3, 6, 97, 148, 154, 155, 159, 174, 227
Kean, Edmund, actor, 172
Keate, George, explorer, 10
Keats, John, 16
Kendrick, John, trader, 116
Kent, John, surgeon's mate, 131, 135
Kew Gardens, 27
King, James, lieut., 6, 14, 29, 52, 71, 74, 75, 85, 89, 96, 148, 150, 153, 154, 156, 161, 169, 226
King, Philip G., Governor N.S.W., 39
Kippis, Andrew; *Life of Cook*, 216-17
Kitson, Arthur; *Captain James Cook*, 216-17
Klipstein, F.A., 136
Koah (Koa), priest of Hawaii, 154
Kodiak Is., 69

Korea, 52
Kotzebue, Otto von (O. Ye. Kotsebu), navigator, 123, 125
Krenitsyn, Peter Kumikh, capt., 65, 79
*Kreyser* (ship), 124
Krusenstern, A.J. von (I.F. Kruzenshtern), Russian explorer, 123–5
Kruzoff Is., Alaska, 105
Kukulaimoku, Hawaiian god, 227
Kurile Islands, 63
Kuyper, Jacques, 203, 204, 206; *De Mensch...*, 203, 204
Kwakiutl Indians, 92

Labat, Père, 131
La Billardière, Jacques de, navigator, 203
La Pérouse, Jean François Galaup, Comte de, navigator, 5, 6, 12, 19, 109, 110, 114, 133, 153, 199, 203
La Roché, Antoine de, navigator, 49
Latin America, 55
Law, John, surgeon, 148, 154
Lazarev, M.P., navigator, 124
Ledyard, John, marine, 6, 154, 155
Lémontey, Pierre; *Eloge de Jacques Cook*, 163–66, 180, 183–84
*Léon* (ship), 49
Lessing, Gotthold Ephraim, dramatist and critic, 168
Levashev, Mikhail, lieut., 65, 79
Le Vieux, Lucien, sculptor, 175
Lichtenberg, Georg Christoph, scientist, 227
Lincolnshire, 37
Lind, James, physician, 135, 142–47; *Health of Seamen*, 147
Linne (Linnaeus) Carl von, botanist, 26
Lipperheidesche Kostumbibliothek, West Berlin, 207
L'Isle, Guillaume de, cartographer, 64, 76
L'Isle, Joseph Nicolas de, cartographer, 64, 76
Lisyanskiy, Yu. F., navigator, 123, 124
Lithuania, 211
Lloyd, Christopher, 145
Loire, the, 164
London, 12, 49, 51, 66, 68, 106, 213, 221, 227

*London* (ship), 42
Lono, Hawaiian god, 182, 184, 227
Louis XV of France, 162
Louis XVI of France, 164
Low, C.R.; *Collected Voyages*, 172
Lowes, J.L., 15
Lunar Society of Birmingham, 26
Lyons, 164, 166
Lysaght, Averil, 214

MacBride, Dr. David, 137, 143, 144; *Essay on Scurvy, Experimental Essays*, 144
McCluer, John, captain, 54
McClure, Robert, explorer, 145
McIntosh, Alexander, carpenter, 149
McIntosh, John, A.B., 148
Mackay, David, 2
MacLean, Alistair, author, 217

Macon, France, 199
Madras, 42
Madrid, 100, 109, 113
Magellan, Ferdinand, 218
Magellan, Straits of, 147
Magidovich, I.P. 127
Mahoney, Mortimer, cook, 131
Major, R.H., author, 55, 57
Malaria, 139, 140, 141, 143, 144
Malaspina, Alejandro, navigator, 5, 36, 114–15, 118
Malay Archipelago, 41, 42, 43, 53, 54
Maldive Islands, 56
Manila, 113
Mannevillette, M. D'Aprés de, geographer, 49
Maoris, 21, 48, 132, 133, 151, 152, 190, 196, 202, 204
Maquinna, Nootka chief, 90, 111, 116
Marechal, Sylvain; *Costumes civils*, 199
Marquesas Islands, 13, 132, 190
Marseilles, 166
Martin, Admiral, 135
Martínez, Esteban José, navigator, 103, 104, 110–14, 116
Marton, Yorkshire, 216
Marx, Karl, 125
Maskelyne, Nevil, astronomer, 43, 44
Masson, Francis, botanist, 5

Maty, Matthew, secretary, Royal Society 68, 71, 74
Mavor, William Fordyce; *British Nepos*, 173
Meares, John, trader, 116
*Medical and Physical Journal*, 129
Melville, Henry Dundas, 1st viscount, 142
Menzies, Archibald, botanist, 29, 30, 31, 32, 38
Mercator's "Sea Chart of the World," 50
Metz, Frederic, 55, 56, 57
Mexico, 99, 108, 118, 164
Mexico City, 109, 112, 114
Milan, 206
Millar, John, 142, 143
Milton-Thompson, G.J., 133
Missionary work, 100, 101–2, 103, 107, 116–18
Mississippi R., 112
Missy, César de, 228
Mitchel, Bowles, midshipman, 131
Mitchell, Charles, 174
Moachat Indians, Nootka Sound, 86, 91, 92, 93, 94
Molyneux, Robert, master, 140, 156
Monkhouse, Jonathan, midshipman, 140
Monkhouse, William Brougham, surgeon, 136–37, 139, 142
Montagu, John, earl of Sandwich, first lord Admiralty, 68, 144, 226
Monterey, 66, 103
Montesquieu, C.L. de Secondat de, 184
Montreal, 194
Moorea Is., Society Islands, 153, 155
Moorhouse, Geoffrey, 213
Morehead, Alan, 217; *The Fatal Impact*, 81
Mortality, 140, 142, 148–49, 156
Mount Edgecombe, Alaska, 66, 105, 123
Mount St. Elias, Alaska, 61, 79
Mount Snowdon, Wales, 17
Moziño, José Mariano, 115
Muchalat Arm, 91
Muchalat Indians, Nootka Sound 91, 93, 94
Müller, Gerhard Friedrich, 52, 63, 64, 65, 70, 71, 73, 74, 76, 79; *Nachrichten von Seereisen*, 64
*Nadezhda* (ship), 123

Naples, 151
Napoleon I of France, 175
Narvaez, José, pilot, 112
National Library of Australia, 191, 196
Nature, European perception of, 7–8
*Nautilus* (ship), 29
Navigation, 23, 33, 41, 42, 123
Navy Board, 21, 34, 39, 46
Nelson, David, botanist, 29
Nelson, Admiral Lord, 124, 146, 175
Nepean, Evan, 24, 32, 33, 34
Netherlands East India Company, 147
*Neva* (ship), 123
New Albion, 70
New Britian, 41
New Caledonia Is., 133, 165, 190, 194, 199, 202
New Guinea, 41, 47, 54, 59, 139
New Hebrides Islands, 133
New Holland, 32, 47, 54, 56, 138, 165
New Mexico, 105
New Orleans, 112
New South Wales, 6, 19, 21, 23, 24, 38, 39, 220
New South Wales, Public Library of; *Bibliography of Captain James Cook*, 221
New Zealand, 14, 51, 163, 165, 167, 190, 196, 202, 204; Cook charts, 6, 59; Cook on coast of, 19, 48, 96, 98, 130, 138; Furneaux on coast of, 132, 152; preserves memory of Cook, 1, 182; Forster forsees its development, 212; scholarship in, 214, 219, 220
*New Zealand Listener*, 221
Newfoundland, 22, 35, 78
Newton, Sir Isaac, 19, 26
Nice, 148
Niger R., 6
Nile R., 16
Nootka Indians, 4, 84–98, 104, 204; *see also* Moachat and Muchalat Indians
Nootka sound, 1, 4, 55, 66, 71, 72, 80, 81–98, 99, 104, 106, 107, 109, 110–15, 153, 202, 206, 207
Nootka Sound crisis, 31–32, 55, 104, 111
North, Frederick, Lord North, 49, 50
North America, 5, 10, 19, 29, 31, 32, 34, 60, 64, 67, 68, 70–72, 74, 77, 78, 79,

North America (*continued*)
81, 85, 100, 124, 207, 212
Northeast Passage, 60, 224
Northeastern Geographical and Astronomical Marine Expedition, 122
Northwest coast of America, 4, 6, 34, 53, 54, 55, 60, 62, 66–79, 80, 81, 98, 99–119, 201
Northwest passage, 3, 29, 56, 59–60, 46, 66–70, 77, 79, 99, 105–06, 112, 145, 224
Norton Sound, Alaska, 75

Omai, of Huahine Is., 150
*Orange* (ship), 51
Orient, 43, 53
Ortelius map, 50
Oxford, Earl of, 56

Pacific; general, 1, 3, 6, 13, 19, 21, 22, 34–36, 42, 43, 45, 48, 49, 50, 52, 54, 57, 59, 64, 68, 70, 81, 94, 99, 100, 105, 106, 118, 122, 127, 151, 152, 159, 160, 162, 166, 168, 180, 187, 207, 212–14, 217–18, 220, 226–27; north, 3–4, 53, 60, 100, 101, 109, 110, 112, 113, 119, 121–22; south, 3, 4, 14, 51, 53, 59, 66, 76, 79, 88, 137, 138, 190–91; people of, 118, 182, 184, 185, 188, 196, 199, 202–04; its impact on Europe, 3, 210
Page, engraver, 188, 199
Paintings of Cook, 168–83, 195–96
Pallas, Peter Simon, naturalist, 5, 227
Palliser, Sir Hugh, 21, 136, 144, 226
Paris, 22, 64, 79, 164, 194
Paris, Pierre Louis, 166–67
Park, Mungo, explorer, 6, 7, 10, 12, 17, 29, 30
Parkinson, Sydney, artist, 140, 149; *Journal*, 204
Parry, Sir W.E., explorer, 29
Parsonson, Gordon, 227
Patten, James, surgeon, 132, 133, 134, 142, 152, 154, 155
Pelew (Palau) Islands, 202
Pelham, Henry, secretary Victualling Board, 145
Pérez, Juan, navigator, 66, 84, 92, 101, 103, 104, 107, 111

Perry, William, surgeon's mate, 136, 137, 142, 143, 144
Peru, 164
Petropavlovsk, 121, 123, 227
Philipp, Dr. Ernest, 130
Phillip, Arthur, Governor N.S.W., 23
Phillipines, 165
Phillips, Molesworth, lieut. marines, 169
Phipps, Constantine John, lord Mulgrave, 22
Phipps, John, captain, explorer, 5, 6, 67–68, 147
Pingré map, 50
Pirates, 53
Pitt, William, 19, 31, 39
Plain language, 15, 160–61
Plant transfer, 21–24, 28, 38, 39
Plymouth, 133, 135, 144
Plumb, J.H., historian, 227
Point Grenville, 105
Poissonière, Dr., 147
Polynesia, 81, 97, 98
Poole, Thomas, 9, 19
*Porpoise* (ship), 21, 22, 24, 25, 30, 39
Port Egmont, Falkland Islands, 145
Portlock, Nathaniel, navigator, 35, 36, 97
Portsmouth, 144
Potatow, (Potatau), of Tahiti, 191
Poverty Bay, N.Z., 96
Prince of Wales Is., Alaska, 61, 66
Prince William Sound, Alaska, 72, 202
Prince's Is., *now* Panaitan, 139, 140, 143
*Princesa* (ship), 107
*Principe* (ship), 101
Pringle, Sir John, pres. Royal Society, 129, 133, 134, 135, 142, 144, 145, 147, 155; *Diseases of the Army*, 135
Privy Council Committee for Trade and Plantations, 37
*Promyshlennik* (ship), 64
*Providence* (ship), 34
Public Record Office, 217
Purchas, Samuel, explorer, 10, 14

Queen Charlotte Islands, B.C., 66
Queen Charlotte Sound, N.Z., 131, 136, 149
Quiros, Pedro Fernandez de, navigator, 13, 218

*Radja* (ship), 139
Raiatea Is., Society Islands, 153
Raleigh, Sir Walter, 180
Ramberg, Johann, painter, 174
Ratmanov, M.I., 125
Reardon, John, bosun's mate, 138
Rennell, James, geographer, 32
*Resolution* H.M.S., 6, 21, 23, 27, 29, 34, 81, 85, 94, 96, 121-2, 162, 169, 174, 211, 214, 215, 219, 222, 226; health aboard, 2nd voyage, 129-35, 142; health aboard, 3rd voyage, 147-57
Resolution Cove, Nootka Sound, 81, 91, 92, 93, 96
Resources, exploration for, 28-29, 30-31, 36, 49, 99
Revesby, 27, 39
Revillagigedo, Conde de, Viceroy, 112-15
Reynolds, Joshua, artist, 174
Rickman, John, 72, 73; *Journal of Captain Cook's last Voyage*, 226
Rietz, Rolf Du, 212
Rio de Janeiro, 107, 137, 153
Riou, Edward, midshipman, 36, 73
Roberts, Henry, lieut., 72, 80, 148
Robertson, Dr. R., surgeon, 130, 135, 151
Robinson, Will, illustrator, 172
Rodney, admiral lord, 145
Rollin, Dr., surgeon, 132
Romantic poets, 8-19
Rome, 165
Ross, John, capt., 29
Ross, Sir John, 124
Rousseau, Jean-Jacques, 183
Royal Academy, 168
Royal Academy of Florence, 162
Royal College of Surgeons, 148
Royal Institution, 26
Royal Navy, 2, 3, 19, 45-47, 50, 51-2, 124
Royal Society, 6, 15, 25-6, 27, 42-7, 50, 51, 56, 68, 77, 129, 144, 147, 160; *Philosophical Transactions of*, 25
Royal Society Club, 48, 52
Royal Society of Arts, Manufactures and Commerce, 26, 180
Russia, 3, 68, 109, 122, 125-7, 165
Russian Academy of Science, 5
Russian American Company, 122
Russian exploration and expansion, 60-65,

Russian exploration (*continued*) 100, 103, 104, 109, 110, 122
Russian navy, 122-23, 124
Ryukyu Islands, 52

St. Helena, 133, 219
St. Jago, *now* São Tiago, Isle of, 130, 135
St. Lawrence R., 175
St. Petersburg, 66, 100, 122, 227
St. Petersburg Academy of Sciences, 64, 68, 79
St. Sauveur, Jacques Grasset de, 190, 194-95, 202-03; *Costumes civils*, 190, 194-96, 199; *Encyclopedie des voyages*, 194, 196, 202
*Salisbury*, H.M.S., 144
Salisbury Plain, 16
Samgoonoodha, Unalaska, 153
Samoa, 153
Samuel, Richard, artist, 188
Samwell, David, surgeon's mate, 118, 148, 150, 153, 155, 161
San Blas, 101, 104, 105, 107, 109, 114, 118
San Diego, 103
Sandwich, earl of, *see* Montagu
Sandwich Islands, 153, 165, 196; *see also* Hawaii
Sandwich Sound (Prince William Sound) Alaska, 72
*Santigo* (ship), 101, 103, 104
Saussure, Horace-Benedict de, author, 7
Savu, Indonesia, 139
Schlegel, Frederick, critic, 218
Science and empiricism, 25-27
Science and exploration, 5, 29-30, 31, 32, 38, 45, 100-101, 105, 109, 114
Scott, commander *Porpoise*, 24
Scott, James, lieut. marines, 131
Scott, Robert Falcon, explorer, 224
Scurvy, 3, 35, 105, 130-39, 144-49
Sea otter, 29, 36, 88, 90, 98, 109, 112, 113, 118
Second voyage, 5, 6, 13-14, 29, 33-34, 35, 44, 52, 59, 121, 124, 127, 128, 130-36, 152, 154
Seward, Anna; *Elegy on Captain Cook*, 167
Sexual contact with indigenous people, 93-96, 118, 138, 148-54

Shank, Joseph, lieut., 130
Sharp, Andrew, 214
*Sheerness* (ship), 144
Shelvocke, George, privateer, 14
Ship Cove, Nootka Sound, 81
Shokal'skiy, Yu. M., scientist, 126
Shumagin Islands, Alaska pen., 61, 63, 65
Siberia, 6
Sicily, 146
Sick and Hurt Board, 136, 137, 143, 144, 145
Silver spoons at Nootka, 92, 106, 110-11
Simon Fraser University, 1
Singapore, 42
Smith, Adam; *Wealth of Nations,* 179
Smith, Bernard, 2, 3, 7, 187, 214; *European Vision and the South Pacific,* 3
Smith, Christopher, scientist, 29
Smith, H.M., 151
Snagg, James, surgeon's mate, 148
Society Islands, 132, 138, 153, 190, 202
Soho, 183
Solander, Daniel Carl, botanist, 5, 27, 140, 215, 226
Solomon Islands, 41
*Sonora* (ship), 66, 104
South Africa, 164
South Sea Company, 55
Southern continent, 59
Southey, Robert, poet, 8, 12, 15, 16, 18
Soviet Union, 125
Spain, 67, 99, 100, 104, 105, 109, 113, 114, 118, 119, 162
Spanberg, Martin, captain, 60
Spanish exploration, 4, 31-32, 65-66, 76, 79, 99, 100-119, 122
Sparrman, Anders, natural historian, 5, 6, 130-34, 215
Spencer, first lord Admiralty, 32
Spöring, Herman Diedrich, secretary, 140
Sprat, Thomas, *History of the Royal Society,* 160
Stählin, Jacob von, map and account of Russian discoveries, 52, 68, 70, 74-77, 78, 79
Staten Island, 214
Staten Land, 61
Stephens, Sir Philip, secretary Admiralty, 49

Still, John, gunner's servant, 140, 156
Stokes, J.F.G., 184-5
Storsch, Baron von, 145
Strachan and Cadell, publishers, 179
Strait of Juan de Fuca, 71, 114, 207
Straits of Anian, 72
Strange, James, fur trader, 35
Struyck, Nicolas, 53, 56
Stuart, Martinus, *De Mensch,* 203-04
Sulu Archipelago, 42, 44, 45
Sumatra, 6
Surveying, 35, 42, 54-55, 65, 70
Sutherland, Forby, A.B., 138
Svet, Ya. M., 127
Switzerland, 164
Sydney, Aus., 221
Synd, Ivan, lieut., 65, 68, 69, 77, 78, 79
Syria, 10

Table Bay, S. Africa, 140
Tahiti, 9, 51, 81, 96, 131, 132, 136, 138, 147, 149, 155, 167, 174, 222; people of 84, 137, 190, 202; introduction of syphilis, 150-53
Tahsis Inlet, Nootka Sound, 87
Tanna Is., New Hebrides, 202
Tasman Sea, 167
Tatarinov, M., major, 122
Tayeto (Taiata), of Tahiti, 140, 156
Taylor, Isaac, mariner, 132
Télémaque, 59
*Terra Australis,* 6
Texas, 100
Thames R., England, 46
Theoretical geography, 35, 43-44; of Arctic regions, 54-55, 64-65; of New Holland, 56-57; of North Pacific, 52, 59-60, 68-69, 74-79; of southern regions, 49-51
Third voyage, 3, 4, 5, 29, 33, 52, 53, 60, 61, 64, 70-78, 80, 81-98, 121, 127, 148-57, 190, 226-27 Tierra del Fuego, 133, 137, 166, 191, 214
Timor Is., E. Indies, 139
Tobin, James, 9, 18
Tom, Henry, Commissioner of Sick and Hurt, 144
Tonga Islands, 149, 150, 155, 202
*Torbay* (ship), 144

Torres, Luis Vaez de, explorer, 47, 50
Toynbee, Arnold, historian, 182
Trade, expansion of, 28, 38, 53, 55, 164–65, 179–80
Trafalgar Square, 75
Transit of Venus, 42, 44, 166
Treasury, 38
Trevenen, James, midshipman, 122, 149, 153
Tristan da Cunha, 53
Trotter, T., 136
Trusty, H.M.S., 148
Tuberculosis, 156–57
Tupia (Tupaia), of Tahiti, 138, 139, 156
Typhoid fever, 142

Unalaska Is., Aleutian Islands, 65, 69, 75
Unimak Is., Aleutian Islands, 65
United Kingdom, 31, 172

Valdés, Cayetano, Spanish explorer, 114, 119
Vancouver, George, captain, 5, 6, 7, 12, 19, 30, 31–32, 34, 36, 55, 74, 121, 210
Vancouver Is., 1, 76, 80, 119; see also Nootka Sound
Van der Sluis, I., 151
Vassenbosch (ship), 56
Vatoa Is., Fiji, 225
Venereal disease, 94, 131, 132, 138, 147, 149–54, 155, 185
Vessels employed in Pacific exploration, 34
Victualling, 34, 130–33, 137, 143
Victualling Board, 137, 143
Viero, Teodoro, 190, 194, 195; Costumes religieux & dignitaires, 194; Raccolta di... Stampe, 190
Villiers, Alan, 217
Vilna, Lithuania, 211, 213
Virgil, Georgics, 162
Vladimirov, V.N., 127
Voyage or journey motif, 11–12

Wales, William, astronomer, 219, 222, 223, 228
Wallis, Samuel, captain, 5, 6, 81, 138, 143, 145, 146, 150, 151, 219

Wallpaper, 199–203
Warrington, 222
Warwick, Henrietta, 19
Washington, State of, 105
Watman, William, A.B., 148
Watt, Sir James, 2, 3
Webber, John, artist, 93, 169, 172, 195, 206, 207
Weir, Alexander, master's mate, 137
Wellington, N.Z., 220, 221, 228
Wells, Spencer, surgeon, 147
West, Thomas, 7
West, Benjamin, painter, 175
West Berlin, 207
West Indies, 25, 124
Whaling, 36, 37, 49, 53, 77, 165
Whitby, 216
White, Gilbert, naturalist, 22
Wiles, James, scientist, 29
Wilkinson, Francis, master's mate, 137, 140
Williams, Glyndwr, 3–4
Williamson, John, lieut., 85, 97, 150, 169
Wilson, William, commodore, 41, 51
Windham, William, 19
Wolfe, James, general, 175
Woollett, William, engraver, 175
Wordsworth, William, poet, 8, 9, 11, 12, 15–18, 161; The Borderers 10–11; Lyrical Ballads, 161; The Prelude, 10, 12, 16; The Recluse, 9
Wyatt, H.V., 146
Wye valley, 16

Yedso Land, 61, 63
Yefimov, A.V., 65, 69, 78
Yorkshire, 2
Young, Alexander, surgeon, 145
Young, Arthur, 27
Young, John, surgeon's mate, 135
Young, Rev. George; Life and Voyages of Captain James Cook, 216
Yuquot, 86, 87, 89, 90-93, 96-98; see also Friendly Cove

Zoffany, Johann, artist, 174, 182

# THE EDITORS

## Robin Fisher

Associate Professor, Department of History, Simon Fraser University, Burnaby, Canada. Program Chairman for the conference Captain James Cook and His Times. Author of *Contact and Conflict: Indian-European Relations in British Columbia, 1774-1890.* Dr. Fisher also contributed a paper to this collection.

## Hugh Johnston

Associate Professor, Department of History, Simon Fraser University, Burnaby, Canada. Author of *British Emigration Policy 1815-1830: Shovelling Out Paupers.*


# THE CONTRIBUTORS

## Christon I. Archer

Associate Professor, Department of History, University of Calgary, Calgary, Canada. Author of *The Defense of Bourbon Mexico, 1760-1810.*

## Terence Armstrong

Assistant Director of Research, Scott Polar Research Institute, Cambridge, England. Author of *The Northern Sea Route, Russian Settlement in the North,* other titles.

## Alan Frost

Senior Lecturer, Department of History, La Trobe University, Melbourne, Australia.

## Howard T. Fry

Senior Lecturer, Department of History, James Cook University, Townsville, Australia. Author of *Alexander Dalrymple and the Expansion of British Trade.*

## Michael E. Hoare

Formerly Third James Cook Fellow of the Royal Society of New Zealand, now Manuscript Librarian, Alexander Turnbull Library, Wellington, New Zealand. Author of *The Tactless Philosopher: Johann Reinhold Forster (1729-98).*

## Rüdiger Joppien

Curatorial staff member of the Kunstgewerbemuseum (museum for decorative art) in Cologne, and author of a number of publications on eighteenth-century art, including *Drawings from Captain Cook's Voyages.*

## David Mackay

Senior Lecturer, Department of History, Victoria University of Wellington, New Zealand.

## Bernard Smith

President of the Australian Academy of Sciences and formerly Power Professor of Contemporary Art and director of the Power Institute of Fine Arts, Sydney, Australia. Author of *European Vision and the South Pacific, 1768-1850: A Study in the History of Art and Ideas.*

## Sir James Watt

Retired Medical Director General of the Royal Navy and Dean of Naval Medicine at the Institute of Naval Medicine.

## Glyndwr Williams

Professor of History, Queen Mary College, University of London. Author of *The British Search for the Northwest Passage in the Eighteenth Century.*

Printed in the United States
24511LVS00003B/225